D1389120

AN END
OF WAR

AN END OF WAR

FATAL FINAL DAYS TO VE DAY, 1945

KEN TOUT

These are the researches published in the hope of preserving from decay
the remembrance of what men have done… and of preventing the great
and wonderful actions from losing their meed of glory.

(Herodotus, 440 BC)

Front cover images: (*Above*) German SS troops double across a road in a staged photo after the
destruction of an American convoy of jeeps and half-tracks in the Ardennes, 16 December, 1944.
(*Courtesy of the Imperial War Museum. EA 47962*). (*Below*) Troops stop for tea in Kranenberg, next to a
large circular swastika emblem, 9 February, 1945. (*Courtesy of the Imperial War Museum. B 14402*)

First published in 2011

Spellmount, an imprint of
The History Press
The Mill, Brimscombe Port
Stroud, Gloucestershire, GL5 2QG
www.thehistorypress.co.uk

© Ken Tout, 2011

British Library Cataloguing in Publication Data.
A catalogue record for this book is available from the British Library.

ISBN 978 0 7524 5913 4

Typesetting and origination by The History Press
Printed in the EU for The History Press.

CONTENTS

ACKNOWLEDGEMENTS

This book is intended as a collection of the everyday experiences of frontline soldiers, rather than as a work of military history supported by eyewitnesses. I therefore greatly appreciate and thank all those veterans who, directly or indirectly, contributed personal memories to the book and whose names are noted. Especially kind are those who agreed to allow the use of quotes from their own published memoirs where a particular incident seemed to fit into the narrative.

A number of friends helped in the search for new material and made my task easier at a time when the pool of veterans still able and willing to contribute is rapidly diminishing. Most of my books have started out from my own experiences, extended to those of comrades of my regiment, 1st Northamptonshire Yeomanry (1NY), and then reaching out further, through 51st Highland Division, to other units. It is doubtful whether compiling another such book will be feasible in the second decade of the century.

Valued help came again from Canada, thanks to Shelagh Whitaker, Maj. Bob Bennett, Bud Jones, Capt. Tim Flowers, Terry Copp and, before his departure from this mortal scene, George Blackburn. Old Poland spoke through Capt. Zbigniew Mieczkowski and Jan Jarzembowski. Dutch help came from Ger Schinck, Anthony van Vugt and the Soeters family, Jan Wigard, Marius Heideveld, Bea Dekker and Hans Gootzen. On behalf of Germany, Hazel and Manfred Toon-Thorn were again able advisers. And from the USA, Col. Hal Steward and Gloria and Joe Solarz came to my rescue.

Eminent among sources in the UK was the Second World War Experience Centre, where director Cathy Pugh and volunteer Ernest Tate (like me a post-war KDG) found no request too burdensome. Capt. Ian Hammerton, David Fletcher, the late Bill Bellamy, Caroline at Aces High Gallery, Stan Hicken, and the late Rex Jackson were among those who helped me extend my contacts. Jo de Vries at The History Press was always encouraging, helpful, and patient; as was my wife Jai, in whose case the patience had to be inexhaustible. The book was written amid the shambles of packing up, removing from Essex and renovating our new abode in West Sussex, where I shamelessly found it impossible to handle a screwdriver and a keyboard at the same time.

MAPS

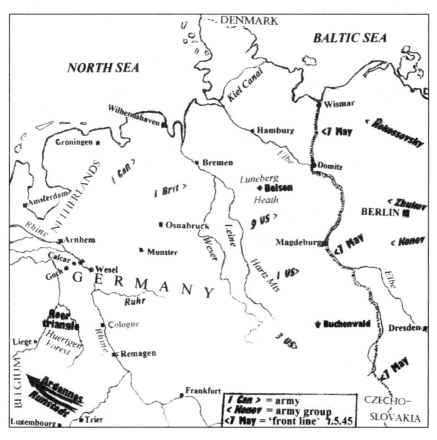

1. North-West Europe, January-May, 1945 *(Tout)*

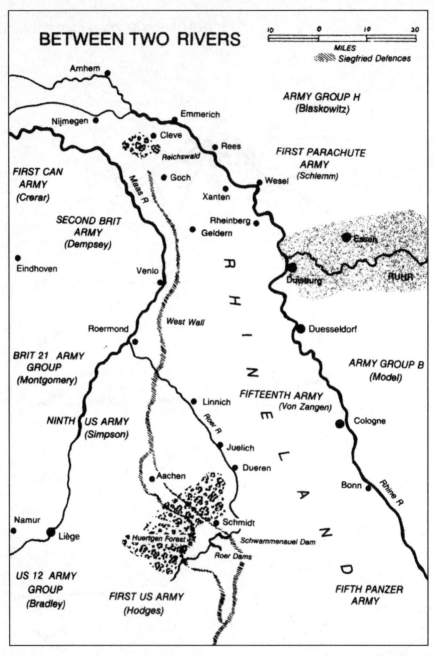

BETWEEN TWO RIVERS

10   0   10   20
MILES
▨ Siegfried Defences

Arnhem

Nijmegen

Emmerich

Cleve

Rees

Reichswald

FIRST CAN
ARMY
(Crerar)

Goch

Xanten

Wesel

Maas R

SECOND BRIT
ARMY
(Dempsey)

Rheinberg
Geldern

Essen

Eindhoven

Venlo

Duisburg

RUHR

Roermond

West Wall

Duesseldorf

BRIT 21 ARMY
GROUP
(Montgomery)

R
H
I
N
E
L
A
N
D

ARMY GROUP B
(Model)

Linnich

FIFTEENTH ARMY
(Von Zangen)

Cologne

NINTH US ARMY
(Simpson)

Roer R

Juelich

Aachen

Dueren

Bonn

Rhine R

Namur

Liège

Schmidt

Huertgen Forest

Schwammenauel Dam

Roer Dams

US 12 ARMY
GROUP
(Bradley)

FIRST US ARMY
(Hodges)

FIFTH PANZER
ARMY

ARMY GROUP H
(Blaskowitz)

FIRST PARACHUTE
ARMY
(Schlemm)

2. Rivers Maas and Rhine, 1945 *(Whitaker)*

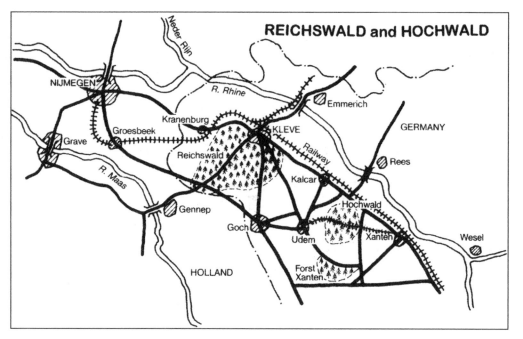

3. Reichswald and Hochwald, 1945 *(Hammerton)*

PROLOGUE

Christmas is coming,
the goose is getting fat:
please put a penny
in the old man's hat.

It was the familiar Christmas jingle, but instead of the old man's hat it was a tank trooper's beret which was collecting donations of the pretty Occupation Money banknotes. This was going to be the Christmas party of all Christmas parties.

Our tank squadron of 1st Northamptonshire Yeomanry (1NY) was laagered in a group of recently liberated Dutch villages; the villagers ecstatically joyful after years of Nazi oppression. But many of the smaller children had never experienced a real Christmas with all the delights and celebrations, toys and sweets, presents and decorations, which we ourselves had so recently known as children.

When we liberated Vught our burly Regimental Sergeant-Major (RSM), George Jelley – boy soldier of the First World War and 'uncle' to the raw recruits – had driven his jeep into the town centre and found himself surrounded by excited civilians. A local father had hoisted his 6-year-old son into the jeep and onto George's lap. George had produced a purple-wrapped bar of Duncan's blended chocolate (the nearest to milk chocolate in wartime), and offered the bar to the boy. He had been astonished when the boy screamed, struggled and pushed the sweet away.

'He has never seen chocolate', explained the father. 'Never in all his memory.' It was only after George and the boy's father had each chewed a piece of chocolate and twisted their faces into expressions of intense delight that the boy had deigned to savour the strange treat.[1]

Now all the village children would share such pleasures. Hastily scrawled (and mercifully uncensored) letters from troopers to mothers and female relatives demanded urgent parcels containing fruit cakes, sweets and children's toys, which Post Corporal 'Topper' Billingham would chase at the divisional sorting office. Affable Cook Corporal Jack Aris, abetted by Harry Claridge and 'Scotty', now served reduced rations of dessert at the improvised field kitchen and announced that all the American ration canned yellow cling peaches would be reserved for the big party. Three troopers had already dressed up for the traditional Dutch Saint Nicholas ceremony. Father Christmas would be even more benevolent when played by our gruff, elderly Captain Bill Fox hidden behind a mountainous beard of Royal Army Medical Corps (RAMC) cotton wool.

Of course there were less joyful aspects to life in Christmas 1944. The war was still going on, and on, and on. Before D-Day, nearly a year ago, we had been paraded to be inspected by the then General Montgomery. Spit-and-polish parades may have been the daily bread of life for the Brigade of Guards, but for wartime conscripts endless and apparently irrelevant peace-time routines caused much moaning and groaning. Nevertheless, we had put our trousers under our mattresses to obtain good creases, blanco'd our webbing equipment, polished our boots and made ourselves look like real soldiers for an hour or two.

To many of us Montgomery appeared a funny little man with a strange, clipped style of speech. But he handed out free cigarettes so he was a good general. Telling us of the glory days he said that, all being well, the war could be over by Christmas. Subsequently not all went well and it was still not over as we prepared the Christmas parties for our generous Dutch hosts and their children.

We had fought through Normandy, the claustrophobic *Bocage* and the agrophobic crests south of Caen. We had played a small part in the encirclement and disintegration of an entire German army, and had undertaken the heady race across France and Belgium. It had then seemed inevitable that the war would indeed be over by Christmas. The Germans would never be able to recover and resist, even at the infamous

Siegfried Line. But somehow the enemy continued to pose problems in spite of the Allies' overwhelming strength and it was not yet all over.

On the positive side, we had been told that we would have three weeks' rest in these hospitable Dutch villages. Optimistic and beguiling rumours spread that new formations were coming over from Britain to take over the main thrust of the last battles. Had not the 15th/19th come over to replace our battered 2nd regiment? Had not the entire elite Scottish Lowland Division come directly to Holland to replace the Highland Jocks whom we had been supporting? Good news was triumphing over bad news.

Leave had commenced and usually came in the form of a 48 hour pass to Antwerp or Brussels. We heard that our squadron leader, David Bevan, had gone off to Paris for a day or two accompanied by the colonel and the brigadier. Sergeants and lesser ranks had won lotteries for leave to Antwerp or Brussels. Only skeleton crews remained in the squadron lines. As night drew on, most troopers were sat talking and smoking in Dutch houses or singing and laughing at an Entertainments National Service Association (ENSA) concert. Two male 'troopers' of another kind were performing vaudeville acts with a seductive female singer in the borrowed local community hall. Unlucky Tpr Brian Carpenter had drawn the short straw to go on prowler guard among the tanks. An officer and a corporal drowsed in the Orderly Room.

Brian Carpenter was not unduly perturbed about his guard duty. It was much more pleasant here than doing prowler guards in Normandy where showers of 'Moaning Minnie' mortar bombs were likely to descend at any hour of the night. Here he could plod for a little while or lean against a tank and think about his leave in Antwerp coming up in two days time. He could not hear the jokes of the comedians, but he could hear the laughter and imagine the old, hoary jokes told to and by servicemen throughout the ages. 'Why did our colonel [name Forster] go to see the brigadier? Because he was forced-tuh … Forster, see?'

'Prowler guard!' A light flashed on in the squadron office and the duty officer's black bulk showed in the doorway. 'Prowler guard! Emergency! Stop the concert. All crews back to tanks. Pack up! Start up! Ready to move immediately. The Germans have broken through and are encircling us. Stop the concert. Cancel everything. Shift!' [2]

CHAPTER ONE

BRAVEST OF THE BRAVE

Wheresoever ye place us, 'twill be our endeavour to behave always as brave men.

(Herodotus, 440 BC)

An important theme which runs throughout this book is that some of the most bitter and costly fighting of the Second World War took place in the last months. This period needs to be written about more fully, and remembered.

It was a time when the determined German defences might well have been overwhelmed by the massed Allied armies and the road to Berlin opened without much more blood being spilt. It is an era which has largely escaped the attention of the influential Hollywood cinema moguls. Even for serious historians surveying the vast panorama of six years of total world war, it has often been relegated to a brief paragraph or a footnote. Ask a person in the street about El Alamein, D-Day, Dunkirk or 'A Bridge too Far', and a positive response might be expected. Ask about Reichswald or Hochwald and a blank stare results.

Some of these last battles were of minor strategic significance, but immensely important at a local level. Battle conditions were among the worst encountered anywhere. At battalion, company and individual level each action called for commitment as intense and sacrifice as horrific as at any time since September 1939. If this statement appears to be exaggerated then one simple fact underlines its truth. Four days and a few anonymous square miles of earth saw unsurpassed acts of heroism performed by the bravest of the brave.

In two world wars Canadian frontline soldiers had gained a high reputation for bravery. Since D-Day the Canadian Army in North-West Europe had been thrown again and again into virtually impossible missions and had responded with continuing valour at ground level. Over the whole of the war sixteen Canadians had been awarded the highest of honours, the Victoria Cross, 'for Valour'. That might be said to represent rather less than three such awards per year. Now in the brief space of four days, two acts of outstanding self-sacrifice gained the award, and a third should also have been rewarded in the same way. These examples of exceptional service demonstrate the perilous situations in which those brave men found themselves.

Major Frederick Albert Tilston, Essex Scottish Regiment, led his company across flat, open countryside under constant enemy fire. Three-quarters of his men fell as casualties and he was also badly wounded in the hip. He continued to lead, crossing and re-crossing open ground to carry ammunition and organise platoons. Eventually he fell having lost one leg and with the other leg so badly damaged that it had to be amputated. In between losses of consciousness he shouted orders from a prone position, refusing to be evacuated until another officer could come up, be briefed and take over.[1]

Four days earlier and not far away, Sergeant Aubrey Cosens, the Queen's Own Rifles of Canada, had displayed similar disregard for personal safety during an undertaking with rather different physical demands. Taking command of his platoon when it was reduced to four men he, like Tilston, had to cross open ground on foot under such intense fire that every step forward was something of a miracle. Finding one surviving tank from the initial attack, he climbed up and placed himself outside and in front of the turret, totally exposed to the enemy. From there he proceeded to direct the tank crew verbally and his surviving infantrymen via hand signals. After the tank had crashed into the first farm building, Cosens continued to lead his men into further buildings on foot. He was at last shot by a sniper having captured a vital objective, leaving many enemy dead and taking more than twenty prisoners.

In virtually the same place, the same day, and at almost the same time, Maj. David Rodgers performed similar acts of bravery. His citation for the Victoria Cross was approved at battalion, brigade, division, corps and army levels, but was left suspended beneath the strangely hesitant pen of Field Marshal Montgomery himself. There were surely very few examples of such bravery and heroism during the entire war.

To clearly understand the unique conditions which required this outstanding commitment, it is necessary to explain a little more about the history of those soldiers involved, the geography of the battleground and the supreme efficiency of the enemy.

Like so many Victoria Cross heroes, Fred Tilston was not the prototype 'tough guy' mercenary who is so often featured on the cinema or television screen, or depicted in the more lurid war novels.[2] He has been described as a 'mild-mannered, affable, 34-year-old University of Toronto Pharmacy graduate... not perhaps the firebrand the forces were looking for. For one thing, he was too old.' He managed to join up by 'adjusting his age backwards'.[3] He had twice been wounded badly enough to be able to opt out of frontline service and take a 'cushy' job.

The Essex Scots had already rendered service which might be thought to excuse them from any further exposure to ferocious combat. They had suffered badly during the abortive landing at Dieppe in 1942, and in Normandy they had been thrown into the battles around Tilly-le-Campagne and the Verrieres Ridge; later described as the 'worst fighting of the whole war' by captured German SS troopers. As adjutant of the battalion at the time, Tilston would have been aware of this.[4] The battalion ended the war with the highest casualties of any similar unit in the Canadian Army. Before the battalion could go into the action again, it had to be reconstructed by combining the relatively few remaining veterans with large numbers of raw recruits and transfers from other arms.

Little wonder then that, as adjutants were routinely 'Left out of Battle' (L.O.B.), Capt. Tilston felt that he was not getting involved in frontline action as much as he should, or as he would wish. For some time he had pestered his colonel for a move. At last, in the reconstruction of the battalion, he was promoted to major and given command of the lead company for the forthcoming battle. It was to be a very brief but remarkable command.

Whilst the immediate objective of Tilston's company was a mundane border farm set well back over open country, it was an integral part of Germany's great defence line set up to protect the Fatherland. Known in Britain as the Siegfried Line it had been the focus of many feeble jokes, such as the popular song 'We're going to hang out the washing on the Siegfried Line'. In fact it was a masterpiece of German planning, engineering and military efficiency. The Germans had already proven their ability to turn humble Normandy farmhouses into fiercely defended strong points. Here on the frontier, the defences were the result of longer planning and even greater determination to resist. Tilston's farm was like the jutting barbican of some medieval fortress.

In amongst the normal farms and dwellings the German engineers had constructed specially designed linking pillboxes from thick, reinforced concrete. Capt. Ernest Egli, a REME (Royal Electrical and Mechanical Engineers) expert, had the opportunity to examine one such miniature fort. For siting guns there were three slits or embrasures (slits narrow on the outside and wider inside):

> … each embrasure sited to cover together 360°. Each embrasure was made of steel 3" to 4" thick and mounted in concrete approximately 2 feet thick. Behind each one was a concrete room with a steel door leading into a passage with sleeping quarters in the centre of the pillbox. Each room contained a… fast firing m-g (machine-gun) on a mounting…. The outside walls and roof of the pillbox were covered with earth and grass sods for further protection and concealment. A belt of trip wire and mines circled each pillbox in a radius of 50 – 80 yards. Pillboxes were sited to support each other and between each two gun pillboxes was another for control.[5]

As Egli indicates, the ground in front of the pillboxes was treacherous for troops who were involved in many aspects of action: watching for enemy movement, firing, diving for cover, giving orders, liaising with comrades, checking the wounded and so on. But for every walking solider the great fear was of the anti-personnel mine. An anti-tank mine produced a massive explosion, but would not normally detonate under the pressure of a single human body. The more sensitively fused anti-personnel device generated a terrifying blast and a cloud of iron shards. Again Capt. Egli was an eyewitness:

> I saw a group of men at the road verge. Suddenly there was an explosion and a column of debris shot up into the air, a typical land mine explosion. We drove up and saw a soldier with a foot blown off. He had fallen back with his injured leg in the air. You could see the white end of the splintered leg bone, with the sinew hanging down. He was quietly moaning to himself.

If circumstances permitted, the infantry could crawl forward and probe in the ground for mines. Men carrying mine detectors could clear the ground, but only in the absence of enemy gunfire. There were also specialist tanks with chains which beat the ground and set off hidden mines. However, on Tilston's vital day there were neither mine-clearing tanks nor gun support tanks available because continual rain had turned the ground into a bog in which the tanks sank and were unable to get sufficient grip. The timing of the battle and the open nature of the area meant that a quick advance might be more successful than a very slow crawl with men down on their stomachs searching for mines.

As the preliminary artillery barrage ceased, Tilston's company broke through a protective hedge and began to walk forward. The distance to travel was too far to permit even a jogging advance. The major followed his two forward platoons and for a while was able to control them in good order. Seeing one of the platoons held up by a machine-gun at close quarters, Tilston walked forward and threw a grenade, destroying the gun. In doing so he was hit in the ear and the hip. Gradually Essex Scots fell dead or wounded and the major found himself leading the advance. By now the enemy were counter-attacking and the Canadians had to switch quickly from attack to defence. After the counter-attack had been beaten off, they continued to advance. Ammunition was running low.

Reduced now to a few men from the two front platoons, Tilston had nobody to send back for more ammunition. So he walked across a hundred yards of exposed ground to obtain a supply of ammunition from a following platoon. Men were also searching fallen comrades to supplement their own stock of bullets. The crisis was exacerbated because the three signallers who were carrying the wireless sets had all been hit, rendering communication extremely problematic. Rescue services for the wounded at this forward point were limited, so Tilston also supervised the movement of fallen comrades into a captured enemy command post where a German medical orderly tended wounds.

Ammunition within the company was now virtually exhausted so, whilst his survivors lay firing off their final rounds at the slowly withdrawing enemy, the major set out on another quest for supplies from a neighbouring company. As he did so a shell landed at his feet and shattered both his legs. As he lay, between bouts of unconsciousness, he refused to be moved and instead gave himself a shot of morphine and waited for another officer to arrive. Only then, having briefed the new man, did he consent to be carried away. His physical condition was so bad that one of the stretcher-bearers pulled a blanket over his face, thinking he was dead. Fortunately the efficient military evacuation system, by aeroplane directly back to an English specialist hospital, saved his life against all the odds. The quiet, affable man had not been too old for the task in hand.

Fred Tilston's experiences have been extremely well documented thanks to his own conversations in later days with Denis and Shelagh Whitaker. Sadly Sgt Aubrey Cosens did not survive to recount his actions. Much of what Tilston experienced would also have been true in Cosens' case and need not be repeated. That being said, Cosens' activities did require exceptional physical agility and mental determination, and deserve further explanation. It was also an example of how a low-ranking foot soldier could adapt to tank action in a way which was not regarded by higher authority as normal or desirable, nor was it detailed in training manuals. The Germans had perfected the tactic of integrating infantry with tanks; the Americans had gone some way in the same direction. However, the British landed in Normandy with a rigid distinction between infantry and armoured units, and very little training in the combination of the two. Canadians also tended to conform to the British system as dictated by Montgomery, within whose overall command the Canadians served.

Cosens, aged twenty-three, had a much tougher background than Tilston and had grown up and developed his physique in a wild forest region. This preparation was essential for his final acts of bravery. Cosens' battalion, the Queen's Own Rifles, aiming for a tiny hamlet called Mooshof, was quickly shattered by intense fire from well-placed strong points. Supporting tanks of the Canadian 1st Hussars were exposed to the heavier enemy guns. Sgt Cosens soon found himself without an officer and in charge of a pitiful force of four disenchanted survivors. Something spectacular was required to turn rout into achievement. Five men trying to walk the final yards towards steadily firing enemy machine-guns could expect to live for a only few seconds more.[6]

One Sherman tank, commanded by Sgt Andy Anderson, remained in action. Leaving his four survivors lying inert on the ground, Cosens ran through the visible patterns of tracer rounds to the tank. One of his riflemen described the enemy bullets as 'just like bloody rain bouncing off that tank'. Jumping on to the tank, Cosens yelled at Anderson to advance. This required an equal amount of bravery and determination from the tank commander, putting himself and crew at grave risk and also endangering the last of the armoured support.

Now, instead of returning to the ground to present a lower profile and lead his men from there, Cosens remained on the tank and stood up outside the turret. Despite attracting enemy fire he was able to direct the tank commander's aiming as well as encourage his riflemen by hand signals to follow behind the 30 ton armoured vehicle. This required Cosens' unique blend of mental obduracy and physical agility.

Standing on the turret of a tank places a man's eyes about ten feet above ground level. A ground level where nothing could move without being shot at. A tank commander would sometimes be closed down inside the turret and restricted to a periscope view of the battlefield or, more commonly, would only have his skull and eyes visible above the turret opening. Casualties among tank commanders were of a very high ratio. In one instance, the drain on officers and higher NCOs was such that a lance-corporal was left in command of a captain's tank for three weeks before reinforcements could be found.[7]

How much more exposed, then, was a man standing outside the turret and firing his Sten gun at targets whilst waving on his comrades? A tank is not a car on a tarmac road and has an erratic rock and roll motion. Crossing ditches or mounting tree trunks can cause violent crashes. Boots slide dangerously on the armoured surface. When the massive turret swings to traverse at targets a man can be swept off and under the grinding tracks. No infantryman normally chooses to stand anywhere near the deafening, blazing muzzle flash of a large tank gun. Sharp, pointed and polished bullets, which can sometimes pass through a man's body without causing fatal damage, are transformed when ricocheting off a tank's armour into twisted, lethal slugs. At any time, riding on the turret requires at least one hand to grasp some odd projection of the tank for safety.

Sgt Cosens, the tank and the following foot soldiers all miraculously reached the first building. Over the last yards of advance, the very apparition of a small force manoeuvring in such an unexpected way may have caused the defenders to lose aim. The attackers were not behaving in the way in which an enemy marksman's brain might automatically be calculating. Surprise is always a significant element in attack.

At the first farm building, Anderson commanded his driver to continue at full speed and his gunner to fire into the house. As the wall collapsed under the impact, Cosens jumped down, rushed through the door and led his men in a burst of fire; the enemy surrendered instantly. Very quickly the Canadians cleared the complex of buildings, taking many astonished and petrified prisoners. It was a moment of high triumph as Cosens ordered, 'Take up defensive positions'. At that moment an unseen sniper, with time to concentrate, fired a shot and killed Cosens instantly.

Yet more evidence of extreme bravery was found only a mile away. Maj. David Rodgers, the Queen's Own Cameron Highlanders of Canada, and like Tilston newly promoted, was clearing another farm complex of almost the same size in a manner strikingly similar to the attack by Tilston. Some time later, the fully authenticated and approved citations for three Victoria Cross awards lay waiting under the pen of the final authority, Montgomery. For no other apparent reason than a fear of devaluing the award, Montgomery signed off only two awards. On Rodgers' document he scratched out Victoria Cross and amended it to 'Immediate Award of the Distinguished Service Order'.[8]

These rare examples of extreme bravery and self-sacrifice were necessary in some of the bitterest fighting of the entire war.

The attacking forces were not only facing an organised, experienced and skilled enemy, enjoying superior defences and weaponry, but an enemy inspired by the final defence of their homeland.

CHAPTER TWO

WHEN HELL FROZE OVER

The whole district has winters of exceeding rigour and those who dwell
inside the trench make warlike expeditions on the ice.

(Herodotus, 440 BC)

After the disrupted ENSA concert and the cancelled Christmas parties for Dutch children, Brian Carpenter's diminished squadron 'stood
to' for an immediate march. And was promptly 'stood down'.

The comedians and the female vocalist were instructed to gather
their props and leave without so much as a cup of coffee or a *ginever*.
Some Dutch people, who had been sharing in the concert, wandered
bewildered back to their homes. Skeleton crews, shepherded from the
concert hall or dragged from beds, did double work packing everyone's
gear, loading Sherman tanks, starting up the engines, testing the wireless
set and turret traverse. A few abruptly awakened sergeants shouted and
pointed whilst one or two puzzled lieutenants assumed *sang froid* and
cantered about, tapping their bums with riding crops. A few moments
later the order came through on the wireless or was shouted from the
squadron office, 'Switch off. Dismount. Unpack. Back to billets and get
some kip.'

Regimental second-in-command, Major The Lord George
Montague-Douglas-Scott, was summoned suddenly into the presence of the corps commander. Lord George, although a son of one
of the largest landowners in Britain and linked by marriage to the
royal family, had the professional soldier's sense of trepidation when

summoned to appear before such a solemn and exalted potentate. Anxiously he searched his conscience to uncover what misdemeanour he might have committed. But there was no time to meditate and, shouting for his jeep driver, he hurried to corps headquarters (HQ).

He was shown straight into a large conference room filled with imperious senior officers wearing red tabs. Maps were scattered on a large table. The general was speaking as he turned around. 'This is an emergency. Von Rundstedt has broken through the Ardennes. The American line has collapsed. May 1940 all over again. Take this map reference. Go there. Recce in each direction. Report if it is a suitable place for a last long-stop before Brussels. Or for counter-attack. Most immediate. There and back as quickly…'. And without waiting for a reply or salute the general continued issuing further orders to those about him.

At the correct map reference Lord George realised that he would not need to recce in each direction for he was standing 'on a huge memorial mound which provided a magnificent OP [Observation Post] for artillery observers. The name on the map… Quatre Bras. Suddenly I knew that the X on my map was none other than the centre of the Battle of Waterloo.' This was the place of Wellington's great victory in 1815, and which condemned an earlier dictator to solitary confinement on a remote Atlantic island. For a moment Lord George imagined lining his tanks 'turret up' to the ridge and performing heroics to stave off the enemy hordes. But time did not permit delay and he turned from the historic names like La Belle Alliance and Hougoumont, his jeep roaring back towards corps HQ.[1]

Meanwhile, Brian Carpenter and the skeleton crews enjoyed a few hours sleep before shouting voices and banging tins woke them to further frantic action. Comrades were returning from leave on the Liberty trucks and were being pointed straight to the tanks in order to pack up again and make them ready to move. Some troopers found time to carry the prepared Christmas party delights to the house of the local doctor. At least the children's Christmas would not be cancelled.

This time there was no revoking of orders. The long column of Sherman tanks was soon out on the road, shunting through other military and civilian traffic, held up where battle damage still closed off portions of the roads and frustrated by the continual concertina effect if one leading tank slowed down. They halted as harassed military policemen made instant decisions as to which urgent batch of traffic might have priority over several other convoys. All headed ominously south and east; towards an enemy as yet far away but already menacing because of the emotive names of von Rundstedt and the Ardennes. Was it not von Rundstedt who had commanded the new *Blitz* style of warfare and erupted from the sparsely defended Ardennes forests in 1940, surrounded the British Army and forced it, ignominiously if heroically, to evacuate the beaches of Dunkirk?

The convoy roared on. But this was no grand prix race and these were not the new German autobahns. This was a sluggish trundle of monstrous armoured vehicles and these were narrow Dutch lanes leading from long straggling village to long straggling village, shunt and stop, jolting and crashing, shunt and stop. The tank radios insisting, 'Keep rolling! Claim priority'. That day Brian Carpenter noted a total distance, hard won at a cost of burned hands, sore elbows and a battered spine, of 86 miles in bitter cold to Quatre Bras. Next day another 86 miles.[2] Riding in a similar artillery convoy, Capt. Jack Swaab noted, '77 miles, 65 the next'. As the convoys neared disputed or vacated territory the difficulties increased. Jack found that the next day took seven hours to complete a seemingly endless 40 miles.

Like so many people, the artillery captain found that Christmas 1944 had been cancelled:

XMAS DAY. *Noon:* The worst ever. Back into Belgium where the enemy is apparently penetrating around Liege. The situation is in fact pretty serious. We had Xmas dinner, a tree, and everything laid on but all has had to be scrapped now, though we are trying our best to get some kind of meal out to the Troops. Still, it's no use grumbling. Heavy frost, sunshine and bitter cold. Tremendous welcome in Liege where we were the first British column into the city. *20.30 at Strivay:* drive of 40 miles in icy weather.[3]

Capt. Hugh Clark of the 6th Airborne Division was rushing by truck from Bulford to Dover. He went via a troop ship to Calais; a transit camp overnight, where he caught impetigo from dirty blankets; on by lorry in freezing temperatures, and spent Christmas Eve billeted with a local family in a comfortable bed. Pressing on during Christmas Day the convoy was inundated with local women bringing out large cups of *ersatz* coffee, which tasted horrible but was most welcome:

Our lunch on Christmas Day was a piece of bread and cheese. After travelling through the night we arrived in the Ardennes at Givet at 06.00 hours
on 26th December. The ground was covered in snow and the temperature
was well below zero. We took over from the Americans and started to dig
our defences into a very rocky hillside. I discovered that there was some
advantage in suffering from impetigo. Everyone else had to shave out in the
open in cold water but I had to report to the Medical Officer to have my
razor sterilised and then shave in hot water before he applied gentian violet.[4]

Gordon Highlander Bill Robertson almost celebrated Christmas. The
regimental cooks had done a marvellous job before Christmas Day,
serving hard biscuits soaked in hot soup against the cold. Food stocks
had been saved for the 25th. Christmas morning started 'full of edible
promise'. A truly traditional meal was served, despite losing some of
its appeal in worn, scratched mess tins. It was enhanced by confections
and good German cigars – source of origin not disclosed. No liquor
was available and indeed in the 5th/7th Gordons the traditional tot
of rum was never served to soldiers under the age of eighteen. Then
'literally half way through our Christmas meal we were told to pack
up and be ready to board TCVs in one hour'.[5]

Back in the columns of 1st Northamptonshire Yeomanry, Don
Foxley's tank had been halted by a traffic jam; the 'umpteenth of the
day'. Whilst his commander walked up the road to find out the cause
of the delay, Don served himself a scrumptious Christmas dinner,
it being that time of day, which consisted of corned beef and hard
biscuit. Sitting on the freezing front of the tank, as an alternative to
the refrigerated rush of air entering the driver's compartment, he
thought, 'at least I can sing myself a carol. Even von Rundstedt can't
object to that'. Avoiding 'Holy Night', he sang a verse of 'Away in a
Manger', but quietly in case anyone should think he was becoming
a psychiatric case.

One trooper who was definitely not singing Christmas carols was
popular Wally Tarrant. He had been sitting in his driving compartment down in the front of the Sherman tank, patiently juggling the
gears to maintain a difficult average speed of about 6 mph. His equa-
nimity was shattered by a loud crash; both heard and felt. The tank
slewed to one side, slid across the icy road and ploughed its way into
a ditch. A link in the right-hand track had broken and the entire track

under tension had snaked off; threatening any lurking human being with instant decapitation. This was the long, immensely heavy steel track which ran from a driving wheel, along the entire length of the Sherman, over a sprocket, and then back along the ground to form a moving roadway upon which the tank's relatively small bogey wheels could roll. Simply to lift the track was a job for several men.

Wally had an on-call armoured recovery vehicle (ARV); a turretless tank equipped with a winch and cables to pull tanks out of this sort of situation. There was also the Light Aid Detachment (LAD) in a half-track, carrying skilled fitters who were able to repair most problems. Urgent wireless messages uncovered that in this thronged, blundering procession one rescue vehicle was far ahead and the other far behind. Wally's tank was now impeding other vehicles. So the crew climbed out and found that, in addition to the normally hazardous task of repairing the track, they also had to dig into rapidly deepening snow. Wally's mood was not improved as tank after tank crawled slowly by; a commander peering out of each turret and watching Wally struggle in the snow. Ribald and sarcastic shouts greeted Wally and his pals, the insults usually rounded off by a chirpy, 'Happy Christmas'. Eventually the normally placid Wally reacted and bawled, 'Bugger off!' A sentiment not usually associated with yuletide carols.

A few tanks back, and wearing his recently awarded Military Medal ribbon, Tpr Rex Jackson saw something which he found disturbing in all this great demonstration of military might. In the mounded snow an elderly, bowed Belgian man was pushing a pram piled high with personal goods. Many civilians were moving away in a piteous procession from the oncoming, vengeful Germans. But each time the old man tried to cross the road the pram became stuck in the snow and he had to wait for another tank to go by. As the tank in front of Rex's edged forward, the man made a further dash for the other side of the road. The pram wheels caught in the furrowed snow again and the huge, threshing tank track caught the pram and hurled it away, spilling clothes and bags all across the road. The old man staggered away and fell into the ditch. There was nothing Rex, a kind-hearted lad, could do. His own tank was crashing relentlessly forward, crunching under its 30 ton weight and whirling tracks anything which hindered its progress. Rex cursed the robotic stupidity of war.[6]

RSM George Jelley was using his faster and lighter jeep to dash ahead of the lumbering tanks. Unexpectedly he came into a long section of road which was totally deserted, except for a staff car. A staff captain waved him to a stop. Another tall figure wrapped in a great sheepskin coat and muffled by a long scarf approached George, looked at George's arm badge and the silver horses on his lapels. 'RSM Jelley, I believe?' said the mysterious figure. 'Whatever you are doing, I want you to stop here until relieved. Halt all traffic. Divert them along that side road. There are no defences ahead of us. The Americans have gone. Capt. McGregor will alert your colonel. Good man!' And with a gesture of the hand the figure turned and headed back to the staff car.

Not a little puzzled, George beckoned to the staff captain. 'But who shall I say…? What if some colonel or even a brigadier comes up and refuses to listen to me?' The captain smiled, 'It's the privilege you've waited for all your life, sar'nt-major, to tell colonels and brigadiers what to do. Your orders are from the divisional commander himself, General Rennie. They don't come much higher.'[7]

On another parallel road, one of George Jelley's minions, Sgt Jack Pentelow, ordered his driver to slow down as he noticed what looked like a large airfield beyond the hedges. The map was indicating that the town of Florennes lay just beyond the far bend in the highway. Jack had moved up to take over the role of lead tank and, although there had been no sign or report of the enemy, he was proceeding with due discretion. His tank had been knocked out twice before and he did not wish a repetition of those horrific occasions. A tarmac road ran towards the airfield. A figure in strange uniform was running, leaping, almost gambolling down the road.

It was an American Air Force colonel who vaulted on to Jack's tank and shouted over the engine noise, 'Thank God, you've arrived. You're the best thing I've seen since Texas.'

'Are there any Germans in front?' asked a worried Jack.

'No sight of them, but we have been expecting them any time.'

Jack ordered his driver to switch off the engine and waved his troop corporal through to take the lead. He then listened to the story of the delighted American colonel. All ground troops, low-grade men from a newly arrived reinforcement unit, who should have been guarding the airfield, had simply disappeared, some of them leaving arms and equipment behind them. In despair and lacking any firm information about the enemy, the colonel had sent his pilots away in their Black Widow planes to a safer airfield. Before they went he had taken all the machine-guns out of their planes and, with the remaining air crew and ground staff, had mounted a thinly spaced and all too inadequate guard around the extensive field perimeter. Was he just too glad to see the Yeomanry? A very happy man now, he invited Jack Pentelow to share a Jack Daniels, which caused the English Jack to query, 'Who the blazes is Jack Daniels?' The Bourbon sour mash whiskey and its history of illegal stills were not yet familiar in local pubs around rural Raunds in Northamptonshire.[8]

It was not only isolated American Air Force colonels who were confused about what was happening. Hitler had ordered a final desperate attempt to cut off the British and Canadian armies in the north from the American and French armies in the south. If von Rundstedt's men could reach Antwerp then another Dunkirk-type evacuation might be necessary. Hitler was relying on the sheer brute force of *Blitzkrieg*. His generals added some more subtle tactics to the plan. A German commando officer, Col Otto Skorzeny, was ordered to form a secret assault mission. This comprised American-English speaking soldiers, wearing American uniforms and travelling in American vehicles, infiltrating the rear areas once the American front lines had been shattered. There was even a suggestion that they might reach Paris and carry out high command assassinations.

Confusion was certainly rife as rumours spread that such disguised enemies were appearing everywhere. Fred Leary was driving his NY lorry in the area of Namur when he was stopped by military police and asked for identity papers. This was something which Fred had never previously encountered either in Normandy or on the long-distance supply runs from the beach depots to the Arnhem road. Not content with examining Fred's pay-book the police asked further questions to ensure that he really was British, and also explained why it was necessary. Similar check points situated in Allied territory added to the volume of rumours about Skorzeny's infiltrators.[9]

Sgt Bernard Upson, XXII Dragoons, had been demonstrating his flail tank, used for mine sweeping, to a new American division which was not equipped with that kind of vehicle. He was caught up in the panic. 'The saboteurs infiltrated our area, all sorts of wild rumours were circulating – Germans dressed in civilian clothes, as nuns and priests. "Trigger-happy" GI patrols became even more trigger-happy than before.' Upson was involved in a farcical incident which could have cost him his life. He was billeted on the top floor of a house and, during the night, needed to use the chamber pot. As it overflowed, in desperation he emptied it out of the window. It splashed a patrolling American soldier who immediately blasted the entire side of the house with automatic gunfire.[10]

Well away from the battle, Lieutenant Frank Gutteridge and a friend were on leave in Brussels. They were driving a captured BMW staff car. (Enemy vehicles were often used in this way.) Entering a car park full of American tanks, Frank and his friend suddenly found themselves surrounded by Americans pointing Tommy guns at them and accusing them of being infiltrators. After explaining themselves with some difficulty they realised that they were fortunate not to have been shot on sight.[11]

Soldiers in units flanking the breached American defences were also dismayed by the sight of retreating allies. Canadian soldier Wilf Abdallah remembered a scary moment:

> In this barn, matey gets up to go to the john when he hollers, 'Holy shit! C'mon take a look'. This army walking this way up the road single file, and when you see the army doing that, you know something's wrong. Next thing this American Sergeant-Major come along. He says, 'Guys take it easy, lay low. You're cut off, three sides'. And we, 'Where's the closest enemy?' And he, 'About 100 yards that way'. Well we were somewhat scared and we pretty well hit the deck. It took about three days before we got out of there.[12]

Stan Whitehouse with 1st Black Watch, 51st Highland Division, realised that his unit was taking over from American soldiers. 'A ragged column of about sixty GIs came shuffling towards us'. Stan expected the usual banter to be exchanged between the two forces. 'The sullen GIs trudged wearily past us, faces swathed in scarves and balaclavas and buried in greatcoats'. When Sgt McKenzie stopped the American sergeant and asked where the enemy was, the

American replied, 'Gee, Sarge, I truthfully don't know. My guys are so shattered I couldn't ask them to shove out on patrol.'[13]

It wasn't only Skorzeny who was causing confusion. The BBC newsreader also added to worries. Capt. E.A. Egli had parked in Dinant when the driver of his wireless truck rushed up in panic, relaying the latest news from the BBC that German advanced elements were already in possession of Dinant. Egli was only reassured when he looked up at the citadel on a high rock face and saw that it was the Belgian flag flying from the flag pole, and not a swastika.[14] Egli later saw advancing tanks spinning 'like curling stones on ice'.

Even without Skorzeny the German breakthrough was enough to amaze and shock most opponents, although they might have been encouraged to learn about the negative opinion held by German commanders. Advancing with the Waffen SS, Manfred Thorn was involved in the initial strike:

> The weather was the worst it could be. It rained, it snowed, was icy cold and foggy and the whole operation was to be held as secret as possible. This weather was a blessing as far as air attacks were concerned, but when one had guard duty the cold kept you awake. We used the protection of forests – Blanken and Schmidtheim where all tracks had to be disguised. No fires were to be lit, no loud conversation and there was definitely no singing.

This account contradicts many descriptions of storm troopers singing martial songs as they attacked. What Manfred did not know, and the same applied to Eisenhower and Montgomery, was that von Rundstedt himself did not believe the plan could succeed. He possessed neither the armour nor the manpower for such a huge undertaking. Later he said, 'not one soldier believed reaching Antwerp was feasible. It was however impossible to protest, for Hitler would not listen.'[15]

Most soldiers involved in the battle remembered not the panic or the bitter fighting, but the cold: the sheer, unparalleled, unmitigated, relentless, freezing cold. Some Canadian units, like the Winnipeg Rifles, might have been accustomed to intense prairie cold and mountainous snowdrifts. But for the vast majority of

British soldiers it was a unique experience; preferably never to be repeated. A 1NY tank corporal, sadly killed in the fighting amid the snows, remarked, 'I always believed that Hell fire was hot. Now I know it is freezing cold'. Another said, 'fighting in a Sherman tank, waiting for instant cremation, was always Hell. But this was the day Hell froze over'.[16]

Cpl Johnny Johnson, 1NY, thought that the fierce cold weather would make a good subject on which to write home to his mother. He found his old post office style pen-holder with its steel nib and his bottle of royal blue ink. Opening the bottle he discovered that the ink was frozen solid. Already he and others had bartered cigarettes in exchange for eggs at a local farm. On return to the tank they found that the eggs were frozen solid inside the shells. Seaforth Highland despatch rider Charles Dunesby and comrades were in agonies stumping along in solidly frozen boots, and 'we were all walking stiff and splayed legs like a squad of Charlie Chaplins'.[17] Many soldiers like Cpl Don Ward, Military Medal, of the Airborne, and Cpl Doug Austin of the REME were regretting having to leave warm billets with very hospitable Belgian families and venture into this arctic waste.

Cpl Percy Sumner, 1NY, squatted beside his tank to lace up his boots. The frozen leather laces snapped. He tried again but every time he put pressure on the laces the leather broke apart. In frustration he cut off a length of electric cable to tie on the boots. Inside the freezing tank Stan Hilton, on night wireless watch, had invented his own way of keeping frostbite away from frigid toes. His mother had sent a parcel containing night lights; small squat candles intended to comfort children in the night. Now Stan listened in on his wireless set with a night light burning under each foot.[18]

One of Jack Swaab's colleagues, who treated his hair liberally with Brylcreem, woke one morning to find the Brylcreem frozen solid to his scalp. A few evenings later Jack found that his bedding roll was frozen solid and would not unroll. Water had frozen in the jerry can. On 15 January the steering of his jeep had frozen up, as had also the fan-belts and brake drums.[19] Brian Carpenter, like many others, developed chilblains due to the cold weather and inadequate warming facilities. After a while the chilblains broke. When he thawed his boots the leather dye ran onto the chilblains and they began to ulcerate. The Medical Officer produced an ointment which improved the condition and Brian felt that the problem had been sorted out. Unfortunately it would cause pain much later on.

Capt. A.E. 'Sandy' Saunders, 1NY, wrote in his diary, 'It is cold! It is bloody cold! It is ★★★★★ COLD'. He had congratulated himself on inventing a sheltered bivouac; a tarpaulin spread from the side of the tank and supported above by the considerable weight of a spare bogie wheel. Unfortunately the enemy chose to bombard the area. With each concussion the bivouac slipped a bit. Then, to the amusement of the crew, the bogie wheel came crashing down on Sandy's head. The NY diary said tersely '30° of frost'.

The frost was no laughing matter for infantryman Cpl Stan Whitehouse. It seriously affected his equipment:

> Our personal weapons froze up and to cock a rifle we had to hammer the bolt in position with a piece of wood, a stone or any other handy object. We were issued with graphite grease to rub on the mechanism but it too froze. The ground was frozen solid and digging out of the question.

When Stan and his mates were on sentry duty, which often required lying prone or standing still to avoid attracting enemy fire, it was decided to relieve each sentry every twenty minutes to avoid the body, and especially the firing fingers, going rigid with cold.[20] An artillery officer dictating notes to a signaller noticed that the man spent more time blowing on his frozen fingers than actually writing.

Metal shrinks as it cools and the huge steel medium and heavy guns suffered far more significant shrinkage than rifle bolts when temperatures dropped below zero. In normal weather a 25-pounder gun could hit its target precisely with the first or second shot. Now in the Ardennes, artillery observers were noting that metal contraction was causing the first ranging shots to fall a considerable way short of the targets. Conversely, as the metal warmed up with firing, the guns adjusted. This demanded an early morning adjustment for 'shorts' and then a gradual return to normal ranging. These short-falling shots were a serious concern not only as a waste of ammunition and time, but also as a danger to forward outposts.[21]

The Germans were also suffering from the continuing cold. Manfred Thorn noted that, whilst the weather, ice, low clouds and fog had favoured their initial advance, it was now working against them:

> Our group in La Gleize had in three days had no warm meal and iron rations only which had been quickly eaten. Some had not even eaten or slept for days and morale was at rock bottom. There was no strength for fighting, no desire to shave or wash, many had inflamed eyes from the bitter cold, or colds and bronchitis plus minor wounds. The American pincer gradually surrounded La Gleize as we wished each other 'Merry Christmas'.
>
> That group was cut off, but some managed to escape through the thick forests as counter-attacks intended to rescue them withered away. The survivors had marched through deep snow, through forests, waded through the icy high water of swollen rivers, marching fourteen miles at night. Of thirty lost men most had drowned. The fast flow of the water tore the men away. The men… emerging from the woods all looked ten years older.[22]

Perhaps the most bizarre instance of the impact of ferocious cold upon friend and foe was witnessed by Highlander Bill Robertson of the 5th/7th Gordons as they advanced to retrieve occupied ground:

> Coming to a small village our passage through the snowscape was uneventful for the village was not defended – a fact we had to ascertain the hard way by checking every building. The detritus of enemy occupation lay all around… took up positions at the edge of the village in darkness in some abandoned trenches which must have been dug long before the sub-zero temperatures. One or two were awake on watch at a time but it was impossible to snatch more than a few minutes at a time with the ever-present thought of a counter-attack. The dawn came to an almost lunar landscape.

The dawn revealed a sight which first alarmed and then shocked the tough Gordons, and revealed a mystery of war which has never been fully explained:

> To our astonishment and trepidation we saw a German half-track static about 200 yards away and previously unseen when we arrived in darkness.

There was no activity around the vehicle but it certainly looked lethal, for we knew it by reputation. Two of us were sent forward to investigate; it was a short journey during which we kept the regulation 5 yards distance apart, just in case! We reached the [covered] vehicle without incident. It was on the tarmac and its angled sides closed everything from sight, as did the rear closed door.

The 'reputation' of the half-track related to its multiple uses. It had two front wheels with a driver's seat above, but the covered rear section sat above a tractor system which gave it more mobility and turning ability than other vehicles. It could tow an 88mm anti-tank gun, carry mortar tubes, have a rapid firing machine-gun cleverly concealed and ready to fire, be full of waiting infantry or be empty and booby trapped. All German troops were trained to wait for the enemy to pass by and then emerge with the element of surprise. So Bill and his companions trod cautiously:

> Eventually we swung the door open and looked inside. To our horror twelve Waffen SS men sat there rigid, unmarked and stone dead! They sat on both sides of the vehicle heavily armed with everything from MP40 machine-pistols, the highly lethal MG42 machine gun, 'tattie-masher' grenades and P38 pistols. I had never seen men armed with such quantity of weapons. Each man was at least 6ft tall, well muscled and in their mid-twenties. There was worse: for the bodies had the genitalia reaction of hanged men.
>
> Eventually we entered through the steel door into a nightmare scene, almost expecting them to come alive. But they were frozen stiff beyond resuscitation.[23]

As there were no survivors and no apparent physical marks, either on the bodies or on the vehicle, the Gordons were unable to explain what had happened and had to resort to conjecture. One suggestion was a blast from a low-flying rocket attack by a Typhoon aeroplane. However, the blast and resulting shrapnel would have left clear evidence. Another possibility was that the vehicle had halted in no-man's-land waiting for daylight. The soldiers inside had gone to sleep and been frozen as they slept. A sentry should have been posted but there were instances of elite troops becoming somewhat arrogant and, having survived many battles, taking risks in a situation with no imminent danger.[24]

From a purely military point of view Bill Robertson was fascinated to see that these were not the kind of soldiers the Gordons were expecting to encounter. They wore special camouflage overalls. Each soldier carried a paybook with a picture of Hitler in it and wore the name of Adolf Hitler on a sleeve. Only three elite SS divisions carried this decoration. Some German infantry divisions were only qualified for frontline defence. Attacks and counter-attacks were mainly carried out by the panzer divisions with combined tanks, infantry and artillery. Some of the panzer divisions were an integral part of the *Wehrmacht*, the regular army. However, a score of divisions had been raised under the aegis of the SS: Himmler's peacetime military police and Hitler's bodyguard. Although coming under the command of regular generals like von Rundstedt, the SS divisions were administered separately and enjoyed the priority and choice of equipment through Himmler's intervention.

The dead men Bill had discovered were members of the 1st SS panzers. But the vehicle sported *Wehrmacht* markings rather than SS signs, which led the Gordons to question where it was going and what it was doing beyond the normal military tactics. Yet another mystery! One thing was certain: the simple rifles and elementary Sten guns of the Scots, perhaps supplemented by the six-shooter revolver of the nearest officer, would have left the platoon in danger of being wiped out if it had openly confronted the group of SS men and their superior armoury. In addition, most of the SS men would have had years of war experience in the toughest of situations, whereas Bill and several comrades were recent graduates of a relatively brief training at the Gordon Barracks in Aberdeen.[25]

It might be relevant at this point, having described the vicious winter snows of 1944, and having enlarged on the sufferings of the troops on both sides, and having mentioned warm Belgian civilian billets, to refer briefly to something terrible which was happening to another civilian population at the same time. Only a part of the Netherlands had yet been liberated. A large area was still occupied by the Germans. Due to circumstances which will be expounded upon later, Dutch civilians in the large western cities were afflicted by a sudden and traumatic famine which is forever remembered as

'*De Hongerwinter*'. Its impact was so horrific that it has become a classic study for academics looking at the effects of famine on the human body. Again, as for the soldiers, so for the civilians involved it was the worst winter weather in living memory: a time when the human body could least support the denial of nutrition to an unprecedented degree.

Battle drove soldiers to seek cover within the earth itself. Defending troops often had time enough to prepare their bolt-holes. Advancing troops needed to dig in rapidly at every pause, and sometimes several times a day. Lance-Bombardier R.W. Deans, an artilleryman with the 51st Highland Division, found it very frustrating that the ground was too hard to dig, yet enemy fire urged people to try desperately to delve for shelter. At the same time, digging did at least help to keep the body warm. In the emergency he saw prisoners of war also being used to dig, and equally for them this was not only a forced duty, but a means of staving off death by freezing and ensuring refuge from their own artillery.[26]

Bill Robertson, relieved to have escaped from the menace of that lurking half-track, was involved in a digging incident which was both cruel and comic: 'black humour in a white wonderland'. First of all, the company was 'debussed' from their lorries, told to parade as in barracks and then 'Mark time!' marching on the spot, 'get those knees up!' An apparently senseless reversion to peacetime military formalities, until the young lads realised that wise old Company Sergeant-Major Aitkenhead was merely restoring their blood circulation after long exposure without movement in the confined back of the lorry.

There followed another perceived insult. Around their adopted empty house, previously occupied by the enemy, there were odious yellow and brown circles and lumps in the pristine snow. Enter a 'little Lieutenant' who yelled, 'Corporal Clay, get these men to clear up this shite!' Normally such an order would set privates digging and sweeping. The officer seemed unaware of the psychological implications of his order. There was a pause; Clay responded, 'Sir, we have been fighting these bastards since France and I'm not asking my lads to clear up their mess.' The lads growled their agreement. The inexperienced officer, not much older than the majority of the men and younger than some, stormed off shouting, 'You are all on a charge in front of the CO'. End of incident, or so Bill thought.

One man who found a grain of comfort in the appalling conditions was Despatch Rider Duchene who had been issued with a new form of garment. This was designated by the quartermasters, in the quaint military idiom, as 'suits, tank, troops for the use of'. Until then he had faced the icy weather with the addition of a new winter issue of underwear, hand-knitted scarf and gloves termed 'comforts for the troops' from a women's group at home, and an ill-fitting leather jerkin. Not ideal for racing along frozen roads at 60 mph against biting headwinds. The new top garment was:

> ... one piece but clever. The front had zips, two in number, each starting from the ankle and going right up the front to the collar. It was liberally scattered with various sized pockets. It had a detachable hood and was warmly lined. Though not entirely waterproof because of the zips, it was showerproof and windproof.

The DR found that 'when issued it cheered up life enormously for those in forward areas' and, no doubt, encouraged Duchene to add another 10 mph to his speed in tail winds.[27]

Meanwhile, the initially successful German attacks, after smashing through weak American divisions, strung out widely along what was thought to be a quiet zone, had run into tougher American troops standing firm at vital transit points like Bastoigne. British divisions were being brought back to reinforce the Americans. The attackers were soon outnumbered. The alarm bells had rung as far away as Bulford camp in England. There, at very short notice, 6th Airborne Division's Capt. Hugh Clark and his men were suddenly summoned and surprisingly sent, not in the accustomed Horsa gliders, but by train and sea ferry to the continent, and rushed as further defensive cover along the flanks of the advancing panzers.[28] The experienced airborne troops were soon switched from defence to counter-attack as fortunes swayed between the opposing armies.

The tank lads of 1NY had honed their skills on the fairly level fields and gentle turf of Normandy. Now they faced sterner challenges on the spiral ascents and downward chutes of the narrow, densely forested Ardennes trails. The regimental diary recorded, '27.12: home leave started. Tanks down forest tracks so steep in parts that all vehicles skidded to the bottom and could not have returned if necessary.'

Driver Stan Hicken in C Squadron had been to collect a replacement tank, which proved to have steel track pads instead of the preferred rubber:

> … and it was like putting on a pair of skates at an ice rink. Where the snow was packed down on the roads it was terrible, so the tank slithered along the sides of the road, knocking down loads of fir trees. We came to the top of a hill and there was a convoy of Canadian trucks lined up waiting at the bottom. Down the hill we went and the tank slid this way and that, turning around 360° in the process, hitting the bank each side. Nothing I could do. Rex and the others got crowbars and logs and threw them under our tracks to try to get a grip, but we crashed down to the bottom into a clump of trees. Fortunately the Canadian lorries backed out of the way otherwise we would have wiped them out all along the line with our 30 tons of uncontrolled Sherman like a wrecking ball.[29]

Brian Carpenter driving in B Squadron had similar problems, but perhaps at greater risk to himself. He had just successfully steered past a column of shuffling infantry retreating in the bitter cold; men so haggard that Brian, not for the first time, pondered about how the craziness of war made people suffer so much. The troop of tanks then had to make a rush at a steep frozen slope. Some did not make it to the top but slid back down again and again, tracks failing to bite into the ground. Brian reached the summit:

> Then I saw a column of small 15cwt trucks emerging out of the fog and coming towards us. There was no room to pass in the road without striking these trucks so I pulled over to the side, jumping a ditch, smashing into trees and back on to the road. Only to see another convoy of these small, harmless trucks in front. Again on the treacherous slope I tried to swing over but this time crashed into a larger ditch, went nose up, hit a telegraph pole and came to a halt. The pole was jammed between the steel tracks and miles of wire fell festooned over the tank and around the tracks.[30]

What neither Stan nor Brian mentions is that even the well-engineered Sherman tank was lacking in the springs normally found in a car. Every violent departure from the tarmac road, encounter with a ditch or stubborn trees, or shuddering to a halt at the bottom of a hill meant painful concussion of the neck and spine. One of the men cited would himself suffer debilitating freezing of the spinal column many decades after these incidents and as a direct cause of them.

Like many infantrymen, Bill Robertson appreciated the firepower of tanks in action, but was very wary of the huge, churning machines out of action. Near the village of Hodister, he and his platoon were advancing through ice and snow along 'a route at the base of a hill when I heard our tanks coming along the ridge upwards on our right... the next thing I knew there was much engine noise and the 40 ton tank was sliding, skating down straight at ME. We scattered from the path of the tank and watched it slide helplessly by like a wounded monster.'

Lieutenant-Bombardier Bill Lowe found it every bit as dangerous in the cab of a wheeled vehicle as in the driving compartment of a tank. He was already disheartened because he and his mates had just suffered one of the greatest blows to morale a soldier could suffer: his beloved regiment had been broken up to provide reinforcements for other unknown units. Like many artillery units it was an old territorial yeomanry regiment equipped with bigger guns than of yore. One man per gun had been summoned to a cinema where the colonel had announced the bad Christmas greetings: the evocatively named South Notts Hussars, after 150 years, would disappear forthwith and be forgotten, except by its veterans. Lowe and others would go to the less emotively titled 127 Regiment, Royal Artillery (RA).

Now fetching petrol from a depot, his lorry came to a snow-covered hill 'sliding and slipping all over the place', but kept going to the top. Going down was worse, the truck gathering speed in spite of the brakes, which only locked the wheels and spun the vehicle. Suddenly an officer stepped out from the trees and waved Lowe to stop. By some miracle of skating-on-ice lorry ballet the bombardier managed to slither to a halt inches from crushing the officer under the wheels. Lowe was justifiably furious when he discovered that the officer's message was, 'You can't get down this hill!' and, soldier fashion, the driver proceeded to prove that an artilleryman certainly should, could and would get down any hill in the cause of duty, and cussedness![31]

Not all snowbound problems were of the more humorous type. The Christmas battle was not an event of clearly distinguished battle lines or neatly advancing tanks and infantry. The 'Battle of the Bulge' title was somewhat of a misnomer. On the maps the German advance looked not so much like a distended stomach, but as open, probing fingers. A more apt description would be of three powerful battering rams crashing through a thin wall, and then diverging into empty spaces. In those areas of void little was certain, and danger was ever present at a personal level. Nothing illustrates this more than the fate of Sgt Huitson.

He was commanding the lead troop of four tanks because of 1NY's lack of officers; killed, wounded or sent off on what were deemed essential upgrading courses. In a trackless, hilly forest there was little to differentiate between 'lead', 'support' and 'rear' echelons. The first tank had adopted the now customary method of hill descent: the driver taking his hands off the braking levers, accelerating gently and closing his eyes. The trend of the slope sent the Sherman plunging down into a deep snowdrift, which was masking a large pit of some kind. The driver changed into reverse gear and set the engine roaring, but to no avail. The tank was firmly trapped. Huitson pressed his microphone switch and ordered the stranded tank to sit fast, await a tow-rope, and then prepare to reverse slowly. Calling his own co-driver out, Huitson unhitched his tow-rope and shuffled towards the other vehicle.

The Germans in the Ardennes were well supplied with the *Nebelwerfer* – a highly mobile bomb-discharge machine which could send batches of bombs high into the air. These 'Moaning Minnies', with tiny sirens attached, could come down vertically, shrieking loudly, in a neat pattern of six to enclose a tank's shape and blast everything within yards. *Nebelwerfers* and hidden observers lurked everywhere in the Ardennes.

Huitson and his co-driver managed to hitch their tow-rope, actually a strong steel cable, to the stranded Sherman. 'Go back to the tank', the sergeant ordered the co-driver. 'Tell the driver when I raise my arm, take the strain. If I drop my arm, stop!' The trooper 'waded back through flurries of snow to their own tank, in that grim murk a figure like Captain Oates going out into Polar oblivion.' Sgt Huitson raised his arm. As though coordinated, two things happened. The tank engine thundered to take the strain, but with tiny sirens screaming a batch of mortar bombs descended precisely around the two tanks. One batch of bombs. Two batches! Three! Huitson was flung to the ground. He did not get up.[32]

Whilst some British units did become involved in brief, bitter battles of a more formal nature, for other units it was a slow, frustrating advance. They slowly bled casualties, although without major tragedy, and this added to the attrition which some units had suffered all the way from the Normandy beaches. Indeed, for the Highland Division, all along the route from El Alamein. In the two weeks of a not-at-all merry Christmas and Hogmanay, 5th Black Watch lost six men killed plus forty wounded, and another forty-two evacuated with severe frostbite or pneumonia. Every batch of reinforcements inevitably diluted the vital battle experience and skills of a battalion as a whole.

In 1st Black Watch, Stan Whitehouse witnessed another savage example of a solitary casualty. As his platoon advanced through the icy fog into a village, an unknown British officer stepped out into the street in front of them. Before anyone could speak a sniper shot the officer; he fell in the middle of the street and tried to crawl away. Whilst the advancing men stood for a moment indecisive, an enemy trooper walked from behind a building, threw a grenade and retreated quickly. The grenade exploded against the officer and killed him instantaneously. The Black Watch men could not fire because all their weapons were frozen up. (The Germans and Americans had a better anti-freezing substance than the Scots' graphite grease.)[33]

Like many soldiers who had experienced battle during more normal weather, Bill Robertson was awed by the extraordinary silence which prevailed for much of the time throughout this Christmas card scene. When the usual battle sounds were absent:

> …there was a strange, palpable silence for the blanket of snow muffled everything. The pine trees were laden and even when a tree divested itself of snow it took place in silence. On many occasions we moved forward through waist-high snow and often found ourselves struggling with snow up to the oxters [armpits]… had been issued with rumpled white camouflage overalls which made us look like prime targets [against the smooth white of snow] and there was resentment that the Germans and Americans blended well into the countryside with their 'whites'.

The familiar crunch, crunch, crunch of infantry boots on gravel roads was muffled or absent. Even the sliding of steel-shod boots on ice was quiet, a scraping, whistling and ghostly sound. The only clear sound was the inevitable strident siren of a Moaning Minnie falling through the crisp air. Correction: choirs of six or ten Moaning Minnies in horrid chorus.

CHAPTER THREE

UNHAPPY NEW YEAR

At once they were eager to engage, fearing the enemy would fly, and
hoping to capture them before they should get away.

(Herodotus, 440 BC)

New Year 1945 appeared to bring better tidings to the beleaguered
Allied armies in the Ardennes. The tide was turning; the enemy attack
was petering out. The very impetus of the initial breakthrough had
left some German units almost stranded. They were now in danger of
being cut off by the pincer movement of the ever-increasing Allied
forces in the region. Hope was in the air.

The German New Year's greeting to the Allies, however, was a nasty
surprise. REME Sgt Ken Cardy noted:

31st Dec overnight stop on an airfield north of Maastricht. 1st Jan '45 a
bright morning. Suddenly the air shattered with jet aircraft – German!
About a squadron and shooting. Several tanks struck. Luckily only machine
gun ammo and not cannon. All over in a flash. New type of Planes.[1]

Wing Commander Jerry Easton, a Typhoon pilot, was also waiting on
the ground and astonished at the sudden, unexpected events:

1st January 1945 was when our wing (146) was based near Antwerp. The
German Air Force made a last big effort to destroy our aircraft on the
ground by making a strong attack on our airfields. Our Wing was on the

ground waiting for ice on the runway to go when we saw the swarm of aircraft suddenly appear attacking us. We only lost two aircraft. The attack failed mainly because the German fighters did not seem to be under good control for such an attack.[2]

The Luftwaffe had been able to fly from well-established military airfields in spite of the weather, but many Allied squadrons operated in relatively makeshift conditions and were more prey to its effects.

Jerry Easton's wing were fortunate because the Luftwaffe, for so long thought to be broken in spirit and lacking in power, had made a huge and devastating attack on that New Year's Day. Statistics later revealed that almost a thousand planes had been assembled for the massed, coordinated swoop named Operation *Bodenplatte*. The operation targeted sixteen Allied airfields and at 09.20 hours, using, according to the type of plane, cannon, rocket and machine-gun fire, attacked undefended planes unable to take off because of the pervading ice. In a few moments 240 Allied aircraft were hit, many of them totally destroyed. It is difficult to portray the impact of such an attack made at speeds in excess of 300 mph. Many planes had dived, fired and flown away before ground defences could make any kind of response. Some reports tended to validate the suggestion that the attack had been timed to coincide with the 'night after' hangovers suffered by many Allied personnel who had celebrated New Year's Eve in the time-honoured way.

One German squadron had a nasty shock according to RAF Regiment records. The Luftwaffe squadron attacked an airfield at Grimbergen only to find that it was disused. Furthermore, a flight (platoon) of the RAF Regiment in transit, well equipped with various calibres of machine-gun, had chosen to sleep on the airfield overnight. Quickly alerted the RAF's own infantrymen brought down four of the twenty-four fast-flying FW 90s and badly damaged four more.

It was a harrowing and unsettling experience for flyers like Jerry Easton, but in the long run proved to be relatively more costly to the attackers. In spite of the element of surprise the Luftwaffe lost about 300 planes in the action. Massed anti-aircraft fire quickly opened up and proved dangerous to the later planes, and those ordered to dive more than once. Allied planes were able to fly from some of the airfields and counter-attack. As with tanks, the Allies were able to replace damaged or lost planes much quicker than German industry, which had been seriously handicapped by prolonged Allied bombing.

It was a strange coincidence that, on the same day as the Luftwaffe strike, an RAF officer was winning the country's highest award for valour. Flight Sergeant George Thompson had been operating the wireless set of a Lancaster bomber as it flew in and dropped its bombs on the Dortmund-Ems canal ahead of the Allied armies. Almost at the moment the bombs were released a heavy shell struck the 'Lanc' and caused an intense fire. Gaping holes appeared in the nose of the plane, above the pilot's head and in the floor. Ammunition started to explode. Thompson could see the mid-upper turret gunner engulfed in fire. He rushed through the flames, pulled the gunner from his perch and dragged him around the gaps in the base of the plane to comparative safety. Thompson then observed that the rear turret gunner was in a similar predicament. Again, crawling the length of the huge burning plane he dragged the other man forward to where the icy wind rushing through the broken screen at least drove the flames back down the tunnel inside the aircraft.

Having beaten out the flames in his comrade's clothing with his bare hands, and now at risk from frostbite, he then dragged himself forward to report to the pilot. The flight sergeant was so badly burned that the pilot did not recognise him. Forty minutes later the pilot was able to make a successful crash landing. In his journeys through the plane, which had lost radio connections, the rescuer would have been unable to hear orders to abandon plane, and was at all times severely risking his life as the plane disintegrated. One of the gunners died of his wounds, but the other was saved. George Thompson himself succumbed to his painful injuries three weeks later.[3]

Down on earth, the wider picture revealed fresh American divisions hurrying up from the south, and more British units reinforcing the Americans in the north. Hitherto victorious German vanguards ahead of the main army were now themselves in some jeopardy. Many of those leading troops were extremely experienced. Some had already walked out of Russian encirclements and had escaped from the Falaise Gap disaster. They would not panic, but would take advantage of the terrain and the continuing bad weather to find ways through the labyrinth of forest tracks. More and more Allied advances would become frustrated. British and American troops might link up, but there would be no great triumphal moment.

The 1NY war diary revealed an advance averaging three-quarters of a mile per hour, contact with an almost invisible enemy, and then another slow push forward. The weather was closing in. More snow and lower temperatures. And, 'in addition to the usual mines under the ground, booby traps were found all along the route'. Equally frustrating was the fact that 'end connectors for tank tracks', (essential for gripping in snow) were 'received only 8 Jan', nineteen days after the regiment was ordered to move. Someone in the supply system had not been studying the snow on the Christmas cards.

A brave airborne soldier who was denied the advantage of speed, Capt. Hugh Clark, Military Cross, had a similar trek through a frozen wasteland:

> We seemed to be on the move every two or three days. We carried out long reconnaissance patrols but with no contact with the enemy. The weather continued very cold with a lot of snow, which was often more than a foot deep. Once we were scheduled to carry out a silent night attack on a hill but this was cancelled when German tanks were reported on our start line… much to our relief, as it would have been impossible to dig in on top of the hill because of the rocky terrain and depth of ice. But before the attack was cancelled I thought it a wise precaution to fill out my will on the form provided.[4]

In spite of the constant invisibility of the enemy, due as much to his military skills as to the vagaries of climate, the persistent, slow bleeding of frontline units continued. Stan Whitehouse's Lt Robinson was such a case:

> 'Come on, you dozy buggers, let's get moving', he exhorted us, dancing on top of a heap of rubble. 'There's snipers about, sir, snipers,' several of us warned him. 'Snipers? There are no bloody snipers. Get up! Follow me!' Reluctantly we began to rise when a single shot rang out and Lt Robinson rolled down the rubbish heap, shot in the back. I never heard whether he survived his terrible wound.

Once again Stan found his platoon without an officer. One evening a new officer had visited each slit trench to introduce himself to the troops. He was never seen again, having been shot whilst attending to his ablutions at dawn. Senior sergeants took over and also fell by the wayside. In spite of his reputation for eccentric behaviour Stan found himself unwillingly promoted to corporal so that he could pass on the fruits of his experience to fresh recruits.[5]

Not all tactical surprises drew blood. Capt. Charlie Robertson was most concerned about the feeding of his company of 7th Black Watch. Unlike their tank friends, who could light a primus stove, even if illegally, on the turret floor of a tank, the 'footsloggers' had no way of providing their own adequate hot meals. Charlie had therefore undertaken the role of lead 'Meals on Wheels' man, carrying hot meals in his jeep up to forward posts which the cooks or quartermaster might not locate. Trying to take a short cut through the trees his 'mad driver' did a racing turn around a bend in a narrow lane and braked violently. They were virtually queuing up behind several German infantrymen who were themselves drawing rations from a German vehicle. Charlie's mad driver reversed gear, jammed down the accelerator and shot out of there in faster reverse than even he had ever driven forward. Fortunately the hungry foe did not have time to swap mess tins for machine pistols.[6]

Lt Tony Faulkner, commanding the lead troop of C Sqn, 1NY, was also in for a shock of a more pleasant fashion. Having reached their objective, a farm near La Roche, Tony's thoughts, like those of any soldier, inevitably turned to farm produce. Checking that there was no apparent sign of enemy and always ready to lead, the lieutenant handed command over to his gunner and approached the farm, shepherded by one or two Black Watch privates. He made his way cautiously to a barn that might be housing chickens. Suddenly the door opened violently, as though thrust aside by the muzzle of a machine-gun. A moment's pause! And then an attractive 16-year-old girl emerged, followed by a priest and a dozen civilians. Tony was amazed to learn that the young woman was a renowned Resistance leader who had contrived to shelter the endangered group from retreating enemy rearguards.[7]

Often the furthest soldier forward was the artillery observation officer; his title abbreviated to FOO and commonly known to ordinary soldiers as 'our Foo'. In the uncertain battle situations, the bleak winter and appalling terrain in the Ardennes, the very act of finding his vantage point could be difficult and dangerous for the FOO. On one particular day this proved problematic for Jack Swaab in his jeep. His diary recorded, '10 January. 1300. Warizy. Nightmare day yesterday. We set out at 0800 and eventually after much ditching, sliding and cursing reached our mountainous O.P. [Observation Point]. The snow was knee deep but at first visibility was clear and we had a fine view.'

It had been a difficult journey, but it was to get worse. As so often happens in the frontline, there was a change of orders and Jack was required to move from his recently possessed OP to another observation point. This entailed a trek down the mountain, across open ground under fire and up another perilous ascent; all the time in advance of the waiting lines of infantry in their slit trenches. Jack reached the new start line; his wireless promptly broke down. He was following a bulldozed track through an area full of knocked out enemy tanks and bodies still unburied. In his laconic way he wrote that 'a few German tanks threw high velocity shells about the place'. That meant that guns large enough to knock out a 30 ton tank, and accurate enough to hit first time at 1,000 yards, were firing at and just missing his fast moving vehicle. Freezing conditions played havoc with over-heated engines, so Jack ran out of oil and had to stop and top up: an exposed target. His engine boiled over and he needed to find water. It took him forty minutes to refill the radiator. They had been moving since dawn and now night had fallen.

The new observation point was still ahead and much higher yet. Searchlights playing on the clouds made ghostly reflections:

> The artificial moonlight cast a glow over the snowy wilderness and dark patches of Christmas trees. Twice we got ditched and twenty times nearly ditched. I was driving the jeep and had Butcher and Allen with me. We hadn't eaten or brewed since 0730. The track was bloodier every minute. We reached here about 2200. Ronnie's half-track turned up and soon after midnight we had a meal.

This saga of patience, endurance and sheer contempt of danger merely constituted Jack's journey to the start of his observation duties. It would then be necessary, at any time of day or night, to observe the direction from which any enemy guns might be firing, and to watch constantly for furtive movement of ground troops. Just another day and night along the route from Normandy to the German border.[8]

Even in the frontline the average officer or NCO was still burdened by the chores of normal military routine. REME Capt. E.A. Egli was struggling with problems of compassionate leave. Officers still had to censor letters, although at this stage of the war, and with the armies in daily hand-to-hand contact, such censorship served little purpose. Often the censors became aware of family circumstances which would eventually evolve into a request for leave. Two cases were emerging for Egli's consideration. One tank mechanic told him that his young son was seriously ill and asking for his father:

> I immediately took the matter up with [34 armoured] Brigade.... As the Brigade was in action there was reluctance to let anybody leave. This man was an excellent tank mechanic and we were all working hard trying to keep the Brigade up to strength. In the meantime the man was getting letters from home describing the worsening condition of his son and he himself became very distressed before we could arrange his leave. I heard afterwards that he got home just before his son died.[9]

The other case was quite a frequent family situation. A tank mechanic had been advised that his wife had left him and was living with another man. A very human story, but in the welter of battle it was not sufficiently important to merit leave. Egli and his colleagues were left with a different kind of problem. The brigade workshops were sited beside an icy, fast-flowing river and the worried trooper began to walk beside the river in obvious distress whenever he was free from duty. The only thing Egli could do was to set up a watch among the man's comrades to ensure that he did not commit suicide. Fortunately news came that the wife had repented and returned to the family fold.

Capt. Sandy Saunders, 1NY, was faced with a language problem. He was approached by a distressed elderly Belgian man, beckoning urgently and mumbling in a strange rural dialect. The words which Sandy could comprehend were, '*Trente-quatre... trente-quatre... trente-quatre...*' Sandy sought enlightenment, '*Quels trente-quatre? D'ou? Qui est-ce que?*' The man continued with his plaintive routine until the exasperated officer bellowed, 'Thirty-four what, for God's sake?' But the old man was leading him through a door, down into a cellar. Bodies lay in a pile. All males. All shot through the head. All shot by pistol at powder-burn range. Forcing down the rising vomit, Sandy counted. 'Thirty-four'. Leaving the man there still mumbling, '*Trente-quatre*', Sandy hurried to report. He was hustled to higher authority, told to write a report and keep his damned mouth shut.[10]

By this time the German movement had reversed into overall retreat. American troops from the south hurried to meet British, Canadian and other American troops in the north in an effort to cut off lingering enemy units. The German vanguard had become a rearguard, almost as invisible as in the initial surprise attack: all too evident in massed attack; only too elusive in well-trained retreat.

The NY diary recorded, '14 Jan. 2 Derby Yeo met Americans. White camouflage paint only just arrived near Hives on River Ourthe. Every day frustrating sounds of Pzs but no sightings. Infantry dashing from copse to copse in heavily wooded country.' 2nd Derbyshire Yeomanry were the reconnaissance regiment of 51st Highland Division and had met with American infantry near La Roche, closing off any enemy troops inside the pincer. Wally Tarrant's tank, 1NY, had ploughed through the snow to halt outside the Hotel de Liege. Having advanced all that way in a huge, armoured monster, and exposed in vivid Normandy camouflage paint against the pure snows, Wally and friends had the inspiration of invading the hotel, 'borrowing' white sheets and adding some measure of snow camouflage to the tanks. They were not to know that the imminent arrival of white paint would coincide firstly with the sullying and browning of the snow, and then with a local thaw; colours changing back to black and green.

Forward units might have been frustrated in their often unsuccessful attempts to locate German troops. They may have sensed that the 'Battle of the Bulge' was phasing out. But there was still time for death, in ones and twos, usually in a remote, anonymous patch of woods and often not by the route normally taken by a fatal bullet.

A German Panther tank had at last been brought to bay by 1NY on their last day of fighting in the region. The Panther was the tank most feared by many Allied tank crews. Slightly smaller than the Tiger, but much more mobile, it could still offer to the Allied guns a front shield of armour too thick to penetrate. A gunner would aim at the almost invisible join between hull and turret or hope that his commander could manoeuvre to obtain a side view of the Panther.

This enemy tank was skilfully hidden in woodland. The muzzle flash and smoke as its gun fired were much less noticeable than that of hidden Shermans or Cromwells. Tpr Phil Bonney had only recently joined 1NY and wanted to prove his capability. Here was the golden opportunity. His eye was quick enough to spot the gun flash as the Panther fired across the open snowfield. With only a moment's adjustment of traverse and range, Bonney fired. His red tracer sparks sailed in the customary slight loop and impacted in a tiny shower of fire on the weak point of the enemy vehicle. Bonney was rewarded by the sight of the resultant explosion, smoke rising from the target and distant bodies vaulting through the air and scurrying for safety.

Tommy Tucker, wireless operator on the troop corporal's tank, loaded the 75mm gun after his gunner too had aimed at the Panther. Tommy said to himself, 'That's finished for the day'. Rarely, at that date, had enemy tanks appeared as more than a single quickly vanishing gunshot or two. Cpl Hughie McGranahan, popular regimental middleweight boxing champion and a scholar who could quote Greek poetry, ordered, 'Keep watching' as, with eyes just peering above the turret rim, he suited actions to words. At that moment heavier German artillery from a distance calculated the approximate range of the British tanks and fired unsighted. Most shells fell short and threw up large clouds of snow. One rogue shell screamed through the trees, smashed into a branch above the tank, exploded and battered McGranahan's head with huge steel and wooden splinters.

Tommy Tucker was distraught. Good companions after many months of battle, crew mates often broke the strict rules of discipline. Before the battle Tommy and Hughie had disagreed over when to eat the day's rations; Tommy being known as the hungriest man in 1NY. Tommy, yielding to Hughie's decision, had said, 'Oh, go to Hell, Hughie'. Now he had to help extract the flaccid, bloody body of his commander and friend through the narrow turret ring. This was always a physically difficult and emotionally fraught task. He could hear his own words ringing again and again in his mind, 'Go to Hell, Hughie'.[12]

Death also stalked areas away from the frontline. A distressed private of the Gordons, wearing the Africa Star which marked him as a remarkable survivor of years of battle, decided to desert to the safer haven of Antwerp. On the run from the military police he sought shelter in a cinema. A German V1 flying bomb, timed so that its engine would cut out over the city, fell on the cinema, the roof collapsed, the building caught fire and very few people escaped. The Gordon private did not.[13]

On a more legitimate visit, 1NY's Sgt Danny Danson, Tpr Blakiston, Tommy Tucker, 'Shorty' Coleman and others had been transported by a regimental lorry to Antwerp on a forty-eight hour leave pass. Shorty had decided to do a 'crawl' around the Salvation Army, YMCA and other canteens. Tommy went to do a lone 'recce' of the red light district to complete his education. Danson and Blakiston wanted to see the Wild West film in the cinema. As they were watching, the even wilder west of actual battle burst in on them in the shape of that same V1 bomb. They were numbered with the Gordon private and several hundred others.

Life was also hazardous for the civilian population in the Ardennes. Bill Robertson, who had enjoyed Belgian hospitality behind the battle lines, observed:

> The population of the Ardennes were understandably cautious for they had been occupied by the Germans for some years, then liberated by the Americans, only to be reoccupied by the Germans, sometimes with drastic consequences when revenge killings of Resistance people were carried out by an SS execution squad.

As 1NY tanks, now resplendent in redundant white camouflage paint, pulled out of the Ardennes sector, Capt. Michael Rathbone noted a similar attitude among civilians. He was leading the column with orders to entrain at the railway sidings in Ciney. Although not the type of person to consider himself a conquering hero, the modest schoolmaster might have expected a cheer or at least a friendly wave from local people. But the streets were almost deserted. He saw 'pale Belgian faces peeping out through windows at the retreating

Shermans. Retreating?' He understood their reticence even more when a young Belgian waved to him, jumped on the tank and said that although the SS had been in the village for only a few hours, they had dragged out and shot suspected Resistance men. Now the liberating Shermans were visibly leaving again.

Still awaiting orders for another possible battle, Bill Robertson and his fellow malefactors were surprised and worried to be summoned before the Gordons colonel in regard to the earlier incident described on p. 41. Battalion commanders normally only judged very serious offences. However, the men had disobeyed an order 'in the presence of the enemy', even if it was only to do latrine duty for that enemy. 'I'm surprised to see you here, Clay', the colonel said to Bill's corporal, but then, fully aware of the idiosyncrasies of soldiers, the commander proceeded to unravel the sequence of the 'shite' incident. Finally he decided to change the 'in the presence of the enemy' charge to a minor offence and routinely asked if the men would accept his punishment. 'Yes, sir', they chorused and were promptly deducted four days pay. Later the miscreants were pleased to hear that their lieutenant had received a discreet private lecture.

As the troops withdrew to fulfil new missions back in the Netherlands, artilleryman Jack Swaab would sum up the sentiments of many on both sides of the firing line:

> I shan't forget for a long time the red blood on the white snow, and the tanks splattered with blood where the A.P. shot had riddled them. Or the nights of agonising cold and fear with the battle loud and angry on all sides as 'ignorant armies clashed by night' – the numbness and pain of feet, the drenching tiredness, the twinges of fear, and the night sky lit by flashes, and the whistle of shells nearby as one crouched in the snowy ditch, soaked and tired beyond belief.[14]

Throughout their time in the Ardennes, British, Canadian and Polish troops had been holding long defence lines, often indistinct amid flooding waterways and unfortified other than with impromptu trenches and barricades. In spite of the concentration of elite forces in the Ardennes, *Wehrmacht* troops elsewhere continued to be aggressive, even at this stage of the war, patrolling and probing at weak points in the Allied dispositions. There were sudden raids by small groups, constant observation by snipers and the ever-present danger of the shrieking Moaning Minnie mortar bombs. From time to time sweet revenge was taken.

Capt. Joe Brown had joined up in 1939 as a private in the 8th Territorial battalion of the Royal Scots. He had then been promoted to signaller; to signals officer; to intelligence officer; was now a captain with 7th/9th Royal Scots and would become a major. As they held a supposedly quiet stretch of the River Maas, a patrol encountered two male civilians ostensibly escaping from the German-held far bank in a small boat. A fluent linguist in the Royal Scots Intelligence Section was suspicious of the men's accents. They were arrested for further questioning. Word eventually came back that they were soldiers of the 'Brandenburg Sabotage Division', a unit of which Joe had never heard. Their mission had been to infiltrate Allied positions and cause mayhem by any and every means. Joe never learned the infiltrators' fate: soldiers wearing civilian clothes were likely to be summarily shot. Sinister impostors at first sight, they were in fact very brave men.[15]

On 30 December Joe's battalion had been redeployed to a place called Bruggerhof, naturally named by the troops 'Bugger off!' There they were constantly harassed by the Moaning Minnies. One evening, as Joe started a two-hour duty officer shift, the field telephone rang. An anxious voice said, 'Is that Mr Broon, sir? I have a compass-bearing of a mortar firing tracer'. Joe quickly contacted other forward units and asked for immediate compass-bearings on the mortar tracer. Plotting the various angles he was able to call artillery fire down precisely on a location which on the map seemed to be a likely place to hide a mortar. The mortar firing ceased.

The battalion commander was pleased with the presumed result. It so happened that an artillery Lysander aircraft was available nearby. The Lysander was a light plane with an exceptionally low minimum speed; it could remain in the sky at speeds when other aircraft would have stalled or entered into a fatal spin and fallen to earth. On the strength of the captain's skill in locating the mortar, the colonel was able to arrange for him to go up in the Lysander to check on the result of the action. Whilst Joe was delighted to be able to see the 'totally pulverised target scene', the Lysander flight had another pleasant significance. 'This was only my third flight in the air: the first was on a five-shilling trip during an air circus which flew round the hills of Peebleshire when I was 17; the second in a glider on air-transportable training.' For most British foot soldiers in 1945 a flight in an aeroplane was still a very heady experience.

After six years of fighting and several promotions Joe was still innocent enough to record, 'it was an eerie feeling flying over the enemy in such a flimsy aircraft: I was careful about how I moved my heavy army boots in case they pierced the thin skin of the aircraft's frame.' At about the same time he was instructed to parade at a large hall where officers were to be addressed by FM Montgomery. Typically Monty's opening remark was, 'Have a good cough and then no more of it!' He then charged that officers, in spite of the shock of the Ardennes breakthrough, were to return to unit and tell their men, 'that I, Monty, am in charge and all is well'. Brown himself thought that to tell the braw Jocks such a thing would merely cause ribald amusement. On the contrary, the lower ranks were impressed and encouraged by the message.

Much of an infantryman's daily life revolved around endless patrols. Whilst often proving frustrating and yielding no apparent gain, these had a dual purpose: to correctly map the enemy's positions and to keep the enemy, and perhaps one's own troops, on their toes at all times. One routine patrol was described by the scribe of the Royal Regiment of Canada, and aptly includes both the boredom and the sudden tragedy of such enterprises:

> The regiment was holding positions near Groesbeek on the forward edge of a gentle ridge facing flat low fields, on which fortifications of the Siegfried Line could be vaguely descried and beyond that the vast black shadow of the Reichswald Forest, historically an area where legions have disappeared since Roman times. Some of the Royals were in cellars and others in trenches. Because of the close proximity of the enemy, movement in daylight was most dangerous so patrols took place at night. On the night of 12 January Lt George Fleury, already twice wounded, was ordered to take out a patrol supported by C48828 Sgt Ed Retallick, also previously wounded. Their group would include B67191 Cpl Tom McIntosh, who had been with the regiment since 1939, served in Iceland before landing in Normandy. B42754 Pte Ed Wells had also just returned from hospital

after wounding, whilst B126811 L/Cpl Bert Bainerman, M104753 Pte Bill Bellingham and M42884 Pte Buddy Jones fell in behind.[16]

Bud Jones was one of the most remarkable characters in the Canadian ranks. He was the grandson of an slave who had escaped from the southern states of the USA and made his way, via the escape network of those days, to Canada. Bud was a middleweight boxer of Olympic champion standard and was only denied a gold medal by freak circumstances. He served on in Korea and was a fitness fanatic who ran marathons into old age. It should also be remembered that, at this stage of the war, all the Canadians were double volunteers. As Canada had no conscript system in 1939 each man had to volunteer for service and then, as no Canadian could be compelled to fight overseas, he had to volunteer a second time. Only in January 1945 was the new type of conscripted soldier finding his way up to the Royals as reinforcement.

At the time of Arnhem, months earlier, gliders of 82nd US Airborne Division had crashed or been shot down near Groesbeek with their occupants still inside. They had lain undisturbed in this no-man's-land until now. 'The objective tonight,' said Lt Fleury, 'is to quietly occupy one or two of those gliders and use them as forward observation posts', without disturbing the bodies which would now be a familiar sight to the German troops. Dress would be snow parkas, advancing in total silence in monkey crouch or belly crawl. Mines hidden by the snow might be lying in the way of the patrol, but it was hoped that, if a mine detonated, its force would be reduced by the covering of ice-solid snow. One or two privates were tempted to respond, 'Some hopes!'[17]

The patrol set out at 20.00 hours with Fleury and McIntosh leading. After a long, slow, silent crawl the first glider was reached, as Bud Jones described, 'still half full with ghostly soldiers sitting as though awaiting our arrival. An eerie presence.' Worse still, all the bodies had been booby-trapped with explosives. The patrol would have to find an empty glider. But at that point a flare shot up. Every one hugged the ground. 'BOOM! Cpl McIntosh had activated a Schu-mine' as he plunged down to the ground. The entire area was immediately drenched with machine-gun fire from all angles, but it was random fire and not aimed accurately at the hidden patrol. As the first flare died down, Ed Wells crawled forward with the stretcher he had been carrying and tried to attend to McIntosh without rising too much from the concealment of the snow. More flares and machine-gun tracer illuminated the scene. 'During an excruciatingly long wait we had to suppress the absurd but horrific feeling that the dead Americans were watching us in our plight, willing us to lie doggo.'

George Fleury then gave the hand signal to abort and withdraw. Sgt Retallick ordered Bellingham to push on ahead and warn the Royals behind them that they were withdrawing. Jones joined Wells in dragging the wounded McIntosh through the snow, knowing that as it became light their tracks would be clear to the machine gunners. Retallick stayed as the rearguard until the others were under some kind of cover and within reach of anxious comrades. It was now well after 03.00 hours.

The lieutenant watched as Wells, with enough space to do a thorough examination, checked the wounded man. Wells sadly shook his head. The snow had not given any protection from the limb-shattering blast of the anti-personnel mine. 'Tom McIntosh was dead. Wells delivered the body to the Medical Officer, Retallick notified Padre Appleyard and Fleury reported to the Commanding Officer the failure of the patrol.' It is unlikely that the colonel would have been surprised. Nothing achieved and one more man dead. Duty had been done. Just another day.

After the distraction of the Ardennes campaign three British divisions (7th Armoured, 43rd Wessex and 52nd Lowland) were now launched into Operation Blackcock; the battle of the Roer triangle.

The offensive aimed to clear a maze of waterways and villages around the fortress town of Heinsberg – a strategically important area for the crossing of the mighty River Rhine. The Roer battle is a contender for the title of least known, but relatively most important battle of the war. An official report stated that 'it proceeded from stage to stage almost entirely as planned and was successfully completed with minimum casualties'.[18] This might explain its lack of publicity value, but that was no consolation to the large number of soldiers and civilians wounded, and the relatives of the considerable number killed.[19]

It was in this area that Capt. Joe Brown saw an act of extreme courage, and also became prey to the dangers which constantly beset footsloggers of all ranks. Moving towards Heinsberg, Joe was accompanying his colonel in trying to link up with another battalion on the flanks of their advance. They had a machine-gun in the protection group, but unexpectedly 'shared the unforgettable experience of being sniped at across a large stretch of open ground by an 88mm dual anti-tank/aircraft gun' capable of knocking out Allied tanks at 2,000 yards range. They then ran into an enemy infantry group in snow smocks and supported by a 54 ton Tiger tank, also sporting an 88mm gun. By 'fire and movement', no doubt some of the movement quite rapid, the HQ party crossed the open ground.

Where there should have been defences manned by an entire company of another unit, they found in the trenches only one survivor. He was a badly wounded signaller with both legs missing, but still contriving to send wireless messages back to the artillery and valiantly assisting the platoons forward of his trench. 'He somehow survived and was awarded the Distinguished Conduct Medal but... he should have received the Victoria Cross.'

Later, again crossing open ground on his own and without hearing anything, 'I was amazed to suddenly see, a mere footstep in front of me, that the ground had opened up and earth, stones and shrapnel were flying around me; immediately thought "minefield!" until the whine of another shell followed, and another'. Joe then knew that he had been wounded and deafened by the direct hit of a large shell at his feet. The Royal Scots RSM had seen what was happening, ran up and lifted Joe on to his shoulders, hurrying with him to the aid post. He was evacuated by an ambulance shared with a wounded German. After attention by a surgeon, he was transported back to a large hospital in Brussels; from there by air ambulance to Wiltshire; then on a stretcher train to Worcester where 'all the voluntary helpers swooped down on our stretchers and delightful ladies made sure we had filled in a post-card to our loved ones... if our labels [large luggage labels attached to the battledress pocket] said that it was in order, we were given cups of hot sweet tea.' The hospital evacuation service was possibly one of the best organised systems in the army.[20]

Lt Eric Smallwood commanding 3 Troop, A Squadron, 1st Royal Tank Regiment (1RTR), found that a sudden local thaw brought no easier progress than the previous icy snows. Tanks tended to wallow and sink in deep mud when leaving the road. The troop was tasked to advance to a crossroads at Schilberg. A Crocodile flamethrower, also a large armoured vehicle, was moving in the same direction and halted at the crossroads. 'In quick succession a jet of flame was followed by two explosions and the Crocodile rocked... caught fire, killing the crew instantly... an enormous explosion followed and the turret of the tank was blown off... thick black smoke laid a perfect smoke screen across the road.' The Crocodile had been hit by a lone Tiger tank. The mighty German tank had already knocked out a Cromwell tank from another squadron, which had been reduced from nineteen to six tanks. [21]

1RTR had Firefly tanks available – Shermans equipped with a much larger 17-pounder gun and able to kill a Tiger. But essentially their main tanks were the lighter and relatively thin-skinned Cromwells, and easy prey for a Tiger's 88-mm cannon. The Cromwell was, however, very fast and surprise sometimes was the only weapon against the big beast of the battle.

Smallwood tackled the Tiger in a game of cat and mouse. The Tiger was able to destroy any of his Cromwell tanks at 2,000 yards, and here they were moving amongst trees and houses at a couple of hundred yards range. Firing was coming from several directions. Smallwood instructed his four tanks to wait hidden until the Tiger's gun swung towards another direction. Then they would move into the open, fire and, if the Tiger's gun traversed towards them, reverse back behind houses. The Cromwell also had the advantage of a much faster turret traverse than the bigger tank. The RTR gunners gained several hits at 100 yards but without 'brewing' the Tiger, which they found to be like 'a slow moving pillbox with thick blocks of reinforced concrete fixed on its already massive front.'

At this point accurate mortar fire began to rain down on the British troop, although there were no German infantrymen in sight to direct such fire. It was apparent that there must be observers in the church tower able to see across the town and spot the British tanks. Solution: shoot up the church tower. However, the standard Cromwell 75-mm gun had restricted elevation ability and could not be raised high enough to hit the top of the church tower. Fortunately 1RTR had a special Cromwell available, mounting a 95-mm Howitzer and able to lob bigger shells higher. Lt Smallwood left his tank and climbed into a nearby attic to direct the fire of the Howitzer which, with three shots, rendered the tower inhospitable for observers. Meanwhile the marauding Tiger, possibly itself wounded, crawled off into the smoke eddying over and through the streets.

While the tank men enjoyed some kind of cover inside their vehicles, until the vehicles themselves became mobile crematoria, the infantry were out in the open streets. The thaw had muddied fields and flooded streams, and in certain places where the tanks could only halt and give supporting fire, the infantry had to wade on.

The Royal Scots platoon, which included Fusilier Dennis Donnini, left their trenches, but was pinned down by concentrated rifle and machine-gun fire emanating from enemy hidden in houses. Donnini was shot through the head and knocked out. After a while, with the reduced platoon still motionless, he recovered consciousness, rose and charged along the street for 30 yards in order to throw a grenade through a window. Shocked, the soldiers in the house ran out into the back garden and were pursued by the fusilier and two comrades. When one of the fusiliers fell wounded, Donnini, himself bleeding profusely, carried the man back to a barn, found a Bren gun and again charged forward, firing as he went. He was wounded again, but refused to retreat until a tragic, freak incident intervened: an enemy bullet hit the grenade which he was preparing to throw, exploding the grenade and killing the fusilier. He was awarded the Victoria Cross posthumously.[21]

Before D-Day, tank men were trained to shoot their big guns at ranges of 500 to 1,000 yards. Quickly, like Lt Frank Gutteridge, they found that battle was to be much closer than that. During Operation Blackcock it was at close-quarters for everybody. Frank was standing by the turret of his tank to observe in the normal manner when 'something roared over my head and smashed into the roof of the barn behind me, blowing off my beret'. It was a solid shot capable of piercing inches of armour plate.

Frank continued:

Then to our total surprise two German officers came walking down the road, heedless of our presence until they realised who we were and dashed into a corner house. They popped out again and we let off at them, my sub-machine gun jamming as they got away, one probably wounded. At 13.30 my sergeant's tank was stalked by a bazooka man [extreme range 50 yards] and hit in the front. A brother officer in a light, thin-skinned Honey tank was fired at by a big SP gun and drove behind a house for refuge. The SP destroyed the house. The Honey sped behind another building. The SP smashed down that building, Another house to shelter behind. Another quick demolition job. Then the Honey commander put his trust in the vehicle's high speed, racing across open country, pursued unsuccessfully by tracer from the SP's armour-piercing shots.[22]

Even closer danger was experienced by Pte Webster of the Durham Light Infantry (DLI). During intense fighting in the vital town of St Joost, and up against skilled German paratroopers, the company of the DLI had been reduced to only thirty men; a third of the start-line strength. A few survivors had sought shelter in a loft and their opponents were firing through the roof tiles. These bullets, super-heated by their speed through the air, set fire to straw in the loft. The five Durhams had to yield to an overwhelming force. In the chaos Webster managed to escape and scramble through the buildings. Seeing a large industrial boiler he managed to climb inside. There he waited patiently until another attack by his own side allowed him to emerge, soaking wet, but free to fight again.[23]

Tpr Robertson of 2nd Lothian and Border Yeomanry (L&B) had a similar experience in the confusion which prevailed on both sides of a very indistinct line. Two L&B flail tanks were knocked out and surrounded by Germans. Although wounded, Robertson was marched away after having wounds roughly tended. A heavy British artillery 'stonk' caused the captors to dive for ditches. When they emerged, Robertson stayed put. Left alone he began an incredible wandering adventure. He walked in between Germans who were intent on man-handling big guns in retreat. Then he spent the night on a haystack 'where I was wretchedly cold. Next morning half-starved I set off again'. Robertson's wounds had been dressed but he was still in pain. Coming to an empty farm he found some bottled cherries on which he feasted; his first food for twenty hours. Seeing a group of men in the distance he reeled towards them, not knowing whether they were friend or foe. They proved to be medics of the 52nd Division who laid him on an old door and carried him to an ambulance.[24]

The frontline Germans also suffered and in some instances more than the attackers. One of the scourges for them was Canada's answer to the Moaning Minnie: the 'Land Mattress'. This was a mass of rocket tubes mounted on a lorry, each cylinder carrying ten pounds of explosives. To give this fearful weapon even more impact, ten lorries were positioned as one weapon and all their rockets fired as one salvo. Unlike the vertically falling *Nebelwerfer* bomb, the rockets had a direct trajectory. They emitted a terrifying sound akin to the rushing wind of a hurricane, coupled with an instantaneous, ground-shaking thunder and lightning effect. Prisoners taken after being subjected to a multiple rocket discharge of this type were variously reported as 'limbs paralysed, demented, incontinent, weeping, screaming'.

In situations like this the highest quality of leadership was required; even to the point of deliberately risking ones own life with no tactical objective other than to steady the troops. Maj. Peter Duckworth of the Royal Inniskilling Dragoon Guards was impressed by his colonel, Victor Paley, who had displayed an unusual version of disregard for his own life. As enemy shells fell, Paley would enquire in a loud voice, 'Are they coming or going?' When someone, on cue, replied, 'Coming!' Paley would take off his soft hat and put on his steel helmet. Then he himself would shout, 'No, going', and swap the helmet for his hat.[25]

With 8th King's Royal Irish Hussars in St Joost, the firing from both sides was so intense that tank crews were ordered to stay in their tanks. However, to help morale, Maj. John Gwynne called Lt Bill Bellamy out and proceeded to walk up and down an open stretch of road, discussing the squadron's next move with Bill who:

> ... found it difficult to concentrate on his conversation. Shots were whistling past us, over us and ricocheting off the road. I knew I could not lose face by suggesting to this tough fearless little man that our talk would be more meaningful in the shelter of a tank.[26]

As the author himself had experienced on a similar occasion, the response of rankers was that 'if the major can walk about in the open like that, I can at least sit firm in the tank and get on with my job without thinking about ducking out.'

Freakish happenings occurred in battle and injuries from accidents were frequent. Bill Bellamy, just promoted to captain, recorded that on the morning of 21 January a dense fog blanketed the battle area. The battle still had to carry on. The fog rolled back for a moment revealing three German anti-tank guns. One shot hit a Sherman Firefly as the fog closed in again. As the Firefly driver lost control, the 30 ton tank smashed through the walls of a house. The wooden floor collapsed and the tank crashed down into a deep cellar, its great gun twisted beyond repair. It was what might be called 'a home-made tank trap!'

With 1RTR, after a long spell of firing, Cpl Reg Spittles and crew were boiling out the big gun. Having completed the cleaning, and being in a counter-attack position, they then re-loaded the guns. As could happen, a machine-gun bullet 'cooked' in the breach of the gun and the shot sped down the street. It entered through a window and wounded a lieutenant who was taking part in an officer's conference. Reg would later receive a severe reprimand, not because the gun had misfired, but because the bullet hit an officer.

An even more painful episode for Reg occurred during another close-quarters fight. The turret of Reg's Cromwell had two escape hatches. Reg was standing with his head out of the commander's hatch and the wireless operator's hatch was closed down. The enemy infantry then started throwing grenades at the tank. Reg immediately ducked down and closed his hatch. But the operator, Tpr Baggully, heard the thuds above his head and thought that Reg was calling him to open up. So he did. And two grenades promptly fell into the tank. The sad toll of that freak error was that Baggully was wounded in the legs and lower body, Reg received shrapnel damage to his legs and abdomen, and Tpr Garrett had head and shoulder wounds. Tpr Wells had bailed out of the tank, but was lying in the road motionless. The corporal moved Wells into the ditch for safety and then turned to Garrett, only to see that the man had a piece of steel protruding between his eyes. In that moment of desperation Reg pulled the shrapnel fragment out of Garrett's head and applied a field dressing as the blood spurted forth. Remarkably this act of impromptu surgery had a successful outcome.

Even more inconsonant with frontline realities were absurd intrusions of peacetime military etiquette. L/Bdr R.W. Deans was astonished and frustrated to be withdrawn from his frontline signalling duties in order 'to take an upgrading test in appalling conditions… fortunately it proved to be a very fair test and we all passed out as Class II DOs' (driver operators). He was annoyed because he, and the other men tested, had been carrying out their duties under pressure to save their own lives, and that of those affected by his signals, in conditions that no formal test could replicate.[28]

Lt Frank Gutteridge had just lost two tanks, with two men killed and another two wounded, when he was sent back to Malines 'immediately' to pick up replacement officers. There he encountered an old style colonel, often characterised at the time as 'Colonel Blimp', who bawled out, 'Gutteridge, where's your belt?' Frank responded, 'Sir, I have come straight out of action and my belt is in a pack in B echelon'. The Colonel snorted, 'You are scruffy and a disgrace: I have a mind to have you arrested'. Then he huffed and puffed and shouted, 'Get out! Get out!' Frank could only imagine what his own colonel would have said if, desperately short of officers, he had learned that one of his troop leaders had been arrested for not wearing a largely ceremonial belt.[29]

Doughty warrior Bud Jones, Canadian Royals, was sitting in his slit trench near Groesbeek when the mail corporal delivered a thick envelope from Bud's mother. It contained the official notice that, as conscription had been introduced in Canada and as Bud was of the appropriate age, he must immediately report to his nearest barracks in Canada, on pain of severe sanctions. Bud toyed with the idea of asking his colonel for leave to go home and sign on. He was further disillusioned about the efficiency of the authorities when, on volunteering for service and checking birth certificates, he found that he was just one month older than his sister: a medical miracle, but obviously bureaucratically acceptable.[30]

At five foot six inches tall Ken Cardy, REME, was attached to the Guards and affectionately known to his six foot, six inches tall RSM (a familiar figure on guard at Buckingham Palace) as 'you 'orrible little REME man'. Oily and weary in his demanding mechanical recovery and repair duties, he received an urgent summons for all officers and senior NCOs to 'report forthwith!' Anticipating another major battle conference, he was astonished to be told to clean up and draw the best uniforms from echelon lorries. He and the others so summoned were then taken to Nijmegen and paraded at the local football stadium to be inspected by Montgomery and photographed by the press corps. 'Oh what a lovely war!' thought Ken, long before a film of that name was made.[31]

Back in the real world of battle, the NY diary read, 'Jan 25. Still cold. 46 degrees of frost. Regt alerted to hand in Shermans and train on amphibious carriers'. This presaged the operation of crossing the mighty River Rhine, but not until 24 March.

Peter White, a captain in the King's Own Scottish Borderers (KOSB), had suffered in another type of infantry carrier, the hastily assembled Kangaroo. This was a self-propelled tank with the gun taken out to make room for ten men:[32]

> Once seated, shivering and doubled up on the floor of icy steel we were soon wishing ourselves marching again. To touch the metal of these giant ice-boxes stung, and gloves damp with perspiration froze and clung to metal and weapons. Each Kangaroo had a girl's name. Mine was 'Lucy'. A brother officer was heard to remark 'Esther was the coldest b★★★★★ woman I have ever met'.[33]

White had good grounds for comparison because on another occasion 'we had been lying for three hours... part submerged in icy water and would be pinned into freezing immobility for a further ten hours... our rifle bolts kept freezing solid.'

With 2nd Ox and Bucks, Capt. Hugh Clark, MC, and his men had been issued with white camouflaged snow suits. However, there were not enough for everybody and had to be shared by those going out on patrol. 'The frozen snow the suits collected had no time to thaw and dry out and... were stiff and heavy', impairing movement. After 'a week the thaw set in and the frozen ground turned to mud'.[34]

Whilst others struggled to progress through snow or mud, Ken Cardy, back in denim overalls, found the conditions caused a different problem for his vehicle and his repair crew. As the thick snow disappeared, tank tracks began to dislodge and pick up cobblestones in village streets. The stones were either thrown into the air or spun into the track mechanism itself, clogging up the bogey wheels and causing the vehicles to slow to a halt. The mess of churned stone and damaged steel caused the engineers new headaches.

As the advancing troops gradually cleared the Roer triangle, casualties continued to mount daily, mostly due to accidents or enemy action. Signaller R. W. Deans, back from his trade test, heard over the air that 'German' tanks were approaching. After a moment of apprehension the message was changed to 'Sherman' tanks, and those tanks were from an American unit approaching from the south. Deans had no way of contacting the Americans directly. Suddenly those friends began to bombard the British unit, faintly perceived through smoke and fog. In a moment of real peril Deans saw Lt Bernaby-Atkins running forward and 'waving something on the end of a stick' to catch the attention of the Americans. Only recently troops had been deceived in the Ardennes by similar tricks perpetrated by the enemy. Fortunately the Americans gave Bernaby-Atkins the benefit of the doubt and ceased fire.

Peter White, a toughened soldier, saw savagery at its worst. When 800 yards forward of his position stood 'an isolated, white-draped Sherman... had struck a mine... the crew crouched against it trying to repair the blown-off track'. Two explosions, a 'black tumbling pall of smoke', and the crew scrambling for safety indicated that the Sherman had probably been hit again by shots from an unseen enemy tank. One of the crew, obviously dazed, tried to run back down the open road. Two shots rang out. He tried to double back to take cover by the tank. 'Another crackle of fire and he crumpled and rolled, skidding in the snow'. He tried to get up. A longer burst of machine-gun fire 'spun his over-clad body, and he lay still'. Several mortar bombs were then brought down on the place where the body lay.

Not far from that road, L/Cpl Henry Eric Harden of the Royal Army Medical Corps saw three marines of his 45 Royal Marine Commando fall; seriously wounded. In situations like that witnessed by Peter White, Harden went out to tend the fallen men. Whilst doing this he was shot in the side. Undaunted he carried one man back to safety. Then, gathering a stretcher party, he went out again across the open ground. Sadly, as they were nearing safety a burst of machine-gun fire killed the commando they were carrying. Harden still went back to care for Lt Corey who had insisted on being tended last. Harden managed to bring the lieutenant within reach of cover when he himself was shot through the head and killed. He was awarded the Victoria Cross posthumously.[35]

If soldiers were suffering and dying, many civilians were in an even worse position, often without recourse to rescue and first aid. In Sint Odilienberg a family trying to escape on a horse-drawn wagon had suffered a direct hit by a German shell. The elderly driver and the horse were killed and the others injured. There being no local hospital available, Doctor Harry Stapert had turned his large house into an impromptu hospital and became a local legend for his bravery and medical skill. The German evacuation officer had already visited the house and ejected anyone who was not wounded, including the anxious parents of injured children. All civilians had to depart the town immediately. Dr Stapert then witnessed an exceptional event which revealed the occasional chivalry still found in war.

Two German paratroopers burst into the doctor's house carrying a comrade badly wounded in the knee. Dr Stapert led them to the makeshift operating theatre in his basement. As the two fit men departed hurriedly, he heard the wounded soldier say '*Schreibst Du meiner Frau was passiert ist?*' ('Write to my wife and tell her what has happened'). Almost as soon as the two fit soldiers had left, and while the doctor was working on the wound, he heard shouting from above – 'The Tommies are here!' Dr Stapert went up to investigate and encountered a British officer who was insisting on examining all the patients to see if there were any enemy soldiers lurking there. They descended to the basement. They checked the patients one by one until they came to the operating table, on which lay the helpless and now terrified German.

After a moment's pause, the British lieutenant took a pack of cigarettes from his pocket, lit one and offered it to the German.

'You'll be alright, boy', he said. 'And as quickly as he had appeared the British officer was up and gone into the battle that was still going on'.[36]

A comparison of casualty statistics is revealing. In one town only, Montfort, the number of civilians killed was 186. Throughout the battle the highest number of casualties suffered by any division, 52nd Lowland, was 101.

This does not include the traumas of forced evacuation without destination, which in the case of Roermond alone numbered 12,000 women, children and elderly men. There must be added to this 'the senseless destruction of churches and windmills' (although some were used as observation points by the enemy), the great number of houses rendered uninhabitable, and 'many acres of farming land become useless as a result of a seemingly unlimited use of minefields'. In spite of all this the Dutch civilians remained 'hugely supportive to their liberators'.

The stubborn defences in front of the River Roer had been overcome. Roermond itself 'was left behind as a ghost town, populated by only a handful of adventurers who dared to stay'.[37]

Another river, the mighty Maas provided an almost insuperable problem. The 51st Highland Division needed to cross near Gennep against bitter opposition. However, the Maas can flood and vary in width from 200 yards to 1,300 yards. The lives of many men depended on the correct calculation of the bridge needed to cross the river.

When Den Bosch was liberated RE Maj. Ted Hunt, a D-Day landing-barge expert, went to the former Nazi HQ at the Town Hall and rescued the vital plans of Dutch waterways before they could be pillaged. His colleague Constant Lambrechtsen, a Dutch waterways engineer, reconnoitred despite the risk of capture and inevitable torture by the Gestapo. Together they calculated that on the day of the attack, 20 February, the river would be a massive 1,334 yards wide as the winter snows thawed. A bridge of linked floating barges was constructed in seven days, enabling the Highlanders to cross dry-shod and fight a successful battle at the cost of forty-six killed.[38]

CHAPTER FOUR

THOSE FATAL FORESTS

They cut down trees for the horsemen to ride over. They dug trenches, laying leaves on them that they might not be seen.

(Herodotus, 440 BC)

'Sappers of the Royal Engineers worked around the clock clearing mines and laying timber across muddied tracks. Signalmen toiled to lay lines. At the sharp end men crouched in their slits. Runners became mired as the mud sucked at their boots. The rain had become incessant.'[1]

'The Churchills had been compelled to sit on log platforms to avoid bogging down.' Some tanks had already bogged down to turret-top level and had been left for weeks before special equipment could be obtained to recover them. Some tanks had turrets lifted, either by mud or fallen trees, or traverses wrecked by guns hitting trees. This, as technical officer Egli reported, combined with mine casualties reduced the regiments (of 34th Armoured Brigade) to about one-third of their original strength.[2]

Tpr A.J. Carder of 5th Inniskillings Dragoon Guards (7th Armoured Division – the 'Desert Rats') was reluctant to sleep under his tank for it was rumoured that one tank sank down onto a sleeping crew and killed them. Normally the crew would dig a hole about 2 feet by 6 feet, put the bedding into the hole, and then run the tank over the hole to give cover from airbursts and mortar fire. On one occasion 'it rained so heavily that at 3am we woke up in 3 to 4 inches of water.

All our bedding and ourselves were soaked. We looked more like drowned rats than Desert Rats.'³ The solid ground of ice and snow had suddenly been transformed into treacherous swamp.

To Ken Cardy the whole scene seemed like a comedy film. Responsible for recovering other brewed or blundering tanks, Ken also became a victim of the extraordinary conditions in which Operation Veritable was launched in February 1945:

> In a short time the first troop crossing over what appeared good ground, turned out to be a bog, thick gluey mud and were all bogged down. We went to the rescue… and got bogged down too. The C.O. arrived and he went down. With the help of an artillery tractor, our pulley block and our longest cable we got out, caked in mud.

As his Guards unit continued to advance there was nothing more of comedy. They were in 'very hostile country, heavy shelling, mortaring and booby traps everywhere and the enemy being mostly SS Panzer Grenadiers.'⁴

Higher ranking officers like Lt-Col Denny Whitaker were now aware of what had happened. The Germans had 'detonated holes in the Rhine's winter dikes, allowing the already rain-soaked marshlands to fill up'. He remembered that 'on February 7, D-minus-One, the men of 1st Canadian Scottish climbed out of their bunks and gazed with wonder at the surrounding fields. "The Tide's in!" they exclaimed'.

The immediate objective of Operation Veritable was to clear the land between the Rivers Maas and Rhine. This meant breaking through two areas of thick forest: the Reichswald and the Hochwald. Forests are always hazardous traps for advancing troops. In both world wars forests had been defended until all the trees had been razed to the ground. And long before 1945 the Germans had constructed solid defence works to further increase the difficulties for attackers. Yet an advance beyond the forests would make it possible to mount a crossing of the Rhine, opening the way to the best terrain for a fast advance into Germany and quickly ending the war.

Corps commander Horrocks had climbed into a windmill which Capt. George Blackburn was using as an artillery OP, and had viewed the planned battlefield whilst the snow still lay smooth and serene:

Across the silent white valley, dotted here and there with lifeless farm-houses, the dark evergreen mass of the Reichswald frowns down from its ridge; mysterious and formidable – so dense and easily fortified that it forms the lower bastion of the Siegfried Line.[5]

It was impressive for a mere captain to squat alongside a corps commander, and even more exalted luminaries later on, and help plan an attack. However, to battle-wise George Blackburn it was even more ominous when lower ranks intruded on his windmill sanctuary:

But when company commanders returned with platoon commanders, maps were marked with razor-sharp pencils. Huddling over their maps before the window of your mill with their subalterns, not speaking for minutes on end as they peered out at the ground they knew they'd have to cross – where even a fold in the ground could turn out to be of ultimate consequences to their lives and to the lives of their men – they would sometimes ask, in a quiet voice, barely above a whisper, questions like, 'Is that a ditch out there, running left at 11 o'clock from that last glider with the broken tail?'

Capt. Jack Swaab, at an artillery briefing, heard that 1,000 guns had been assembled for a barrage which Montgomery himself said would be bigger than the bombardment at El Alamein. The artillery would be charged with destroying five fortified towns.[6] George Blackburn noted that there would be a rolling barrage and that yellow smoke would be fired to alert the infantry at the moment when the barrage would be making a leap forward. The 15th Scottish Division would be advancing in Kangaroos, tanks, mine-sweeping flails, flame-throwing Crocodiles and AVREs, the latter armed with mortar petards or carrying devices for bridging and ditching.

A system had been developed whereby, when a planned barrage was not involved, a FOO could radio and cite a point on the map and call for a Mike, Uncle or Victor target. For a Mike target twenty-four guns would fire immediately. An Uncle target seventy-two guns would respond, and at the call of a Victor target 216 guns would be used, giving speed and accuracy at the shout of one man of subaltern rank. This was a system evolved by a British officer, Brig. H.J. Parham and, according to George Blackburn, would allow a lieutenant or captain to wield an artillery concentration 'beyond the wildest dreams of even field marshals and five-star generals of other nations'.

Both the infantryman on the ground and the tank commander ordering 'Driver, advance!' were concerned about the possibility of mines where it had been impossible to check the ground immediately under the noses of the enemy's guns. Capt. Ian Hammerton and his flail tanks of XX Dragoons had cleared a minefield and were advancing in a double-width lane at just over 1 mph. This was a desperately slow speed in the face of enemy anti-tank guns but the maximum at which flail tanks could sweep the ground effectively. Ian called for the Guards' attack tanks to pass through but 'they don't budge. They must think it's too narrow to pass through'. So the Crab flails had to repeat their previous risk-laden operation to double the width of the mine-free zone. A little later Ian would see something he had not seen since D-Day, eight months previously. He actually saw Germans in numbers; they were moving in amongst the forest trees. 'Normally the well-hidden enemy were invisible in their camouflaged bunkers.'[7]

The always observant technician Capt. Ernest Egli noted down the procedure for attacking one of the many solid pillboxes of the long-established defences.

> Isolation of the pillbox by wreathing it in smoke on flanks and rear, either from artillery fire or a Churchill Mk V tank which had a smoke-firing 95-mm Howitzer gun.
>
> Other 'normal' Churchill tanks fired 75-mm HE shells through the loopholes of the pillbox. [Sometimes this produced immediate white flag surrender].
>
> With the tank troop covering it, another Churchill, an AVRE [manned by Royal Engineers] fired a projectile 'the size of a small dustbin' to blast open the reinforced concrete around the gun slit.
>
> A Crocodile [Churchill flamethrower] squirted sticky flame into the restricted space and caused fatal burning to any who did not come out into the open and surrender.[8]

Here tribute should be paid to the soldiers and equipment of the extraordinary 79th Armoured Division; a unique formation which never fought as a division, but always in small numbers loaned out as and when needed. It was equipped with special vehicles designed for particular tasks, such as those mentioned above and others including instant bridge building, and familiarly known as 'Funnies'. It was commanded by a man regarded as a mechanical genius, Maj.-Gen. Sir Percy Hobart, and consisted of ten tank regiments, three of them manned by Royal Engineers. At this time it was also taking over other armoured regiments to furnish them with Buffalo amphibious troop carriers for the Rhine Crossing.

There was much open ground to be crossed before clearing the forests and, whilst there were carefully planned mass attacks, equally hazardous small patrols were still necessary. The Royal Regiment of Canada was again required to mount one amongst very many such patrols. Lt Gordon Matheson's 10 Platoon was chosen. Like many small units it was understrength and had to be reinforced from other platoons to a total of forty men for the purpose. The idea was to quietly enter a group of houses situated between the main opposing lines, and, if possible, occupy them.

The patrol set out at 02.30 hours in the night mists and seemed to be progressing well when one random Very light was fired, illuminating the entire area. Matheson charged through a hedge into the house, his men firing on either side of him. Six enemy soldiers lay dead and the rest seemed to have fled. The Royals still moved carefully, stopping to sniff the air. Some soldiers had the ability to smell an enemy. Some males have the ability to distinguish what perfume a woman is wearing and give it a name. Soldiers in battle exuded a much stronger 'perfume'. Even the new battledress blouse and trousers issued to a British soldier were first treated with a highly odorous substance. The stench of this caused many a young soldier to pause before risking an encounter with a pretty girl who might resent the smell. German uniforms carried a very distinctive odour, as did their ration food. Experienced soldiers like Bud Jones or Jack Williams were experts in this smelling-out practice.[9]

Almost as soon as Matheson was satisfied that the house was safe the Germans launched a counter-attack which the Canadians repulsed. The probing patrol now changed into providing a firm base support as Maj. Suckling attacked with company strength, although he had only fifty men remaining in that company. The day brought a succession of counter-attacks by the enemy and reinforcement by the Canadians. The 'Maisies' (Le Régiment de Maisonneuve), a French Canadian unit, came up to enlarge the fight. The furtive patrol had become a considerable battle.

Casualties were relatively light and offset by the greater number of prisoners taken. The Royals were surprised to find boys and old men among the enemy group. Two Canadians, Sgt Krankovich and L/Cpl Wieczorowski, were each wounded for the third time in seven months. Also among the wounded was Cpl Jack Williams, later a Warrant Officer (WO).

Not a belligerent man, but intensely patriotic, Jack had attended a military summer camp at age fifteen and continued his interest in volunteering for overseas service. Enlisting in 1941 he joined the Royals in October 1942 and landed with them on Juno Beach in July 1944. He had served in every action in the anti-tank platoon up until the Matheson patrol. Like many, but not all, frontline soldiers he had for months dealt with his fears by calculating how long it would be before he met the bullet with his name on it. Usually he bet that it was 'Not today'. But by early 1945 he felt that his luck must be running out. Knocked out by his injury, his first thought was, 'I'm alive and going home'. He says, 'I never felt hatred for German prisoners of war and we took many. They were us in different uniforms. They were never treated badly by my comrades.' Just an ordinary soldier, but worth recording as perhaps typical of the very silent majority of survivors.[10]

Among Jack's comrades, Bud Jones had again survived at the sharp end. Like others previously, he too had to patrol the ghostly area where 'the American gliders were still strewn all over the [Arnhem] drop zone'. The sight of the long-dead bodies added to the usual horrors of war.

On a moonlit night, the enemy using small parachute flares trying to spot us. We could only lay there. Trying to stay still. And had to stare at these men through the round windows of the aircraft and wearing Airborne helmets and one of my patrol swore he saw one move. Also a lot of new spruce trees, the size of an average person, when you stared long enough the moonlight seem to jump and run around and it was like being a child shut in an eerie dark closet. And the spruce trees could be enemy soldiers tracking us.[11]

Advancing into the forests with 1st Black Watch, Stan Whitehouse and his mates worked in couples as pick and shovel men. One would carry a pick in addition to the other mass of equipment, and the other would carry the shovel. At a moment's notice the pair could dig a slit trench deep enough to save their lives. Stan saw an instance of the disadvantage which the Allies suffered in a fairly quick advance – the Germans had time to survey and prepare accurate maps of the entire region.

Lt Bernard had instructed them on the next move forward. 'This map has just come up from intelligence,' he said, 'and it shows a 23 feet wide ditch on the edge of the forest'. They would follow a Sherman tank piled high with fencing and this would be tipped into the ditch to facilitate their crossing the obstacle. Moving forward Cpl Aitchison trod on a Schu-mine and blew off his foot. As he fell his Sten gun fired and set off another mine. The wounded corporal waved the leading men on. At last the tank officer halted and said he could go no further into thick trees with his load of fencing. 'Where is that bloody big ditch?' shouted Bernard. A shower of mortar bombs descended, so Stan and mates jumped into a convenient little ditch at the forest edge.[12]

At the inquest on the incident it was found that the hastily printed map had omitted a 'forward slash' and the 23 feet wide ditch should have been merely 2/3 feet wide. In Stan and Bernard's case this resulted in only a little confusion, but it could have caused many casualties. There were many such instances of the advantages gained by the defenders; however, one disadvantage experienced by the Allies in Normandy no longer applied in the Reichswald. In the two months after D-Day the Allies were usually moving south. This meant that the defenders had their backs to the sun and could use their field glasses (the far superior German types) with impunity. Every time an Allied commander lifted his field glasses he risked betraying his position by the brilliant reflection of the sun on the lenses. Now on the German border the movement was generally west to east, eliminating the advantage.

Lt-Col Whitaker with the 'Rileys' (Royal Hamilton Light Infantry) was in no doubt that the Canadian units were at a disadvantage against the Germans and their short lines of supply and troop movement.

New drafts from Canada were now the product of the recently introduced conscription scheme and had not had time to be trained to the level of the superb Canadian battalions which landed on the Normandy beaches. One of Whitaker's company commanders, Maj. Joseph Pigott, reported, 'at least 60 to 70 per cent of my company was composed of men who'd never heard a shot fired in anger… the majority were men from the service corps, ordnance or artillery transferred in without induction training. We tried to teach them elementary tactics… but they were like lambs to the slaughter.'[13]

Meanwhile, in Whitaker's view, both as battle commander and later outstanding historian, the Germans were still as capable of formidable counter-attack as at any time in the war. On 19 February, such a counter-attack revealed the arrival of two crack German formations; 16th Panzer and the Panzer Lehr (training) Division, the latter replete with officers and NCOs of instructor standard. A momentary delay on the part of another unit exposed a wing of the Essex Scots advance. Immediately their positions were enveloped and overrun with 400 men temporarily missing, many having to find their way back through the attacking ranks. After initial shocks and heavy losses the Canadians were able to stabilise the situation and resume the advance.

To hard-pressed infantry and tank men at risk, a most welcome sound was the sudden roar of Typhoon planes arriving with their anti-tank rockets and precisely aimed bombs. John Shellard was one of the pilots who undertook a supremely dangerous task: diving at speed directly at enemy guns. There was great danger in diving straight into the trajectory of enemy fire. There was equal danger in the last-second touch of the controls to pull out from a 500 mph dive.

According to John, the method was to:

… leave the UK at 100 feet to avoid enemy radar, in four-finger formation, at 350 mph. Then over France up to 6,000 feet or higher if there was a cloud cover. Nearing the target peel off into a long line of planes. Dive as near vertical as possible. Aim plane at target. At about 2,500 feet press bomb release and flatten. 'G' force then was high enough to produce a risk of unconsciousness. Then 'home, James!' Time there and back just over an hour to French targets, a little longer to the German border. When armed with rockets it would be a 30° dive at 350mph, firing at 1,000 yards. The rocket itself then accelerated away to hit at near 1,000 mph. Rockets could be fired in pairs or all eight as a salvo.[14]

Down on earth on 15 February, Capt. Peter White and his men of the KOSBs were waiting to launch into a 'mission impossible' and attack a stoutly constructed and strongly fortified building complex – Kasteel Blijenbeek. Even the redoubtable KOSBs were wondering how they could cross the open grounds and storm into this formidable fortress. Their C Company had already lost forty men in a direct assault across a bridge over a moat; the only entrance to the castle. The attackers were allowed into the first courtyard and then the main doors swung back. At 10 yards range the defenders blasted the KOSBs. Sgt Webb managed to shepherd a few survivors back to cover. Then, trying to make contact with the flank company, he was shot in the head and died a few minutes later.[15]

In an almost hopeless situation the KOSBs heard the sound of diving Typhoons. The planes were on a 'Winkle' mission. The army indicated a general area and the Typhoons flew over at 1,000 feet, picking out strong points or transport and attacking them at the flight leader's discretion. Kasteel Blijenbeek was a conspicuous target. This time an entire wing of Typhoons was directed on the area. As Shellard dived in, there were already clouds of smoke rising from the accurate attacks of the previous planes. His orders were to aim at the bits they could see; it was an attempt at total demolition. Credit must also be given to the airmen of the medium bombers, who joined at lower speed, in the work of pulverising the Kasteel. Together with the artillery they turned a mission impossible into a mission highly feasible, and allowed the attack to be completed by the men on the ground with relatively few casualties.

The incredible speed of the Typhoon dive did not protect the pilot from any collisions with the mass of projectiles aimed at it from anti-aircraft fire on the ground. During the battle for Reichswald, Derek Tapson's Typhoon squadron had moved to an airfield near the German border. Attacking a target house nearby, he was the victim of a double spin on the wheel of fate. Approaching the target location the squadron leader radioed that he could not identify the target. Derek's flight leader said that he could see the target and prepared to dive, with Derek following. Then the squadron leader said he could now fix on the house and would lead. Derek's flight pulled out of their attack and climbed to regain position. As Derek kicked left rudder and moved to the left there was a loud bang as his engine was hit by anti-aircraft fire. Seeing his airfield in the distance he thought it possible to reach safety.[16]

This was followed by moments of sheer horror. Fire broke out in the cockpit. The Typhoon had no ejection seat.

> I jettisoned the canopy, released my straps, lent out to catch hold of the back of the wing, so that pushing the control stick and pulling at the wing I could bail out. However, I found that I was not looking at the sky but at the ground. The aeroplane was upside down! I got back in to try to roll the plane. Realising that it had been climbing and losing speed I thought it might any moment go into a spin. Stupidly I pushed the stick right forward. The nose dropped and I went straight out into the air.

At the very least he had escaped from the fire and the inevitable explosion. But horrors had not yet ceased. 'I had hit my head on the front screen, was knocked unconscious and fell some distance, blanked out. But I came to and quickly pulled the ripcord. The parachute came out between my feet, sending me into a loop and a couple of swings before landing in a field.' It was later estimated that the parachute had opened at 1,000 feet: terribly low for a man coming out of an unconscious state. Strange quirks of fate continued.

Looking up, Derek saw a group of German soldiers running towards him and an officer politely asking for the RAF man's pistol. Turning the other way the pilot found himself staring, at a range of about six feet, at the anti-aircraft gun which had shot him down. Perhaps the captors saw the black humour of the situation for they treated the wounded pilot with great consideration, even though a prison camp was to follow the German doctor's ministrations. At this time pilots were wearing khaki uniform, like the original Royal Flying Corps, because the Air Force blue so closely resembled German field-grey that some parachuting RAF pilots had been fired at by their own guns.

On the ground, Sgt Richard Brew of the Somerset Light Infantry noticed the clever way in which the German defenders strongly resisted attacks until a certain climactic moment. They would then just melt away, reform in a new position and again offer determined resistance. He and his comrades had been 'a bit worried' by what they had been told of the Reichswald defences. Reality was worse than the doubts because the area over which they moved was flooded. This made progress more difficult and caused them to show up as clear silhouettes to the enemy. Moving into Kleve, which had been cleared by 15th Scottish Division, 'the Germans had let the Scots through and now hit us hard and we lost a lot of men' in an area where there should have been no danger. A common tactic used by the defenders.[17]

An event which might have seemed farcical to some did not amuse Sgt Brew and friends. They attacked what proved to be a 'lunatic asylum. The liberated patients kept on saluting us, and getting in our way, and doing make-believe military drill, but we felt sorry for them.' Another twist of fate shocked the company.

> Sgt-Major Davies was killed by a shell which landed OUTSIDE the house he was in. A piece of shrapnel came through the wall which he was leaning on and pierced his heart. It was a shocking sight to see our SM standing there suddenly dead. It was appalling what we went through as young men. Pure chance could still get us, no matter how good soldiers we thought we were.

Trying to keep up with, or even get ahead of the infantry, FOO Jack Swaab remembered 'bad weather – rain and cold – the track was appalling' through the thick forest. His jeep became bogged down and had to be towed out, but in the process of towing his brakes were sheared, and so 'onwards! – but without any brakes! At night the forest was damned uncanny… crashes and crumps, and the whole skyline aflame with gun-flashes and bullets whizzing about the place from pockets of enemy holding out'. Rounding a corner they unexpectedly came upon an enemy strong point, but fortunately it was deserted. There they 'accumulated' some useful tools, which included two pairs of the superior German binoculars so cherished by British commanders.

Jack had to travel with the infantry attack over 2,500 yards of open country to attain his next OP. First they had to cross a small bridge which was constantly being mortared. The only recourse was to drive flat out through the mortar bursts and duck down as far as possible. *Spandau* machine-gun bullets, issuing from each gun at over 1,000 rounds per minute, seemed to lead them on and then pursue them; the spurts of dirt clearly visible. The next water obstacle, the River Viers, required crossing on a Duck amphibious truck. But no Duck arrived, so Jack found an assault boat and rowed his party across. As always the Royal Engineers were already on site throwing a Bailey bridge across the river. Reaching Gennep, Jack scaled the church tower to survey the area and direct the artillery fire.[18]

There never was an easy run on the tormented terrain of a battle. However, Sgt Bernard Upson in a XX Dragoons mine-flailing Crab discovered a new hazard.

> Our attack was preceded by an artillery shoot wheel to wheel. We were parked in the streets and gardens awaiting the start signal. We were to advance through the fields of crashed gliders from the Arnhem battle. Unfortunately my tank picked up a nylon glider tow rope. This wound itself around the rear hub of my Sherman [the Crab was an adapted Sherman] so tightly that only one track would turn. Disaster loomed… we are getting potted at by the enemy and only able to go in circles. Jerry was having fun with us until our advancing Guards tanks pushed them on… we hacked at the cable stiff as steel, separating the nylon fibre by fibre, hands bleeding, knuckles broken, tired and exhausted.

Like the earlier patrols, Upson's men were still working under the gaze of the dead American paratroopers at the windows of the crashed gliders.[19]

Capt. Ernest Egli also had a miraculous escape. Needing to cross an uncharted minefield he chose to walk past a sapper kneeling on the ground; he assumed that where the sapper had trodden would be safe. He was about to speak to the man when:

…there was a flash and an explosion that made my ears sing, and to my horror I was looking at a smoking crater six feet in diameter and about three feet deep. At the bottom was a piece of body about fifteen inches by eight inches covered in smouldering cloth. Nothing else. Still wondering if I was mortally wounded I heard an irate voice in the distance shout, 'You engineers should not blow mines when someone is on the road'. It was a staff colonel resplendent in his distinguishing red regalia. I shouted that he too was in the middle of a minefield. I have never seen such a change in attitude, or a quicker retreat.

Egli walked back to his jeep to 'find a shaken ASM Riley'. Riley had seen the explosion and had said to himself, 'That's Egli gone'.[20]

Back behind the lines, far from where Capt. Swaab was paddling a tiny assault boat across a narrow river, Stan Hicken, Brian Carpenter and fellow 1NY drivers were being introduced to a crude iron monster, a Buffalo: virtually an open box on tracks which was supposed to wade across vast rivers like the Rhine. The first trip for each driver was almost as scary as the Normandy battlefield. In his innocence Stan asked, 'where's the outboard motor?' He was told that the tracks spinning around underwater would propel the craft across the river. Having often had to lift the tons of heavy steel which constituted a single track, Stan thought to himself, 'This bugger's going to sink and me with it'.[21]

Meanwhile, the day that Operation Veritable commenced was a significant date for the men advancing into the Reichswald, and also for several Canadians who had been surrounded at Dieppe in 1942. Since then they had been living out the frustrations and helplessness of a prisoner of war camp far to the east, where the Russians were advancing.

Living in a wooden hut without heating in the sub-zero conditions they had been sleeping fully clothed. This was fortunate for at 04.00 hours they were roused 'by goons they had never seen before, soldiers in grey green anoraks, Hitler's nasty boys', driven out into the yard and made to stand there for eight hours. At midday, and without further information, the 500 or so prisoners were ordered to march out of the camp. Weak from lack of nutrition and cramped from standing still in the frozen air, they were marched along a seemingly endless road. As far as they knew the destination might be a remote forest clearing, a hail of bullets and a shallow grave. Nobody told them otherwise, but rifle butts hastened the tardy. They would be walking for weeks.[22]

The troops advancing beyond the fearsome Reichswald Forest now encountered a smaller but equally fatal forested area: the Hochwald. At this point it might be said that human rivalry intervened. The Canadian army commander, Crerar, allotted two corps, one Canadian and one British, but decided to start the operation with equal priorities for both corps. So whichever corps appeared to be making most progress would be allowed to take the major share of battle and the resultant glory, if any. It was asking a lot of career generals that they resist the temptation to prove themselves the more efficient. Therefore, it may be that the costly Canadian attempt to storm the Hochwald owed something to this imperative for speed.[23]

Lt-Gen. Guy Simonds had already demonstrated his genius for unusual tactics. Facing the unconquered Verrieres-Bourguebus Ridge in Normandy he had sent armoured columns at night to drive through the entire German first defence system. Facing a costly sea-borne landing on Walcheren he had decided simply to sink the island. Facing a repeat of the bloody battle for the Reichswald he saw his opportunity clearly lined out on the map. Tanks elsewhere were floundering in an ever-deeper morass in worsening weather, but through the middle of the Hochwald there ran a railway line; solid ground upon which his tanks could race through the forest and surround the enemy within. And leave a ready-made supply highway behind them.

Maj. John Munro of the Canadian Grenadier Guards described the weak point of the plan as the Canadian tanks drove along the railway. 'Part of the rail line was on a high embankment with practically no place to get off. All the Germans had to do was pick off, say, the tenth tank… then knock out the others.' And, of course, if a tank did get off it was back into the mud. Intense enemy fire, rain, mist, mud and thick forest each side of the railway made communications extremely difficult. One participant stated succinctly that 'the fog of war was at its thickest'. When the South Alberta Shermans tried to swing through an underpass in the embankment, the Germans coolly waited for the last tank to emerge, knocked out the first and last tanks, and continued to fire from their hidden fastness in the forest.

For British tankie Alf Gritton 'it became a sort of cowboy country'. His regiment's tanks sank in the mud and so the tank men got out and served as infantry.[24] Canadian Harold Neumann found his battery command post underwater. They spent twenty-two days in the Hochwald area with persistent shelling and little food. 'We didn't know where we were and the mud... your clothes got covered and you had to keep your clothes on all the time. There were guys laying around dead like cord-wood. People killed on both sides.' Indeed when they eventually marched out he saw 'the tops of all the trees were blown off".[25]

The Sherbrooke Fusiliers were a Montreal infantry regiment who had changed to Sherman tanks for the Normandy landings. They had achieved conspicuous success in the fighting there and were supremely confident before they entered the Hochwald cauldron.[26] Typical of this high élan was the experience of John Hale, who, on arriving as a reinforcement was greeted by his new squadron leader, Maj. Radley Walters, with 'Hello, John. Welcome to the Sherbrookes'. He said he knew then that his unit was 'something different'. But the Hochwald conditions treated everybody the same, irrespective of cap badge. John recorded a phase of a night attack as seen by the ordinary trooper in his tight armoured niche.[27]

'A' Squadron of the Sherbrookes, leading the Camerons in three columns, entered a minefield:

...all three tanks struck mines and were put out of the action. Lt Butler left his lead tank and came back to ours, sending our Sergeant forward to evacuate his crew. The driver, Tpr Laramont, his legs were severely damaged as the mine explosion was directly under his feet. Lt Butler reported the urgency of the situation to the 2i/c, who commanded us to 'Press On'. Butler's response was 'How in hell do you press on in a minefield?' he yelled into the open mike. 'Driver, reverse'. We backed up a short distance, to clear possible mines, turned left and in a short distance came to a laneway of sorts and resumed our advance. The Germans hadn't mined this passage through the minefield. All this and the battle had barely begun and we left three disabled tanks.

The Germans were now firing a counter-barrage of shells and mortars at the column of tanks and infantry carriers. The squadron lost many men to this effective barrage when they got out of their tanks to try to dig the stuck tanks out or to evacuate to the rear. Al Dankoff, whom I had joined the Sherbrookes with, was severely wounded by this fire. Lt McAuley was

killed in this confused fighting. The noise, the tank motors grinding away
in low gear, shells exploding all around us, the roar of the massive guns
firing from behind us, buildings on fire, smoke. This has been reported as
one of the heaviest barrages fired in the N/W Europe campaign. It was an
intensity of sounds you could feel on your body.

We moved forward in low gear. Buildings on fire gave us some light.
Then as I looked towards our left flank, I saw two German tanks 300yds
or more distant. They were sharply outlined as they slowly passed a burning farm structure. I called into the mike my sighting. The 2i/c came on
the air saying 'Don't fire! It's B squadron'. Cpl Tourneau came on saying
'They are Germans and I am firing'. The 2i/c did not respond. Tourneau,
an Alsatian, had a distinguishing accent and was easily recognisable. The
two German tanks disappeared into the darkness past the burning barn.
I don't know if they were hit or not. Our job was to press onward to our
objective, the Calcar Ridge. The German tanks had a Christie design sus-
pension, quite easily recognizable in a side view. Whether they were Tigers
or Panthers I am not sure, but both were much larger than Pz KW 4s.

In this spring offensive the stark reality of war struck me. It was a huge
assembly of troops, guns, tanks all pushing forward over sloppy muddy
ground. In this offensive our regiment led this night attack with infantry
in armoured carriers behind us. In A Squadron only seven out of twenty
tanks reached the objective. The others had been lost to mud, mines,
artillery, mortars, Panthers' 75-mm and anti-tank guns.

The infantry dug in. In the grey light of a misty dawning the German
fire started heavily. The Grenadier liaison tank beside us was hit and
brewed up instantly. The impact area of the shot, on the left front of the
turret, was a glowing cherry red about two feet in diameter with a black
hole at its centre. The crew commander was half way out of the hatch as
the ammo blew. A blow torch effect of the fire gushed up around him; he
threw up his arms and fell back into the burning tank. I turned away and
don't know if anyone got out of the tank.

We were being fired upon from the left flank and our front at the same
time. An anti-tank gun was concealed in a barn. The Germans rolled open
the doors and fired at us. Their shot passed over our tank, narrowly missing
us. It was so close it cut off the radio aerial of the tank behind us, at about
one foot from its base. In a second we fired back and destroyed the anti-
tank gun. Did you know that if you are looking down the barrel of an 88
or a 75 when it fires at you, you could see it coming as a ball of fire? I even

ducked instinctively. Then the 17-pounder tank behind us knocked out a German tank on our front. We then took cover from the German fire to our left, behind a barn/farm house. Once our infantry had dug in, our concern was only for ourselves. We had to get out from behind the structures as the German fire was so heavy that the cover was disappearing rapidly.

The quality of the German troops in this engagement was of the highest in both training and motivation. During the engagement we were firing heavily at the German infantry and the gun positions engaging us. Both our bow and our turret machine-guns had burnt out their barrels, then a shell casing jammed in the breach of the 75-mm gun. I pulled out the burnt-out turret machine-gun, throwing it over the side. Two German paratroopers, seeing our vulnerability, rushed the tank. The crew commander, Lt Butler grabbed the Thompson sub-machine gun and blasted the pair. I had never seen anybody shot with a 45 Thompson gun at close range: I swear one of them did a back flip when hit. I pushed the spare machine gun into its mountings, turning to the 75, and drove the stuck round fully into the breach with a hammer. (Yes, we had one for just that purpose; just don't strike the centre firing cap!) We then resumed our firing at enemy infantry positions and at the gun positions on the left flank.

It was time to withdraw. The farm building was being cut down by the German barrage. Butler ordered the other tanks to pull out off the ridge, one at a time under cover of smoke shells we fired for each to mask the left flank German guns. We had silenced the two firing at us from our front and one on the left flank. We saved two smoke shells for our own withdrawal. We fired one: it was a dud. We fired the second: another dud! We had to make our pull out without smoke cover.

We started to make a 'run' down off the ridge. We pulled out from behind cover. The tank moved about 10 meters in first gear but the deep mud halted the tank, and a German shot passed in front of us with a crack. Our driver ripped the gears into 'Bull slow' and we lunged ahead. A second shot passed behind us. Another shot came but it made a different sound. Reaching the down slope we were out of their line of fire. Lt Butler just sagged to the turret floor in relief. He said that their last shot hit an electric utility pole. Three shots missed us as we moved the short run for cover off the ridge. A 75 or 88-mm shot passing close sounds like a whip crack amplified a million times. You knew what it was and that it was damn close.

It is often the case that someone comes forward to fill the gaps of leadership. In this engagement it was our 2 Troop leader, Lt James Butler. We later learned that the Colonel of the infantry regiment was killed and that our squadron commander, Maj. Gould, was wounded and out of action. We had reached our objective, the top of the Goch–Calcar Ridge. Daylight would be upon us shortly. The infantry were not getting out of the carriers and digging in to hold the position. Butler left our tank, climbed on to a carrier and, with his pistol drawn, ordered the men out.[28] Telling them that when the dawn broke the Germans would shoot the hell out of them and their carriers. They got out and started to dig in. The carriers turned back immediately. Butler just got back to our tank when the shooting started. He ordered the 17-pounder Firefly and two others to cover the front and directed the captain of the squadron to take up his troop to cover the left flank. I assume he had knowledge of the captain's newness or inexperience. I don't know. I had never seen or heard of the captain before, nor saw him after the battle. Lt Butler's leadership in this engagement was exemplary and collectively many owed their survival to his courage and command decisions.

Time and place orient us. We know where we are and have at least a general image of what day it is, and the time of day. In heavy combat, with its seeming endlessness, time and place collapse into a maze of feelings and thoughts.

As we descended the gentle slope from the ridge, the shooting stopped. The scene changed from one of a frenzied action to one of tranquillity. It was most strange. The sensation was one that would recur again and again when coming out of action. You feel that you are in some place and you don't know where it is, nor what you are doing there. Are you visiting some strange happening? Yet instantaneously knowing the reality of the battle you had just participated in.

We, the remaining tanks of the squadron, pulled back the same way we had advanced, looking at the ones that didn't get to the objective, stuck in the mud, shot up, with tracks broken off. We reached the position where the infantry colonel was killed. One of our tanks was stopped beside the partly demolished farmhouse. It was Maj Gould's tank. He and the other wounded crew had been evacuated. The body of Tpr Johnson lay where he was killed. Gould had stopped to re-establish communications with the infantry after their commander had been killed, and Gould and his crew were shot up by a German machine-gunner when they got out of their tank.

Sgt Gerow and I rolled the dead body over. He had been machine-gunned in the face and we did not recognize him. I cut off his bottom

'Dog Tag' and read his name - K.R. Johnson. I thought 'I don't know him?' No face! I didn't want to know him! Every soldier wears two 'Dog Tags'. One is cut off when you are killed, for reporting the death, and the other stays with the body. Johnson had been at basic training with me in Fredericton.

We pulled into an orchard, taking up a defensive position under cover of the trees, waiting for the [Canadian] Grenadier Guards tank regiment to pass through us at 09.00 hours to press the attack on further. Our crews were out of our vehicles, relieving ourselves, cleaning the mud and debris out of the tracks. When the leading elements of the 'Grens' appeared in the distance they opened up on us with machine-guns. After scrambling for cover, some of us got back in our vehicles and resumed a firing readiness. We pondered shooting back at them. The big wonder was 'why? - if they thought we were the enemy, did they not fire their main weapons at us?' The Sherbrookes and the Grenadiers were not on the same wireless frequency. The tank knocked out up on the ridge was the Grenadier liaison officer, so we had lost our radio link with the Grenadiers. They finally stopped firing at us, moving up the grade to resume the attack on to a further objective.

We retired further to a rear area. Wandering crews and some recovered tanks came in. Replacement tanks arrived along with personnel to make up our shortages. New guys just like me of a few months ago. You don't yet ask who has gone, or question what may have happened to him. The answer to these questions waits for a quieter time.

When we pulled back to the place where Gould had been wounded a sergeant of the infantry regiment had taken charge of the place. He was dressed in sniper gear, binding on a scoped rifle, just a beret, no helmet on his head. He had the bug-eyed look that comes from being in a tough fire fight. He directed the round-up of the prisoners, placed two of his men to defend the holding and then took off in the direction of the Germans.

I looked over the prisoners, a sad beaten lot, but one big bugger, a paratrooper appeared alert and perhaps furtive. In any case, I don't know why, I chose to search him. He had a field dagger in a scabbard between his legs as I tapped his groin. I jumped back and told him to dig it out of his pants, which he did – appearing now to be quite frightened (knowing the consequences of being caught carrying a concealed weapon). Lt Butler, resting against a mounded potato bunker, said 'Shoot him!' I responded 'If you want him dead, you shoot him'. Butler angrily 'Christ, he could have taken the gun away from you'. I turned, swinging my Tommy gun over the prisoner's head and past him and fired a burst, saying 'No, he would not have'. That sergeant wasn't the only one that was 'hopped up and bug-eyed'. We were all just as jumpy as the sergeant.

Such was the experience of John Hale, a 20-year-old tank loader/ wireless operator with the Sherbrooke Fusiliers, on a typical day trying to break through the Siegfried Line.

Meanwhile, behind the front slit trenches and replenishing tanks, but within constant reach of enemy counter-barrages, the artillery-men were always hard at work. As the Essex Scots went into another battle on 3 March the Canadian 4th Field Regiment's firing duties included two defensive fire targets, twenty harassing fire targets, a quick barrage and eighteen Mike targets called for by FOOs. One such target killed a large number of enemy and 'caught a German company at change-over. Three prisoners of war taken claimed to be the sole survivors.'[29]

An unusual problem for some Canadian attackers was that they were being fired on from all sides, including from behind. This was due to the bends in the River Rhine which they were trying to reach. As they moved forward between two bends, it enabled German artillery on the other side of the river to shoot from behind at ranges of up to 8 miles. Maj. George Cassidy of the Algonquins expected fire to come from in front or from a flank, 'but when it came in over one's shoulder it was unsettling, to say the least. How do you respond? By firing backwards towards your own troops?'[30] One geometric fix on German guns found them firing on target at 11,525 yards.

John Hale's frightening experiences were shared by a more senior soldier, Maj. Crummer, commanding a company of the Lincoln and Welland regiment and subject to the all-round German artillery fire. He was:

> ... in the middle of it, trying to push forward but we didn't stand long. We went to ground damn fast. You can't do anything. You really hunker down and pray to God that you come out of it. Most men had found rat holes. I was buried a couple of times. It was all mud, mud. I remember hearing the shelling and then I didn't hear anything at all. Still saw huge explo-sions all over the damn place. I crawled under a tank to get away from

some fire. Then I could sense the tank settling down in the mud, so I got the hell out of there. There was no cover. Trees were no cover in shelling, for you got limbs falling down on you and shrapnel bursting down on you from above.[31]

The situation for forward men, both of the Canadians crashing through the forest and of the British trying to outflank it, was grim, prolonged and costly. The way ahead lay across increasingly difficult terrain as rain, artillery barrages and tank tracks churned the ground and felled trees. There was not much opportunity for the rude banter which so often lightened the harassed soldier's day, as despatch rider A. Duchene with the XXII Dragoons quickly discovered.

An affable man, he was popular with those he touched on his rounds delivering urgent and sometimes not so urgent messages. Frequently he would be stopped by soldiers asking, 'Are you going anywhere near XY Regiment? If so, tell them Joe Bloggs (that's me) is OK'. In one wrecked village, amid the detritus of battle, he noticed a black silk opera hat sitting on a pile of rubble. 'Why not?' he thought, taking off his helmet and donning the hat. 'Give the lads something to laugh at'. He rode off on his motor bike. The first troops he passed laughed and gave him the thumbs up sign. Unfortunately, at his destination he was greeted by 'a very suspicious Sergeant-Major on the end of a .38 pistol', and as the pistol jabbed into the DR's chest the SM snarled, 'Take that effing hat off. There's a bloody war on'.

Even normally pacific DRs as well as clerks, storemen and cooks had to be co-opted into essential tasks in battle, usually at the call of a sergeant-major saying, 'You, you and you' at random. Duchene found himself in a very small group responsible for herding a very large number of 'singularly unpleasant' enemy prisoners. His group were allotted a field with a gate, a very large tangle of barbed wire and told to get on with it. Whilst guarding the prisoners they had to construct a hasty enclosure. This had to have two sections; one for officers and one for Other Ranks, because some of the German officers refused to co-habit with the rankers. In both cages the prisoners waited in the open field, doing the best they could with their greatcoats to bed down for the night.

Speaking through the wire, a prisoner who spoke excellent English said, 'I am fifteen and my comrade he is fourteen. We are paratroopers but they have not yet let us jump from an aeroplane'. There was only one latrine bucket and the DR, who always saw the funny side of anything, enjoyed one midnight scene. A prisoner was squatting over the bucket as another approached, giving the stiff-arm Nazi salute and calling 'Heil Hitler'. Puzzled for a moment the squatting figure then responded with the regulation salute and the greeting, but still squatting. Duchene commented wryly that 'the niceties had been observed'.[32]

There were fewer niceties in the psychologically stressful battle conditions; as observed by FOO George Blackburn when he called down artillery support for the infantry around him:

> A young soldier, whose closest buddy was killed by a shot from the para-troopers' house before the flame was used, watches soberly as others relieve the prisoners of Lugers, watches and money. He had been promised his buddy's death would be avenged as soon as they flushed 'the sniper' out, and he appeals to Major Bob Suckling. 'Aren't we going to shoot them?' The Major turns away. But a veteran sergeant puts his arm around the boy's shoulders and says quietly: 'We don't do that sort of thing, kid.'[33]

Amid such scenes George, one of the toughest soldiers, was also aware of the havoc his own guns had caused to human beings on the other side:

> At the first objective of the Régiment de Maisonneuve, a tiny crossroads hamlet called Den Heuvel two kilometres northeast of Groesbeek, one officer is able to count sixty-four Germans dead from the bombardment 'without examining slit trenches' for bodies. Survivors still cringing in cellars from the Niagara of shells that recently descended on them, show clear signs of being in shock when flushed out, according to the commander of the leading platoon of the Maisies, Lieut Guy de Merlis. The result is the Maisies lose only twenty-four, including two killed, taking their objective.

As the Allied troops reached their objectives the immensity of the conflict was illustrated by the extent of German reinforcement. On 8 February General Alfred Schlemm had one infantry division available. By the end of the battle he had been able to command eleven divisions, including elite elements such as the paratroopers and Tiger tank units. During the month of action in the Reichswald and Hochwald forests the British and Canadians had suffered 15,634 casualties, to which must be added the American troops on the southern flank who suffered another 7,300. However, the German losses were estimated at 40,000 casualties and 50,000 prisoners taken. In an earlier twelve-week operation to seize the nearby Huertgen Forest, the Americans had incurred another 33,000 casualties, of which 9,000 were due to exposure-related illness.[34]

'Those Fatal Forests' would appear to be an accurate title.

CHAPTER FIVE

DE HONGERWINTER

All that they had in the way of provisions failed. So long as the earth gave them anything they sustained life by eating the grass and herbs.

(Herodotus, 440BC)

The pram had a false bottom and under that thin board, for fear of theft, reposed a Gouda cheese and some bread and butter. These were all the rations for four people on a 200-mile walk. The whole cheese had been bartered at the cost of the family piano. The bread and butter had required the surrender of both the father's and mother's wedding rings. Whatever else they needed had to be begged along the way.

Peter Overliese, a 7-year-old child, would not be walking. He was a skinny boy, unhealthy and malnourished because of the famine. When he fell victim to bronchitis the doctor had ordered that, to save his life, he must be taken out of the city. There were still parts of the country where there was food and where some kind farmer might offer him a home until things improved. That meant a trek of many days, perhaps weeks. Frail Peter would be sitting on top of a pram packed with clothing, bedding and a 10lb cheese. In the case of another child, Tony van Vugt, the pram collapsed after 100 yards.[1]

Peter's predicament was no fault of his parents. It might be said that the fault lay with FM Montgomery's over-optimistic plans and a well-intentioned but fatal error by the Dutch government in exile in London. The Allies had optimistically planned to capture Arnhem and the vital Rhine crossings by a sudden airborne operation in

September 1944. The free Dutch government in London therefore gave approval for complementary action to be taken by the Dutch Resistance in Holland. A vital part of this uprising would be a national railway strike intended to disrupt the reinforcement of German troops around Arnhem. Once able to cross the Rhine the Allies would then storm into Germany; automatically liberating the whole of the Netherlands. The signal went out from London to Resistance groups and a national strike by the rail workers' union brought the railways to a halt.

Two unfortunate things happened: the airborne attempt to capture Arnhem failed, leaving western Holland still occupied; and the reaction of the German authorities in the Netherlands was immediate and cruel in the extreme. Import of food from farming areas to the densely populated western Dutch cities was embargoed. Urban inhabitants had already become prone to malnutrition with average daily calorie intake down to 1,000. Now the flow of supplies ceased. Towards the end of 1944 the embargo was partially raised but by that time the canals had frozen and the barges, so essential in this land of waterways, could not move. The arctic weather which set in was, for younger people, the worst in living memory. Thus commenced *De Hongerwinter:* the Hunger Winter; a time of famine unique in the modern history of Western Europe. Average daily calorie intake would shrink to about 400.[2]

Many men of working age had been carried off to forced labour by *Razzias* (round-ups) or were restricted in their movements. In a land of many bridges the military police simply patrolled these bottlenecks to prevent casual travel. Even when someone was able to make a foray into rural areas in search of food; the prices were exorbitant, and if he were caught he could be condemned to slave labour.

Albertus Franciscus Rijntjes was fifty-one and until the German invasion in 1940 had a comfortable job as a tax inspector. Although now unemployed he still had some savings. When the famine became intolerable he set out to find some food outside the city. He kept a diary of his travels. On one particular day he walked 20 miles, calling at farms and warehouses. He brought home '5 potatoes, 1 cabbage, 4 slices of bread with butter and cheese, 500 grams of tulip bulbs and 1 half litre of milk. Total price – 150 guilders.' Expensive: an average weekly wage at the time was between 35 and 40 guilders. The tulip bulbs were not for planting and next year's aesthetic enjoyment, but to make a watery soup, perhaps with slices of sugar beet.[3]

Now without savings or saleable goods, little Peter Overliese's mother was typical of many desperate parents. Her only recourse was to set off on a long and arduous journey in the hope of finding relief in some remote area where food might still be available.

Mother pushed the pram while father followed at a distance on their *Hongertocht:* or Hunger Walk. Father had been instructed to go to Germany under a compulsory work order but had gone underground, spending all his time hiding. Now he would skulk along the road, keeping his family in sight but only joining them after dark. They walked for six days to take a ferry at a Harderwijk seaport on the IJselmeer. Arriving in Friesland they found a church at Vlagtwedde which had an organisation for placing refugee children (but not mothers) with charitable farmers. Peter's mother was directed to the kind Niemeijers family. For some days Mrs Niemeijers fed Peter six small meals a day, standing over him to make sure that he completed the tiresome task of eating real sustaining food against which his stomach revolted. It was two months before he was strong enough to go to school. Then the truth emerged about the true charitable nature of farmer Niemeijers and his wife.

On a day of great joy Canadian troops arrived and liberated the farm. At that moment a Jewish couple emerged from a hole under the barn. They had been hidden there so effectively by the Niemeijers that even an inquisitive little boy like Peter had not been aware of their presence. One reason why the Niemeijers had taken in refugees was so that they could buy extra rations and thus accommodate the hidden Jewish man and wife.

In the populous cities conditions continued to deteriorate. Peter Overliese's father and neighbours had broken into empty houses, often where Jewish owners had been carried away to concentration camps, in order to tear up floorboards and break down doors for firewood as power supplies had virtually failed. But they were horrified when the neighbour found the head of a dog in his litter bin. Somebody had made stew of the rest of the dog.

Ration books were issued but there was nothing in the shops. Tulip bulbs now became part of the rations and people were also urged to eat dahlia tubers.[4] At age thirteen Jake Bakker noticed the changes:

Before the hunger our pot-bellied stove would be burning red hot with plenty of coal in its belly. Now we could only fire it up once in a while when we had scrounged some pieces of wood. We were always hungry and food was the only topic we constantly talked about. We were always telling each other about what we would do after the war – eat as many pancakes as you desired until you burst at the seams. Big pancakes with bacon! But the main source of heat for warming us or for cooking was a small tinplate stove, called 'little fire devil' which used less wood.[5]

The little fire devil was rendered even more economical by the use of three graduated rings which further reduced the size of the fire according to the meal being cooked or amount of water being boiled.[6]

Dien van der Burgh's family called their little fire devil a 'high hat because it was like one of those old fashioned black top hats'. It had a tiny door and the wood had to be chopped into tiny slivers to fit inside. She said that in the intense cold you sat round it more for mental comfort than for physical warmth. Her resilient mother made the best of available food and invented new menus:

Tulip bulbs were nutritious but you had to peel them first and then you sliced them like onions. The centre had to be taken out because that was poisonous. So you should not just chew at a tulip bulb. When cooked it was a sort of glassy substance you could mash and bake like a bread or mix through any food. People were handed coupons and you could get from the communal kitchen a big spoon of soup or stew and if you added mashed bulbs it was a bit more. Mother would cook anything remotely edible from chestnuts and beechnuts to sugar beet. But salt was missed. That was very hard. Without salt things tasted bland, gooey.[7]

Dien remembered queuing for as much as three hours in the intense cold for meat, but when her turn came the meat had finished. 'Then I know I cried. You could be cross but that didn't help'. Washing was reduced to a minimum when there was no water in the tap, clothes looked greyish, and there was 'the smell of poverty in every house'. Soap was virtually non-existent and many people suffered from head lice as well as lice on non-laundered clothes. In 1939 Holland had produced 24 million kg of soap, but by 1943 this had decreased to 2 million kg. In 1944, due to Allied bombing and

German restrictions, production ceased totally. Rooms were blackened out so that no lights shone out, but often there were no lights to shine out. The family sat around in the dark and told stories. Often the main entertainment was describing recipes for after the war – 'beautiful puddings and apple cakes' – all of which they were going to cook some day.

Another youngster in Amsterdam to whom the shortage of water was a burden, only a turgid flow from the taps and only for an hour or two a day, was Paul J. Coutzen. Later he would discover how the ozone layer is formed and destroyed, and would be awarded the Nobel Prize for chemistry in 1995. Fifty years earlier he could only look on as several of his schoolmates died of hunger or related illnesses.[8]

Freek van der Wulle and his friends did the rounds of the trash cans hoping to find something edible. There was no garbage collection. The streets were full of trash but few food scrapings. When food did become available Freek suffered agonising stomach cramps from eating what should have been a frugal normal meal. He felt there was nothing to live for. The cold was unbearable. 'I didn't get out of bed any more. We were four of us in the bed. That's what kept us warm', and indeed conserved enough energy to maintain life itself.[9]

Albert Schut heard that there were potatoes in a badly flooded field. Standing knee-deep he and some friends trawled the ground and brought up as much water as potatoes. The farmer stood watching and demanded payments in jewellery or bed linen. All the while 16-year-old Albert had to be alert as at his age a German *Razzia* patrol might notice him and take him away for forced labour. Ger Koks' family and neighbours went out at night to saw down a tree in the Dortsestraatweg. It fell down with a loud bang and should have alerted the police, but perhaps they judged it politic to stay out of the way. Then using a large sledgehammer and wedge they cut it into smaller pieces and shared it out. The police may have behaved in a similar way in Amsterdam where people were tearing up the wooden tracks of the tramway system to obtain firewood.

Nelie de Haan's mother swapped all her treasured gramophone records for food. She managed to buy a loaf of bread for 80 guilders, about two weeks wages, and then money ran out. Nelie noticed that at about 2 am there was a tiny flow of gas through the pipes so they got up at that time to make beet cakes; sugar beet mixed with whatever else was available and eaten brushed with cod liver oil. But always her worst memory was of the terrible cold, continuing day after day without relief. She slept in a bed with her brother and her cat until the brother revolted and refused to allow the cat into the bed. The cat stayed in the kitchen. Next morning it was dead, frozen stiff.[10]

Mrs R.M. Bredius remembers on her *Hongertocht*, aged sixteen, walking into Montfort on the way to Gouda and watching the arriving crowds of refugees growing larger and larger as people looked for an overnight stay. They were 'mothers with prams and whole families of kids. Virtually all of them were without a father because the *Razzias* had rounded them all up in November last year.'

Fay Grindron, who was twelve years old, had a lone, horrific experience related to the *Razzias*. Her father had been rounded up but managed to escape and was hiding in the house. Fay was singing a popular song when her father appeared and reprimanded her because he thought the words were unsuitable for a young girl to sing. At that moment there was a crash at the door:

> The SS police instead of ringing the bell had smashed in our door and burst in – three scary men with guns in their hands and big boots on their feet. They grabbed my father by the neck and dragged him down the stairs. The terror within paralysed me while I watched these three strange men beat my father like he was a dangerous beast. My father was struggling but three ruthless men with guns were too much for him. They dragged him into the street and threw him into a truck. I could not comprehend. I pretended that these adults were just playing a game such as I played with my friends in the street.

During her *Hongertocht* Fay again encountered the *Razzias*. There were so many people 'it appeared like the Exodus'. Schools were opened and bags of straw provided for weary trekkers to sleep on. Then 'enemy soldiers came in the dark, broke down the doors and dragged away eligible men from 16 years and older to forced labour camps'. With his family group Henk Meurs, already approaching the dangerous age of sixteen, arrived in 'a small place called Putten' looking for food. But it was totally depopulated. 'The Germans had rounded up all the men as reprisal because the Resistance had murdered a German officer. We all found dark holes to sleep in.

Nowhere was there anything to get. Unwashed and neglected I walked without shoes in the terrible winter cold.'

In addition to the long-distance walks to find shelter for younger children, mothers performed heroic deeds to find food for families remaining in the large cities. Eltjo van Leeuwen's mother, out foraging for food, found the vital Barendrechtse bridge closed by the authorities. Finding a boat she rowed herself illegally across the wide Old Maas river. 'She got up the mornings before the sun rose, left the house without eating, rode great distances on a bicycle without gears and on solid tyres.'

Hundreds of miles were ridden by Cor Valk's mother. Finding shelter for the night with the Red Cross in Zwolle, she counted in the building, '390 women and 110 men under the age of fifteen or above 55 years old'. The physical effort was almost unendurable:

The road from Utrecht to Gouda was terrible. The rain pelted down. We were soaking and so was our luggage. The bag of bread that hung on the handlebars didn't look good either. We couldn't make progress – there were hundreds of people on the road. We unloaded the baggage, dragged the bikes through thick mud down the slope of the dyke, lifted the bikes and luggage over a fence, loaded up and started peddling again. During the morning Jeanne had three punctures which we had to repair from bits of an old tyre.

Still it rained. That night we were allowed to dry out in cow stables. We hung up our clothes to dry and fell asleep on the floor.

Young lads brought up in comfortable homes were harshly exposed to the realities of life. Ger Koks and his brother thought they had done well on the first night of their trek to be offered a bed of straw in a school:

Well that was an experience! We were attacked by fleas and vermin. All night we tried to catch them and then with our finger nails squeeze them to death on the floor. A hopeless task; they were myriad. In the morning there was a lot of blood. Our feet were bleeding too. My shoes were full of holes blocked by cardboard and my brother's boots were made of artificial rubber and two sizes too big.

Jake Bakker 'mumbled many prayers and made many promises to God' on the appalling side roads. They were unimproved sand roads with deep ruts dug by horse-drawn carts, making it difficult and at times perilous to 'manoeuvre your bike through deep ruts with fully loaded side bags and with filled gunny sacks across the handlebars and the luggage carrier'. Jake also encountered a far greater danger than vermin or ruts in the road – the menace of friends piloting RAF bombers in the sky above. The place Jake feared most was:

> ...the big bridge across the Merwede Canal near the Douwe Egberts coffee-roasting factory. RAF planes appeared frequently to bomb targets like that bridge. Therefore when I crossed the bridge I would always scan the skies. If I thought it was safe I would cross the bridge as rapidly as I could. One time I was half across the bridge. The Brits lobbed a couple of bombs towards that bridge. They exploded on the embankment. Luckily I had thrown down my bike and dived down the embankment.

It was an unexploded bomb which sent shivers down Nelie de Haan's spine whenever she thought about it afterwards. The walking had been bad enough; trudging through thick snow in shoes with worn-out soles. She thought, 'oh what misery and no food on the way. Walking and walking.' In Oldenbroek she had tried to cross a bridge but 'Moffen' (German) guards were on the bridge and sent her back. This coincided with an attack by RAF planes and her group had to take refuge in a drainage channel. Finally at Nieuwekerk aan de IJssel there was a bridge open but in the middle of it was an unexploded bomb. The 16-year-old girl had no choice but to walk past the bomb, fearful that the tread of many feet would set off the ugly monster lying a few feet away.

Back in the flooded potato field Albert Schut continued to fear that a *Razzia* might notice him. Now on 2 January, embarking on another *Hongertocht*, he was arrested when crossing a bridge and put on a train guarded by military police. Fortunately the guards on duty were either slack or sympathetic and Albert was able to sneak away and seek refuge at a house in Kampen. With police still prowling, the householders found some spare clothes and dressed Albert as a woman. They also loaned him a bicycle on which, thus arrayed, he was able to ride over the IJssel bridge without being detected. Shortly afterwards free movement over the bridge was ended.

On another long walk, little Lodewijk van Til was allowed to sit in a café. There was nothing to eat and no proper place to sleep but the café owner had said, 'You can sit at a table all night'. Lodewijk noticed an old man sitting at another table who was frail and stooping. His face was grey from starvation and fatigue. Suddenly the old man began to cough blood. The clots of blood increased into a stream. His head fell with a crash on to the table top. The café owner screamed, 'Get that boy out of here! He shouldn't have to see things like this'. But on the *Hongertocht* children were constantly seeing things they shouldn't.

Even young children understood that bombing by RAF planes was helping to end the enemy occupation. They were 'the Goodies'. The children also understood that there was also airborne danger from 'the Baddies'. The Germans were now firing off V1 flying bombs and V2 long-range rockets not only towards London but also at liberated Dutch and Belgian cities, especially Antwerp with its vital and recently opened docks. Near Lettele there was a launching pad for V1s. For Ger Koks it was terrifying as 'first you would hear a loud thundering sound. Then the projectile would burst out of the woods into the air. It was about eight meters long with a large flame thrusting it forward.'

The thundering V1s reminded Inge Vat of the tremendous Luftwaffe bombardment of Rotterdam in 1940 when she was only eight:

Now, one morning in 1945, when another V1 went on its way it went directly over the house where we were staying, bounced in our front yard; it went up again and, after having crossed the road, drilled itself into the bedroom of the farm opposite. Fortunately without exploding!

Trying to find a way to avoid the packed main roads around Deventer, Jake Bakker lost his way as he peddled with his bundle of food through thick forest:

All of a sudden a German soldier came towards me from a small side road. He called to someone deeper in the stand of trees 'Es ist nur ein Kind' [it's just a child]. Then he told me I had better get out of there fast, pointing out the way to take. Slowly I began to realize that the place I had stumbled on was a site from which they launched the rockets. In my childish thoughts I wondered how many Jews were being held captive there, because we had always heard that the Germans used Jews to launch their rockets because of the great chance of getting killed when rockets misfired. Later I heard that this was not true.

With whole battalions of civilians travelling, either seeking secure lodging places for children or foraging for food to take home to the city, their successes varied as they invaded remote regions. Such areas were relatively untouched by warfare and had to some extent been tolerated by an occupying power which was itself in urgent need of food imports. Human nature being what it is, there were favourable responses mixed with stern refusals. As a girl Inge Vat was encouraged when she and her brother were invited to stay and help on a farm near Benschop for a day or two. But then pressing onward towards Twente, she called at another farmhouse and the 'lady of the house' slammed the door in her face, snapping out the word 'Beggars!'

Jake Bakker met some refusals and fully understood that not all pleas for help could be heeded. He also noticed that the worst offenders were becoming very unpopular:

> By that time the heart of some farmers and vegetable growers had turned to stone because of the great number of people that regularly knocked on their doors in search of food. They did not sell anything in exchange for money any more but had set up a barter trade where they exchanged fruit or potatoes for things of value, such as new bed sheets, valuable clocks, watches, marriage bands, etc. Some people asserted that these farmers had become filthy rich.

After experiencing such a rebuff, Inge Vat was scared and started to run because her brother noticed a farmer following them and gesticulating at them:

> I started to cry and we accelerated our pace to keep ahead of the farmer. But, yes, the farmer caught up with us because he had got on a bicycle. He said 'Why are you walking so fast? I've got some food for you'. Both of us got a packet of sandwiches. We were so glad. So that night we slept at the farm in a loft above the cows. In my sleep I rolled over and fell out

of the loft right down on a cow. I started to cry again. But in the morning we were fed and then on our way towards Apeldoorn.

Inge's journey ended many miles farther on when another farmer overtook them, driving a horse and wagon, and gave them a lift. They arrived in Geesteren and were taken to a large house where a crowd of people were talking loudly in the Twente dialect. Neither Inge nor her brother could understand what was being said and were completely bewildered. Eventually another woman arrived on a bicycle and Inge was given to understand that she had been found a place to stay with this woman, Auntie Truo Ten Velde. So Inge was helped on to the luggage carrier of the bicycle and taken off to live with Auntie Truo. She then realised that she had lost her brother who had been taken elsewhere. It was not until the war ended that she learned that her brother had been taken to another village to be cared for.

Many refugees turned to the churches for help. At Uithuzen Albert Schut was directed to the 'Domi'. Who or what might the 'Domi' be? He proved to be the father of the Reverend Gaaikema:

> Everybody went to the 'Domi': Jews, communists, Resistance fighters and other people in hiding. He in turn arranged hiding places with other families in the area. It's incomprehensible the risk this man ran during the war. It was his nature.

It was at a monastery that Henk Meurs found help. It all seemed mysterious to 16-year-old protestant Henk. Apparently only the 'head man' was allowed to speak, although the brothers provided food, attended to Henk's feet and led him to a cell. There were 'statues all over the cell' and Henk was afraid to look at them. Even worse, during the night when he wanted the toilet he had no idea where it was. So he ventured out of his cell to encounter in the darkness ghostly monks going silently to prayers and refusing to reply to him. In desperation he found and used 'a large vase', unaware of its normal use, whether consecrated or not. Only later was the silent, praying Order of the Trappists explained to him.

Henk was also unaware of the fact that the Abbot Gabriel had already been forced to find extra food and shelter for 110 monks expelled from another cloister. One of the monks, Father Desiderius reported:

…thousands of 'food gatherers' arrived at the entrance porch. It was an honour never to disappoint them. We could only keep this up by curtailing our already meagre meals. The people that arrived here usually had covered great distances. Often their feet were open and hurting and we had to look after them.

A letter of recommendation from Dominee Veerhuizen, the preacher at her home church, proved of great help to 16-year-old Nelie de Haan travelling without a parent. When it proved difficult for her to obtain an official pass to cross a vital bridge and reach her intended destination in Friesland, the preacher at Hattem arranged for her to stay at a local farm. Cor Valk's mother at Almelo found a 'reception which exceeded all our expectations' at the Salvation Army. A cup of warm milk preceded a good meal and a guest bed at the home of a local family.

Military duty performed with excessive zeal could appear cruel to children who were forced to watch events which they could only partially comprehend and could do nothing to prevent. Mrs R.M. Bredius remembered as a girl hitch-hiking on a farm wagon to cross an important bridge over the IJssel early in the morning. Each person was closely scrutinised by the German guards. As wagons rolled through the snow and over the bridge the soldiers 'thrust their bayonets into the jute bags we were lying on'.

Fay Grindrod, still innocent at thirteen years of age, was coming to the end of a ten-day walk when two young men came running towards them. Some way behind the lads were soldiers with rifles and an officer was waving his hands. What happened next was truly horrifying:

One young man decided to stop and hide behind me. The other hid behind a cart. I knew from four years of war that they might execute me as well as the young stranger hiding behind me. I almost died of fear as the soldiers stopped and made a line along the road. They pointed the rifles at me. I heard the rifles explode and knew that I had died. When I came out of shock I became aware that I was still alive but the young stranger lay dying at my feet. I heard the enemy soldiers laugh and cheer. I felt great anger and was ready to tear the soldiers apart. My father shouted at me 'Let's run. Let's run!' My shame is that I ran away and left that young man to die on his own.

Eltjo van Leeuwen was approaching the age and stature when he might be viewed as fair game by a *Razzia* patrol. One day their walk had ended by a canal where some small peat-carrying boats were moored; unable to move because of the frozen water. He and his mother were allowed on board one of the boats to sleep. It was a fortunate change of accommodation:

> The next day we heard the Germans had visited during the night all the nearby farmhouses and had rounded up all the people of all ages who didn't belong there. They had been placed on a transport to be sent back. We had been lucky to have been on the little boat which the soldiers ignored.

Sometimes the local population contrived to outwit the occupier. Ed van der Beld's father was directed to work with the Air Civil Defence organisation and, as such, was issued with a large white official helmet. This did not, however, confer much authority upon him. On one occasion a large group of people with handcarts approached the bridge over the IJssel. The guards on duty were elderly and new to the locality. They barred the way to the refugees. Seeing this, Ed's father donned his impressive helmet and yelled to the guards in a loud voice to let the people through. Not only did the guards obey but they saluted the people as they passed by. It was a trick that Ed's father did not dare repeat too often.

Jake Bakker tried a similar trick which failed to impress but had the desired affect. Needing to cross the bridge near the Douwe Egberts factory he found it closed that day to non-military traffic. Only those carrying an '*Ausweis*' in German were permitted to cross. It was possible to be rowed across or be ferried over. However, Jake was in a hurry and thought a cheeky approach might work. Pushing his old bike up the incline he composed a few words in German to ask permission to cross. It was a dangerous tactic. Whether the guard had a sense of humour is not known, but hearing Jake's childish request the guard shouted to his commander, 'Can I let this boy cross?' And surprisingly the commander allowed Jake over.

Some children, wearied from walking vast distances, learned that, if there were bad Germans, there were also kind Germans. Inge Vat encountered Germans in a good mood and they would prove to be her saviours. Her brother and Inge were trudging along after days of walking when a German lorry overtaking them honked its horn and stopped. Soldiers in the lorry helped the children climb in and ride on in relative luxury. But the kindness extended even further:

> The lorry suddenly stopped and the soldiers jumped out. Not us. But then two soldiers came running back, grabbed us, dragged us into a ditch and sheltered us with their bodies. Seconds later a fighter plane flew over and sprayed the lorry with bullets. It couldn't be driven any more and burst into flames. The Germans were conversing with each other. We didn't understand. Then one soldier picked me up, put me on his shoulders and they then went marching along the road.

On arrival at the barracks nearby the children were given a meal, a seat in the kitchen in front of a big real fire and a bed for the night. 'We slept like logs'. In the morning they found their wet clothes washed and dried before eating breakfast and going on. 'It showed us that not all Germans were bad.'

Nelie de Haan saw from close quarters how the enemy in the pursuit of duty could vary from courtesy to violence in a moment. The farmer and his wife where Nelie was staying were away from the house when 'twenty soldiers of the *Feldchendarmerie* [military police] with bayonets fixed on their rifles' burst in to search for illegal refugees. As the eldest youngster there, 16-year-old Nelie told the Germans that she wanted all the children gathered safely around her before they began their search. She realised that 'I had disarmed their aggression'. They allowed her to collect the children and take them aside. But when she told them there were no people hiding on the farm their reaction was:

> ...to throw everything upside down and stick their bayonets into every-thing, beds, cupboards, hay lofts and just about anywhere people could hide. The house was a total shambles but they hadn't found anyone.

They then left leaving me to clean up the mess but I had succeeded in staying alive.

There were, of course, dangers from the country's own 'forces of law and order'. As with Sir Oswald Mosley's fascists in Britain, there were Dutch men of similar persuasion who volunteered for service 'on the other side'. Some served with the Waffen SS and were far away from home fighting the Russians. Within the country itself a 'Home Guard' type of organisation, the *Landwacht*, supplemented the German military police in carrying out political arrests. The regular Dutch police force at the time were also obliged to arrest whomsoever the occupation authorities might indicate. Therefore, it was not only the German uniform which spelled danger to civilians perpetrating such minimal offences as trying to cross a bridge without a pass or 'borrowing' a boat to row across the river."

The exceptional circumstances caused by famine did generate some crime as people became desperate for food. Ger Koks and his brother had been taken in by the Haverkamp brothers at their farm near Lettele. The farm horse was suffering from colic and Ger was about to take the animal for a walk in the dark. He was accosted by 'a guy with a handgun and a searchlight'. The horse was sent back to the stable and the humans were forced down into the cellar:

> Everything was stolen: hams, dried sausages from the attic; all new clothes and all bed linen. Nothing was left. We were ordered at gunpoint to stay in the cellar for 15 minutes, otherwise they would shoot. It was a dangerous experience. I would like to know who were responsible for this hit job [some assumed that it was the Dutch Underground].

Other ghostly figures, young men, used boats surreptitiously for purposes more aggressive than the quest for food. The same elusive individuals were also responsible for what would normally have been described as petty crime; stealing anything from guns to ration books.

In 1945 the geography of the Netherlands did not reveal any area like the French *maquis*; an extensive area of remote, densely forested hills and mountains, and large enough to hide and nourish large groups of Resistance fighters. Eventually known as the *Maquis,* these groups were able to assist the D–Day landings in Normandy by holding up German reinforcements. As interpreted by the Germans, the former rules of war classed such groups in civilian clothes as criminals and subject to capital punishment. Many resisters, both men and women, were indeed captured and shot. But, under the unrestricted rule of the Gestapo, capture could also mean cruel torture.

In central areas of the Netherlands there was no expansive *maquis.* There did exist, however, a much smaller but equally secluded wilderness of water and swamp called the *Biesbosch* (Wood of Rushes). Now a tourist area, in the 1940s it was an almost inaccessible area of islands, swampy reed land, rivers and creeks. Only a few people lived on small houseboats in isolation among the crowding trees and bulrushes.

After the failure to capture the vital Arnhem bridge in 1944, the Allies concentrated on clearing the area within the great bend of the River Maas. Dutch people there in Noord Brabant and the neighbouring areas felt the overwhelming joy of liberation from a foreign oppressor. However, the military planners saw no feasible way of crossing the wide Maas to liberate the remainder of the Netherlands. The joy of liberation in the south therefore exacerbated the frustration and traumas of the rest of the country. And as mentioned, there was no safe area in which large groups of young Dutch men could rally and help the cause of liberation.

Military strategy had also dictated that the new frontline along river banks in winter 1944 should run through the *Biesbosch*. And it was here that a comparatively few but extremely brave young men in groups of two or three could continue to contribute actively to undermining the occupying power. The watery wilderness lay conveniently on the escape route for people with significant reasons for escaping from areas controlled by the enemy. These included Allied airmen who had been shot down, paratroopers who had survived the Arnhem debacle on the wrong side of the river, intelligence agents, and also Resistance workers whose cover had been blown.

Small boats, with one or two men rowing, could do very little to relieve the great famine in the cities to the north. However, there was the opportunity to convey small items like vital medicines on the northward journeys. The remit of the Resistance fighters was to carry out covert operations and help escaping Allied air crews, but at the risk of excruciating torture if caught. It was here that men like Piet van den Hoek and Arie van Driel worked secretly and anonymously on the fringes of normal human society.[12]

On 13 January 1945 Piet and his comrade Thijs were sent in their boat across the *Biesbosch* towards Werkendam, where they were to collect some men. Normally they would row close in to the banks to escape observation. That night there was thick ice at the edges of the stream so they had to travel down the middle. They were observed and gunfire was directed at them from the banks. Piet and Thijs acted according to standing orders: they lay down in the boat and started throwing their cargo overboard, which was already weighted with stones in order to sink in such an emergency. Then they rowed to the bank and tried to escape but found the area was full of soldiers. They tried to run through the thick reeds but a German soldier loomed up in front of them, pointing his sub-machine gun at them menacingly and shouting, 'Hande hoch'.

A *Feldwebel* (corporal) asked them what they were doing, to which they replied that they were on their way to a farm to find food. He demanded their '*Nachtausweis*', for permission to travel during curfew hours, but of course they had no such document. Then the German demanded Piet's binoculars which were hanging on his chest. Piet realised to his horror that he had forgotten to throw the glasses away and that they were British night glasses. Piet was quick-witted enough to claim that he had bought the glasses before the war, but the explanation was not believed and they were arrested; expecting to be tortured or shot forthwith.

Strangely the German commander seemed to be more fascinated by the unusual night glasses than concerned about the prisoners. So they were merely marched away and taken to a labour camp. Here they were made to dig trenches. The camp was overcrowded and the guards were short-staffed. Eventually Piet and Thijs managed to slip away and arrived back at the *Biesbosch* to resume duties just a month after they were arrested. The first night back they did another crossing of the river.

Not every 'crosser' was as fortunate. The leader of the Resistance group was Arie van Driel. Arie and his rowing partner Kees van de Sande were making their 54th crossing with three intelligence agents on board. Unfortunately the much-used boat began to leak badly. Rowing became dangerous and a German patrol boat caught up with them. The boat occupants were transported to Rotterdam prison for interrogation by the secret police. Both Arie and Kees were tortured and did not expect to live. Then hope was born. Allied troops were approaching and the prison authorities were already liaising with the Resistance on a handover deal. The first requirement was that executions should cease. The Germans complied. But there was a last twist of fate. Just as the war was ending and peace was being celebrated in various ways, a drunken German soldier, whose motives can only be speculated upon, shot and killed both men.

The Resistance men had operated in total secrecy, without visible signs of their work and relied upon secret passwords for identification. Advancing Allied troops were able to recognise the Resistance men because they donned orange armbands as the troops drove in. By order of the Dutch government they then became the *Binnenlandse Strijdkrachten* (Internal Forces) responsible in each locality for security as the German-appointed authorities were expelled from the town councils. Piet received the highest Dutch award for bravery and recognition from three Allied countries. He survived the war and later became the longest-living 'crosser' of the *Biesbosch*. Those 'crossers' never had rank or title of any kind during the war.[13]

Meanwhile, on 25 April 1945 Harry Parkins, a Flight Engineer with 576 (Bomber) Squadron, RAF Fiskerton, was ordered to take all the guns and ammunition out of the Lancaster bombers which he and his men were servicing. 'No, the war hasn't ended yet,' he was told. 'You are going to load up with food to drop to the starving Dutch.' Having carried out thirty-nine bombing raids to kill enemies he was now destined to participate in six raids to save the lives of allies.[14]

The famine of *De Hongerwinter* was now so extreme that the Allies decided to take urgent measures; negotiating with the German authorities in the Netherlands whilst the war still continued. This was not the first time such humanitarian arrangements were made during the war. When a famine had threatened in German-occupied Greece, the *Flotmarin* had agreed to allow Royal Navy ships through the blockade with food supplies. This was achieved through the agency of the group which later became Oxfam.[15]

All planned war-time battles were labelled Operation so-and-so. The mission to bring food relief to the Dutch was named Operation Manna after the Old Testament story of the Israelites in the desert saved from starvation by manna from heaven. It was in every sense a 'heavenly' experience for the undernourished civilians in dropping zones such as Delft, Valkenburg and Rotterdam.

After delay due to bad weather, eight fast Mosquito aircraft took off on 29 April to identify dropping zones. The Germans had marked out each agreed landing strip with a large white cross in the middle. The Mosquito leaders radioed in a first force of 242 Lancaster bombers flying as low as might be safe, sometimes below 500 feet, and at the slowest possible speed. As the planes released their loads German ground crews fired green flares if the parcels were hitting the target and red flares when they missed. Arie de Jong, a 17-year-old, excitedly noted in her diary:

> No words to describe the emotions experienced on Sunday afternoon... four-engined Lancasters... suddenly filled the horizon. One could see the gunners in their turrets... One Lancaster roared over the town at 70 feet. I saw one aircraft tacking between church steeples to drop its bags.... everybody dared to wave cloths and flags. What a feast!

In an extraordinary reversal of angles, air crew were looking up to see Dutch people waving; and civilians were looking down to greet the airmen. Having had brief notice of the incoming air armada people had climbed into windmills, church towers and other high points. They found the huge bombers passing by at almost stalling speed below them. A pilot remembered looking up at people on the balcony of a windmill and another saw 'Thank you, Tommy' written hurriedly on a roof.[16]

Altogether over 5,000 flights took place during this relief operation, the majority flown by the RAF. The American Army Air Force also joined in with some 2,000 of those flights. However, the American effort went under the rather more bizarre title of Operation Chowhound. Neutral Sweden sent supplies by sea and land transport. But it would need liberation by ground forces before the main work could begin: reconstructing disrupted transport systems and importing enough food to provide regular and sufficient supplies.

On the ground civilians were making preparations for the dangerous final battles. Ger Koks, staying with the Haverkamp brothers at their farm, found that the brothers were not sure what to do about any impending battle. When they heard the sound of sustained shooting in the distance Ger suggested that they dig a foxhole, place a thick wooden door over it and load the door down with sods. Just behind the farm was a German artillery position and the incoming liberators were targeting that battery. A large rye stack caught fire and lit up the sky as the dry stalks flared high. Ger and the brothers huddled down in the foxhole.[17]

At the convent where Henk Meurs found refuge, the Germans had located a radio communications and listening post in the tower. An artillery battery had also dug in within the cloisters. Father Desiderius was not impressed by the behaviour of the German troops, who would obviously have no empathy with the silent Catholic order. Under the strain of impending defeat the soldiers 'cursed and abused all around'. Sensibly the monks shut themselves in the abbey cellars and settled down for a long wait. Fortunately for the beautiful abbey complex the soldiers were suddenly ordered to withdraw silently on the night of 10 April.

On the farm where she was staying, Nelie de Haan helped to hide the draught horses. The wagon and dray were taken to pieces and also hidden. Then German soldiers arrived on foot and hurriedly searched the farm. Before long they found a horse and the parts of the wagon, which they reassembled. Then, taking anything of use to themselves, they jumped into the wagon and retreated. Nelie later watched in astonishment as girls who had fraternised with German soldiers were summarily punished. They had their hair shorn off. 'Thereafter the German swastika was painted on their heads with red lead paint.' As to people in general, having survived enemy occupation and starvation, 'we were beside ourselves with happiness and our red, white and blue flags flapping happily in the wind'.

If Nelie, Ger and Henk thought that that was the end of the *Hongerwinter* chapter; they were sadly mistaken. It continues. The

Dutch famine has become a classic for health researchers involved in longitudinal studies on the impact of starvation.

Famine normally occurs in undeveloped regions with poor communications infrastructure and primitive health systems. Hospital records tend to be sketchy and soon lost, if indeed they ever existed.[18] In 1945 the Netherlands, in spite of the war, still enjoyed one of the most efficient hospital maternity services and sophisticated health recording systems in the world. New-born babies were measured not only for birth weight but also crown-to-heel length, head circumference and ratios between these. It has therefore been possible to check on the way in which the impact of famine on a newly conceived baby continues to inflict suffering on that individual in old age. Other babies conceived at the time did not enjoy normal longevity due to illnesses deriving from starvation in the womb.

The late 1990s onwards have been the time when babies from 1945 reached ages permitting significant research conclusions to be formed. The *Hongerwinter* was responsible for the fact that many persons born in 1945 suffered in later years from various long-term problems. These include a greater susceptibility to diabetes, three times more likelihood of heart and vascular attacks, exacerbated cholesterol levels, more fatty deposit, kidney disease, breast cancer, and mental problems including schizophrenia.

One summary carries a striking, if academically restrained, quote: 'It now appears that the limited food intake of mothers who were pregnant during this period altered the genetic material of embryos in the early stages of development. The effects of this can still be observed some sixty years later.' That particular research focussed on the 'degree of methylation of a piece of DNA, the IGF2 gene', comparing the subjects with their unaffected siblings.[19]

An indication of the accuracy of health records in the chaos and stress of war is that the studies were able to distinguish between the effect on babies in the first three months of pregnancy, the worst period, and those in the last months *in utero*. In some cases there was a difference between the sexes; for example, in the pronounced tendency of older females to suffer from increased fat deposits regardless of eating habits in later life.[20]

These longitudinal studies do not indicate the numbers of early deaths due to the after-effects of famine and do not include reference to those who died during the famine – often quoted as 20,000. One gleam of medical hope emerged from the food crisis. Children long deprived of wheat were quickly fed extra amounts to help their rehabilitation. This included rich Swedish bread. The frequent and violent stomach reactions which followed prompted a Dutch doctor, Willem Dicke, to identify the cause of Coeliac Disease and prescribe the remedy.

A further sad thought, but not yet substantiated by research, is that if cases of schizophrenia can now be identified in survivors into the twenty-first century. What mental traumas must have been suffered soon after the war and how many suicides must have been the eventual outcome in civilians who escaped the bombs and bullets of the battling armies?

Tony van Vugt endured a gruelling *Hongertocht* but, in addition to malnutrition, was greatly affected by a lack of education. Many teachers had been caught up by the *Razzias*, buildings were destroyed or used for refugees and some schools ceased to function for a significant period of a small child's development. Older children were so scarred psychologically that they remained dumb about their experiences until, in some cases, they relived their *Hongertocht* with other victims in a 2007 reunion organised by Tony and his family.[21]

Fay Grindrod remembers how she dealt with her girlhood fears; especially after such events as the time when the secret police burst into the house and assaulted her father, before carrying him away. That night she went to bed full of guilt for not doing anything to help her father. Then:

> I fell asleep in the arms of an imaginary prince, who I had created some time ago when things were bad. I believed deeply in the story of Cinderella and… her prince who carried her away on a white horse to a safe haven. Imaginary stories for a child in time of despair brings hope and energy in a chaotic world that has lost all its reasoning.

Later, in a more humorous vein, Diet van der Burgh recalled that during the famine she and her family had lived near the famous tulip fields where tulips were intended to flower and bring joy; not to be eaten in some dire emergency. 'We worked out later that our family had eaten a good-sized field of the little red tulips,' during the famine.

A more formal summing-up stated, 'Before the War Holland had been one of the best fed and healthiest countries imaginable. Now in five short years Holland was one of the most miserable places on earth.'[22] However, the nation which conquered the encroaching seas would again show its resilience by rebuilding the country to its former glory and state of plenty.

CHAPTER SIX

RHINE CRUISES – NO MOD CONS

Here are barriers through which you must pass 'ere you can traverse the river. A strong force guards this post.

(Herodotus, 440 BC)

The *Bund* loomed up in the darkness ahead; high, level and solid like the wall of a medieval fortress. The *Bund* was a huge anti-flood embankment. Engineers had blown a gap in the packed earth but a previous vehicle had shed a track, crawled around like a wounded cockroach and blocked the gap. No time to halt and wait for the repair men!

'Try full revs, Mike', ordered Rex Jackson, 1NY, recently awarded the Military Medal and promoted to lance-corporal in command of the clumsy machine. The aptly named Buffalo was not built for hill climbing. Neither did it appear to have been designed for floating, but Rex and Mike had been ordered to drive into the river inside this mechanical monstrosity in total darkness. 'Full revs and keep it going'. The ugly Buffalo turned its nose up, and up, and up, until it seemed it must turn over backwards. Then with the final pressure of Mike Hunt's foot on the accelerator it perched a moment triumphant on the top of the *Bund*, teetering towards the unseen waters of the rushing river.

'Hold it steady. Down gently. Gently!' But as the vessel pointed down, its tons of grinding iron gathered impetus instantly and rushed faster and faster – 'Brakes!' Beyond human control the Buffalo plunged into the dark swirling waters, which sucked it down, and down again. Water rushed into the iron box fixed on top of the now locked tank tracks. 'Pumps!' The squad of infantrymen inside the box seemed petrified, unable to help. Then, after wallowing for a few long moments in the water, the Buffalo began to make slow progress across the wide expanse of merging belts of darkness. Restless waves continually splashed into the box and threatened to overwhelm the simple bilge pump. Gunfire contributed brilliant blasts of light which made the darkness seem even blacker. Eyes could only stare at flashing purple and orange blotches in the blind vacuum.

Rex and Mike followed instructions, 'point nose diagonally upstream at 45 degrees from target allowing for drift', but without much hope. It was with considerable surprise that they were eventually thrust by the river into the far bank. And luckily at a place where tiny signal lights on painted tin unit signs proved that it was a chosen landing beach. They were across the Rhine after 300 yards of mingled frustration and terror. 'Ramp down! Unload!' Duck under a shower of mortar bombs. 'Driver, reverse. Back off. Swing round. Head back home.'

It could have been worse. It did get worse. Arriving on the safe side of the river Rex's Buffalo was hit by another vehicle emerging from the obscurity of night and drifting smoke. The engine cut out. The river seized the unwieldy craft and pulled it back out into midstream. With no proper steering gear the Buffalo turned round and round. Mike managed to start the engine. But where was land? And which land was home? Smoke and clouds obscured the moon and stars and, in any case, their training had been too rapid to allow a true mariner's study of astronomy and navigation. Artificial war-stars of flame were flashing everywhere. They had to steer by sheer blinkered hope.

Briefing had included very detailed scale sand-models of the areas on both sides of the river. Struggling to achieve success with his first command, Rex was still aware that, with a continuing drift, the mighty river would inevitably land him and his human freight on a stretch of bank near Rees held by the enemy. At that moment, off the starboard bow ('starboard' if it had been a real ship) Rex saw, silhouetted against successive shell-bursts, a profile of buildings and spires on the Calcar bank, which he recognised from the sand-models. Breathing a sigh of relief he ordered Mike to stop one track and veer towards the safe haven. Mike himself breathed an even deeper sigh of relief for he was due to go on homeland leave next morning, and a prisoner of war camp was not a welcome alternative.[1]

Given the overall name Operation Plunder, the attempt to cross the last major river-barrier before the German hinterland had been delayed by the Germans' Ardennes advance. Now six months after the failure to cross the same river at Arnhem, it was time to go across before the Allied armies became a laughing stock for the Russians who were advancing successfully across hundreds of miles from the east. Might 'they' even manage to reach the far bank of the river Rhine before 'we' had managed to cross it in full force?

Thus, even in the closing stages of the war, crossing the Rhine would be one of the greatest combined operations of the whole war. The artillery would again be called upon to exceed all previous weight of fire. Airborne troops would come in both by parachute and glider. Infantry divisions would cross the water in small storm boats or huge Buffalo carriers, supported by some swimming tanks. Bombers from the air would saturate target areas. Typhoon dive bombers would stalk and attack enemy armour. Fighter planes would embark on domination of the skies. Even the navy would provide patrols on the river; enabling engineers to throw bridges across for yet more follow-up and echelon traffic to risk the hazardous crossing.

It would be a huge undertaking but the prize would be correspondingly rich. In front of the Rhine the Germans had built the Siegfried Line, now totally breached. Beyond the river the German commanders had argued the pros and cons of trying to establish another firm line of defence. Commanders on the ground knew that there would be neither the time, manpower nor equipment to establish another Siegfried-style barrier. The defence would have to depend on scattered strategic points and immediate counter-attack.[2] A successful British and Canadian breakthrough around Emmerich, Rees and Wesel would open up the hinterland of Germany to the overwhelming Allied armoured columns.

Farther south, due to a freak coincidence of enemy error, attackers' initiative and individual heroism, the Americans had already seized the bridge at Remagen. But that did not open up direct and easy routes for the Allied armour, like those in the north, nor did it provide sufficient roadway for the vast Allied force to cross in attacking formation. In parallel with Operation Plunder, three American armies would exploit Remagen, open other crossings and, with the French Army towards the distant Vosges Mountains, move forward into more difficult battle areas already beyond the Rhine barrier.

1NY had already been warned to trade in their Shermans for the unfamiliar Buffalo carriers in mid-January. 44 RTR were told that they would man DD tanks, the waterproofed vehicles that could swim, as they had on the first D-Day in Normandy. But for most troops the intensive preparations commenced on 12 March.[3]

Mine-destroying Crab tanks (adapted Shermans) were often first into the action. A Crab commander, Normandy veteran Capt. Ian Hammerton, was amazed at the preparations after travelling through floods and 'perpetual oily smokescreen' to the Rhine banks for briefings:

> What caused us astonishment was to see naval landing craft as well as tugs, bridging pontoons, Bailey bridging materials and the like carried along the roads on huge transporters. Enormous dumps of stores, ammunition, fuel and material were being set up in the area adjacent to the Rhine, fortunately without attracting the attention of the Luftwaffe which was conspicuously absent. There was soon going to be another D-Day.[4]

Back in Britain Capt. Hugh Clark, MC, attended an Order Group on 19 March which alerted his air landing unit, 2nd Ox and Bucks in Bulford, to pack up, move to Colchester and be sealed within a guarded perimeter fence for security. There he was introduced to Sgt Norman Elton and Sgt Des Page who were to be the pilots of his glider when they landed 8 miles to the east of the Rhine. Around them parachute brigades and the American 17th Airborne Division would also be concentrating on high ground behind the foremost German defences. Eight gliders were allotted to the company with platoon numbers chalked behind cockpit windows. Gliders one to six would carry the Ox and Bucks company. Seven and eight would hold Royal Engineers provided with explosives for mining smaller bridges if they needed to form an armed camp behind enemy lines. Their air column would consist of 440 British gliders. And 'don't worry about anti-aircraft fire because what our artillery can't deal with the RAF will wipe out'. If the British could be secretive, so could the Germans because, as Hugh was being briefed, the enemy already had 256 anti-aircraft guns waiting for them, and reinforcements were arriving every day.[5]

Frank Gutteridge and his men, in the midst of preparing for the Rhine crossing, were ordered to clean up and parade for inspection by FM Montgomery. Sergeant-majors lined up the men in formal fashion but 'Monty' ordered them to break ranks and gather round his Jeep. 'He gave a short pep talk and then ended with "Well, good luck and good hunting, chaps, and I wish I were with you". This led to some merriment in the ranks and remarks such as "Orlrite fer 'im" and "Oi'll change places wiv 'im" as he drove off to headquarters.'[6]

Lower down the echelon of command Pte Dunesby with the Seaforth Highlanders was in a forest near the Rhine when, on 23 March, the battalion commander called the entire battalion together and spoke to them. His first words were 'to us has been granted the honour of being first across the Rhine'. An infantry colonel would be well up with the men, sharing their dangers, and so his remarks were as much of comradeship as of command. The colonel then outlined the general plan before the battalion broke down into platoons for specific orders.[7]

Meanwhile, training as Buffalo drivers, Bill Mosely and crew were billeted with Ma and Pop Op T'Eindt. He and his pals were popular with Ma and Pop because they had rescued the elderly civilians from a group of drunken Americans waving brandy bottles and yelling, 'Where are all the goddam dames?' Their farewell meal was Ma's speciality, a Belgian fondue. Bill had made it clear that they could not talk about their 'Rhine Transportation Company Unlimited'. They were on a secret mission. No civilians were allowed into the Buffalo training area. To their astonishment Ma and Pop replied that they knew all about it and could recite more details of the coming Operation Plunder than Bill and crew were themselves aware of. So much for all the secrecy, the perpetual smoke screen and Hugh Clark's men shut off behind a fence in Colchester.[8]

On 23 March the NY diary noted that at 17.00 hours the artillery barrage opened up 'with a shattering roar from massed guns' as '120 enemy positions were subjected to a minimum of five tons of shells apiece'. Jack Swaab, directing some of the barrage, was located in a 'smashed attic in a smashed village', which was his OP. The gunfire was so tremendous that 'the whole skeleton of the farmhouse trembles.

Everywhere the ground is pitted with shell holes.' As he was watching 'great smoke pyres rising skywards' and writing down notes for later report, '4 shells landed plumb outside this HQ with 4 sudden crashes – 2 wounded, one pretty badly… Jerry gave us a most savage pasting… and the roof came tumbling in'. It was not just the enemy who wilted under the two-way barrage.[9]

The immense volume of fire also included the 'land mattress' developed by the Canadians and so called because a discharge filled the sky with an almost solid mass of rocket projectiles. For Operation Plunder there were twenty-four rocket projectors; each consisting of thirty-two firing rails. On the word 'fire' the thirty-two rockets on the rails would shoot away together as a conjoined bundle of explosive. Several, if not all of the twenty-four projectors could be aimed and fired together as an even larger 'bundle'. This fearsome weapon was added to a normal gun barrage three times the size of the famous El Alamein barrage (2,645 guns compared to 980).[10]

This display of pyrotechnics served to confirm to the German commander, General Schlemm, of the defending 1st Parachute Army, the general direction and time of the attack. Yet he marvelled that any of his men could possibly survive. His instructions were 'deep and narrow foxholes for one or two men have to be dug. The men have to have nerves of steel'. His *Fallschirmtruppen* were veterans who were either inured to intense shellfire or, in some cases, so mentally damaged as to be immune from any thought of danger that they became almost robotic.[11]

One of the unsung minor players in this action was the unique Canadian Army Meteorological Group. This provided advice on wind and other weather conditions and enabled not only the correct initial positioning of smoke generators, but also, where necessary, a movement of those generators in accordance with varying weather. This improved accuracy and avoided waste as 200 tons of zinc chloride and fog oil were consumed daily to maintain a 30 mile smoke screen over the river. At about the same time during the final assault on Arnhem the smoke screen, perhaps not so well informed on atmospheric conditions, proved to be less than effective.[12]

In the air above the river, following the heavy planes from Bomber Command, was John Shellard in his Typhoon. It was a 'full wing show', all five squadrons of Typhoons aloft at the same time. Ordered

1. 19 September, 1939. At the Tatarska Pass into Hungary, the then Col Maczek (in beret) addresses his troops before leaving Poland to continue the fight. (*Mieczkowski*)

2. Christmas card sent home by NY soldiers, 1944. Unfortunately the war would not be over soon and very few British troops would reach Berlin. (*J. Howell and P. Bonney*)

"Merry Christmas — shan't be long!"

3. NY tanks in deep Ardennes snow. The air intake through the turret hatch, and the 30 tons of steel armour constituted an almost unbearable deep-freezer for the crew to ride in. (*NY archive*)

4. A patrol of the Royal Regiment of Canada in snow suits leaves Nederrijksche Woud, near Groesbeek, to test Siegfried Line defences, as on the Matheson patrol. (*Bennett, Royals*)

5. Bravest of the Brave: four late war VCs whose exploits are mentioned. *Left to right – top:* Cosens and Tilson. *Below:* Topham and Chapman.

6. Tank troopers survey an 88-mm anti-tank gun and gunner knocked out during the Roer Triangle battles. (*Gootzen*)

ATTACK BY CROCODILE (CHURCHILL) FLAME THROWER IN VILLAGE OF UPHUSEN → TOWARDS BREMEN. INFANTRY COOPERATION · 1945

7. Peter White's own impression of a flame-throwing Crocodile in action in support of his infantrymen of the KOSBs at Uphusen, near Bremen. (*White/Sutton*)

8. After the Crocodiles and artillery have wrought havoc, men of the Rifle Brigade tread over the still burning turf, obscured by smoke and mist in the Roer. (*Gootzen*)

9. Engineer Capt. Ernest Egli (here aged 22) was an acute observer of all things military and mechanical, including mines and pillboxes. (SWWEC)

10. A Typhoon dive bomber. The pilot (Derek Tapson) and the pilot's dog comfortably ensconced in the plane's air intake. The plane could dive at 500 mph. (Tapson)

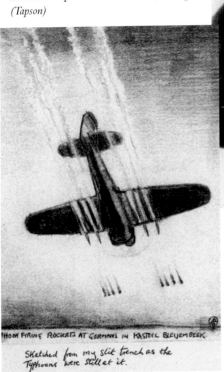

'HOON FIRING ROCKETS AT GERMANS IN KASTEEL BLEIJEMBEEK.

Sketched from my slit trench as the Typhoons were still at it.

11. Peter White saw the Typhoons dive in towards the hitherto impregnable Kasteel Blijenbeek, blasting open the walls. He sketched his view of the epic event. (White/Sutton)

12. Mk IV tank and driver Manfred Thorn, of 1st SS Panzer *Leibstandarte* division, who served in action for three years but was only nineteen when the war ended. *(Toon-Thorn)*

13. Staff-Sgt Ken Cardy, DCM *(right)*, REME and Welsh Guards crews halt for a break during the rush to the Ardennes, at Ciney, Christmas Day, 1944. No time for parties. Photo taken with illicit camera on wartime quality film. *(Cardy)*

14. For the weary footsloggers and frozen tank crews Hongen was just another little village on the road to Berlin. 19 January, and many more villages yet to storm through. (Gootzen)

15. Much maligned (by crews) amphibian Buffalos did splendid service crossing the Rhine, enabling infantry to establish bridgeheads across the river while the bridges were being built. (Tank Museum)

16. After Allied bombers had destroyed Rhine bridges, as on the right, the engineers had to replace them by perilously narrow pontoon constructions. (Solarz)

17. In Dutch communities near the frontier, where German troops were reinforcing defences, civilians were evacuated *en masse*, here from the Venlo area. *(illegal photo, 1945, permission of Beeldbank WO2)*

18. In Dutch towns German troops carried out *Razzias* to round up males of working age for forced labour projects, as shown here during a massive swoop in Rotterdam. *(illegal photo, 1945, Beeldbank WO2/ Schinck)*

19. During the Hunger Winter many urban Dutch mothers walked great distances, pushing prams in search of food or to find temporary homes for their children. *(Beeldbank WO2 per Ger Schinck, himself evacuated as a baby)*

20. During *de Hongerwinter* miniature ovens, about 10 inches high, were produced and were suitable for small portions like soup made from sugar beet and tulip bulbs. Tiny chips of wood heated the food. *(Heideveld, VOGW)*

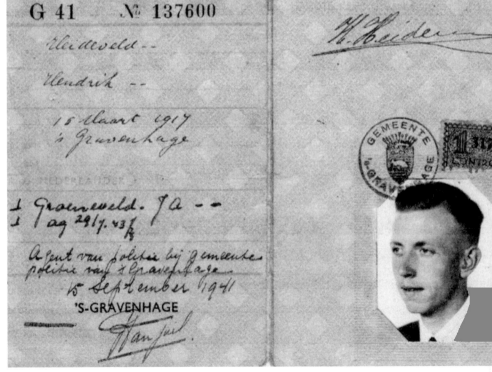

21. Police Constable Heideveld, as shown on his identity card, carried out normal police duties, but was also on call by German authorities to arrest Dutch citizens if required. *(M. Heideveld)*

22. The thrill of liberation at long last: Dutch girls write their names (and at least one address) on a Polish tank which had just liberated their town. (*Mieczkowski*)

23. The threat of invasion in 1940 caused all British road signs to be removed. However, German road authorities left a little guidance for Allied vanguards. Tank with petard. (*Solarz*)

24. Polish infantry with Bren machine-gun await probable enemy counter-attack. Whilst some villages were totally flattened by artillery and air bombing, much fighting took place in partly demolished areas. (*Mieczkowski*)

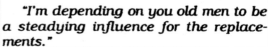

"I'm depending on you old men to be a steadying influence for the replacements."

26. Pulitzer Prize-winning cartoonist Bill Mauldin, himself wounded, caught the spirit of 20-year-olds like Stan Whitehouse who had become the 'old men' steadying new recruits, often older than themselves. *(Hal Steward)*

25. SS General Sepp Dietrich, frequently in the front line, examines the rifle of Pte Wolfsgrueber (2nd SS Panzer, *Adolf Hitler* – name on cuff band). The arm chevron denotes Dietrich was a 'Hitler Guard' before 1933. *(Toon-Thorn)*

27. Lt Maria Milewska reports the Warsaw women's battalion 'present and correct' to Col Stanislaw Koszutski, who led the hazardous drive which unexpectedly liberated the women's POW camp. (Mieczkowski)

LAST BRIDGE of the WAR COMPLETED 0759hrs 5 MAY 1945

28. The last bridge of the war! – but the engineers were still building bridges over numerous rivers and canals well after VE Day, due to the Allied bombing of strategic targets. (Jarzambowski)

29. Personal surrender: a German soldier, typical of many, except that this one was thought to be only 14-years-old and in regular uniform. Many such lads were encountered later in *Volksturm* units. *(Gootzens)*

30. Mass surrender: the commanding officer and burgomaster of Wilhelmshaven surrender the town and naval base to 1st Polish Armoured division. Victory achieved long after its extraordinary odyssey commenced on 1 September, 1939. *(Jarzambowski)*

31. Col Grudzinski *(centre)* and Maj. Gutowski study maps of Wilhelmshaven, paying special attention to minefields. The information was provided by the commander of the German naval base. *(Jarzambowski)*

32. Capt. Bill Bellamy receives his Military Medal from FM Montgomery. The Army Group Commander made a feature of such well-publicised medal award parades 'in the field'. *(Bellamy)*

33. Sgt Jock Sterling's knocked-out tank. The entry hole of the fatal shot is clearly visible on the turret. The AP round, travelling at 2,000 feet per second, went right through the turret, leaving a similar exit hole. Photo handed in by unknown trooper with camera taken from German tank. *(Hammerton)*

34. POW photo of Roland England, 1NY, who was missing presumed buried, but returned like a ghost unexpectedly. The letter from his former commander, Geoff Falconer, expressed delighted surprise. *(NY archive)*

35. Bill Maudlin's cartoon depicts 'cavalryman shoots faithful steed', an ancient tradition at war's end in some horsed units. George Blackburn and Manfred Thorn expressed similar farewell thoughts. (*Hal Steward*)

36. At risk of death, Polish concentration camp prisoners Tadeuse Wasowice, Josef Kachel and Stefan Dziwlik acquired materials and drew scenes of atrocities by SS guards. This drawing was given to Joe Solarz.

37. Like many survivors from the war, Canadian hero Bud Jones, with his wife Joyce, returned to visit the graves of comrades. Here at the grave of his old Royals platoon leader. *(Jones)*

38. The author *(left)*, with 1944 1NY comrade Ron West, officiates at the inauguration ceremony of a 1944 tank set up as a memorial to their regiment by the council of La Roche in the Ardennes, 2004. *(Tout)*

39. Joe Solarz in his nineties is cared for by wife Gloria, having been diagnosed with Brill-Zinsser disease; a long-term recurrence of typhus resulting from concentration camp interpreter duty at the war's end. *(Solarz)*

40. Stan Hicken, 1NY, planned to open a garage with Bill Rawlins, but Bill was killed, his tank burned out. German soldiers buried Bill and chalked on his tank *Du wast gerwerdet* – 'you never had a chance'. *(Hicken)*

to draw the flak at 1,000 feet (assuming that the fast flying Typhoons would be at less risk than the slow tug planes with their gliders) he surveyed the scene:

> The area was full of glider tugs, gliders, Dakotas, supply aircraft (some petrol tankers, I understand) all flying in this murk. The smoke and dust covered a few square miles and rose to a great height. We were supposed to be looking out for flak and then to attack the flak battery, but it was difficult to see one's wingman let alone flak! 'B' flight came out of it at the end and I was most surprised to find us all in the same piece of sky. Later that day I flew another sortie and we 'killed' two enemy tanks beyond the drop zone.[13]

Maj. Lord George Scott, who had had a momentary vision of a second battle of Waterloo, now returned from homeland leave to find that the colonel, Doug Forster, had been seriously injured in a jeep accident and that he was now commanding one of the amphibious river crossings at a few hours notice. He found Lt Owen arranging the lighting and signing of Buffalo routes for two squadrons of 1NY. The routes were to pass through the *Bund* and descend to two launching beaches from which a total of six craft could be sent into the river at one time. By now the crews had obtained some mastery over the strange amphibians, but had not yet mustered any kind of affection for the creature.

Brian Carpenter's Buffalo carried an unusual load. The crews were trained to transport a Bren carrier with four infantrymen and a stack of ammunition boxes. But on their first run they were weighed down with rolls of chestnut palings. These were to be unrolled on the far side of the river for the DD tanks to be able to get a grip on landing. As they were approaching the *Bund* they heard a loudspeaker voice, apparently an urgent signal because they were fitted with wireless for routine messages. 'No vehicles through the gap! Closed by debris. Go up and over the *Bund*'. Like Rex and Mike, Brian contemplated this unwanted venture in hill climbing. However, driver Den Burnand literally closed his eyes and jammed down the accelerator. For a moment their high pile of palings threatened to roll back over them. Then they were up and over and, in spite of Den's best efforts, rushing into the water. The positions of driver and radio operator in front were fitted with hatches which fortunately they had closed. The Buffalo plunged down below their hatch level. All and sundry were doused with oily water and the comments of the Canadians squatting around the palings were unprintable.[14]

1NY carried the 51st Highland Division who, unlike the yeomen, had little opportunity to get to know the Buffalo. Sgt Richard Brew was not attracted to the craft:

> Bloody enormous tanks with the turrets taken out [a slight confusion with the Kangaroo as the Buffalo never had a turret]. They were huge. How the hell they were going to float I had no idea. It was about the scariest thing I had ever done in the war, going over that river in a solid lump of iron that looked like it wanted to sink. When we got to the other side we had to jump out of them and as they were about six foot off the ground it was a wonder that we didn't all break our legs.[15]

The first wave of Buffalos at 21.00 hours on 23 March carried sappers to clear mines. These were followed by signallers to lay wires. Leading 7th Black Watch was Maj. Rollo who would act as beachmaster for the operation. Slipping silently across in storm boats at 22.00 hours was 1st Commando Brigade, tasked to rush inland, ignoring the defences on the far river bank and going on to capture the town of Wesel.

Another sergeant, Andrew Imrie of the Black Watch, felt in retrospect that the hardest part was waiting to start; not an unusual sentiment among soldiers:

> We climbed into our Buffalo at seven o'clock and then began the long wait. Minutes seemed like hours. Bit by bit we crawled to the river. We all wanted to get it over. There'd be spells of quietness and then our guns would lash out. It was in some way a relief when those grand chaps, the Buffalo Boys, started to take us across. I remember how uncanny it was. I know I wasn't the only one to mumble a little prayer. We got across without a casualty. The boys got their first objective, a communication trench. Within ten minutes there was a stream of prisoners. I remember those Jerries' expressions – they were bomb-happy.[16]

At tense times there was often a moment of humour. As Buffalos reached the shore they found the smallest man in 1NY standing in a slit trench which might have been dug for a guardsman. Almost invisible, little Jock McGregor's voice contended with the general cacophony shouting, 'Nae tae the richt. Meens! Stricht aheed. Nae tae the richt'. It might have been comprehensible to the Black Watch but it left some English yeomen scratching their heads.

There was no humour in Rex Jackson's next task. He became a 'grouser' twice over when a collision with another craft damaged the small metal fittings attached to the tracks to give more of a paddle effect in water, curiously named 'grousers', giving him much cause to 'grouse'. Now Rex and Mike had to dismount and carry out repairs with no cover from constant mortar and machine-gun fire. They had to detach some of the grousers from one track and fit them on the damaged track, there being no spares. This involved crawling around in the mud, hammering at recalcitrant bent steel, bruising fingers in the dark and generally cursing the Buffalo as much as the enemy across the river. The light of early dawn was beginning to compete with the fire-work display of the artillery, from both friend and foe. Then, through the noise of gunfire, and like a counter melody, there began the drone of innumerable aeroplanes as the great air fleet approached.

For the soldier on the ground much of war was sheer bore-dom. Even in a planned battle there could be times when nothing happened. Other days were given up to the tiring chores of main-tenance and replenishment. The soldier was left with his thoughts and the hopeful banter of his mates to entertain him. But from time to time he was treated to a free sky display by the Allied air forces. The soldier looked up, wondering and encouraged, as formations of aeroplanes, large and small, filled the skies: the huge Lancasters and Flying Fortresses; the swooping Typhoons; the circling Spitfires and Mustangs, sometimes in their hundreds. And rising dangerously in front of them were the wide beaded curtains of enemy anti-aircraft fire; slowly diminishing under the bombs and becoming sporadic flashes; blinking fiery eyes with furry eyebrows of smoke.

So it was on the banks of the last big river to be crossed that Fred Leary looked up and saw it:

An awesome sight, like a mini-invasion. Hundreds of aircraft took part, wave after wave of heavy bombers droning overhead, many of the planes towing gliders packed with paratroopers as they crossed the Rhine and circled round to return to England. Only on the return trip there were no gliders to be seen and the doors of the bombers were wide open. Leaving it to our imagination...[17]

Capt. Ernest Egli also watched and calculated the odds as they saw the empty aeroplanes returning. 'What we did not know at the time was that the Germans flak concentrated on the Horsa gliders and about half the gliders were damaged in the air and some did not land in the right place.' Nevertheless, his unit was informed that all was going well and that his brigade was in reserve for the time being.[18]

Men in danger on the ground empathised with men in danger in the air. Ian Hammerton, commanding his troop of mine-clearing Crab tanks, watched as Dakotas 'began shredding their strings of parachutists amid black flak bursts'. He then saw heavy bombers towing gliders, 'some towing three in formation', the tow lines loosed and the gliders descending:

> We cheered them on, not envying them their dangerous mission, especially when the flak was seen to touch a plane and send it spiralling to earth. What chance had the men inside? Suddenly a glider, hit by flak, lurched and spilled out a tank. How our hearts bled for the crew in that metal box crashing so heavily to the soil hundreds of feet beneath.[19]

Infantrymen, glad for once to have their feet on solid earth, also surveyed the skies and artist Peter White noted a peculiar beauty in the scene. 'White and black smoke-puffs burst, twinkling prettily to blossom like evil lily petals among dragonflies on a big blue pond.' His soldier's sense of reality quickly supervened on 'seeing such planes hit, stagger and spin down like dead autumn leaves'. One 'crashing glider smashed down', and onto a nearby farm where the adjutant had his HQ. 'A Dakota smoked down to lick in flames just beyond it'. And then 'quiet, suddenly there was an odd silence after the hours of storm'.[20]

Back in England the previous afternoon, Hugh Clark's platoon had pushed handcarts full of ammunition to their Horsa gliders. They indulged in a last few moments of humour by chalking girl's names on the gliders or jokes like 'Horsa keep your tail up' or 'Wot? No engines?' The RAF station commander 'took a dim view' of such pleasantries, as affecting the camouflage of the glider, and the men were ordered to clean off all their witticisms. At 03.00 hours on 24 March a hurried dish of fried eggs, bacon and beans was squeezed in before final loading at 04.00. Take off was at one minute intervals and Clark's towing Dakota, piloted by Sqn Ldr P.A. Clarke, was scheduled to go at 06.02, on a course north towards the Wash. There followed an anti-climax as they flew back and forwards over Essex in order to get the entire column correctly lined up with fighter escorts circling above.[21]

The paratroopers who jumped from their aircraft did not have a comfortable fall. They had to carry heavy equipment and fight as they landed. Canadian Russel C. Melanson carried a kit bag weighing between 75 and 80 pounds with mortar bombs in it. 'When you jumped your chute opened and then you had a 30 foot rope with the kitbag on it, which you then lowered'. As Melanson waited for his chute to open, a piece of flak shrapnel scraped across his finger and cut the kit bag line. He watched helplessly 'all my worldly possessions tumbling – the last I ever saw of them'. He had better fortune and landed in a tree with his toes touching the ground, 'so all I had to do was turn the block of my harness and smack it and walk out from under the tree'. However, his colonel, Jeff Nicklin, landed in a tree directly above a German machine-gun, which immediately shredded his body with a burst of bullets.

Horrifying things continued to happen. Above him the paratrooper saw a fighter plane with smoke streaming from a hit. The pilot rolled the plane over and kicked himself out, but bounced against the tail-plane. The collision seemed to alter the balance of the plane which then nosedived to the ground and exploded into flames. The pilot hit the ground nearby, bounced again, and his body fell into the inferno of fire around the plane. Shocked into action Melanson realised that the only weapon he had to hand was the shovel attached to his body. So grabbing the shovel he ran yelling into action. He was still capable of wondering what the enemy thought of one angry man brandishing a shovel – nobody seemed to be bothering to shoot him.[22]

Another Canadian paratrooper, 27-year-old medical orderly Cpl Frederick George Topham, had been chosen, like other medics of his unit, for his burly size, fitness and stamina. Advancing with his medical kit he saw two other medics mown down by machine-gun fire as they tried to help a fallen soldier. Topham ran through the storm of bullets and, as he worked on the badly wounded man, was himself shot, first through the cheek and then through the nose. For another two hours Topham continued working on casualties. Eventually he was ordered to go back for treatment. At that point a machine-gun carrier was hit and burst into flames. Topham immediately jumped into the carrier and one by one lifted out the three wounded soldiers from the carrier. One man died, but Topham carried the other two men into cover, one at a time. He was awarded the Victoria Cross for working for six hours under fire whilst in great pain, losing much blood and at imminent risk of losing his own life.[23]

Both paratroopers and glider-borne troops had to adapt rapidly as anti-aircraft fire caused the best of plans to go awry. Soldiers had to jump from burning aircraft before reaching their precise jumping point, which resulted in disorientation during the first few moments on the ground. Gliders crashed and caused problems for men trying to exit in a hurry. The appalling mixture of smoke of various kinds, burning planes, the drifting of the original smoke screen, a million explosions and even rendezvous flares made observation difficult.

Cpl Don Ward suffered a similar problem. His light Tetrarch tank was snuggled into a Hamilcar glider in which the pilot could lower struts to the ground for the tank to emerge safely and on an even keel. Bullets and shrapnel had been spattering the side of the Hamilcar, but it descended into a normal dive and slid along the ground as anticipated. Don waited for the pilot to pull the lever and allow the tank to exit. It later appeared that the pilot had died whilst landing. There was no way Don could lower the struts. He ordered his driver to start up. With a roar of the engine the Tetrarch plunged forward and leapt down to the ground from a height of 5 feet, jarring the crew as it smashed down on springs which were never very kind to spines.

The glider had landed in the middle of a parachute zone. Suddenly the tank halted, its engines labouring uselessly, the tracks still reeling, but without forward movement. Don leant over the side of the turret, a prime target for snipers. His tracks were enmeshed in a hopeless tangle of dozens of nylon parachute cords. The crew made a frantic but futile attempt to sever the tough nylon. The tank had now become a target for the enemy from three sides. The crew remounted the tank and opened fire, subduing machine-guns and driving off approaching infantrymen. Only when all the enemy guns within view had ceased to fire could Don move forward on foot to link up with his unit and await the rescue vehicle. Don Ward was awarded the Military Medal for the action.[24]

Battalion commanders landed with the first troops and often took up lead positions in the attacks. Lt-Col Napier Crookenden was a well-known character in 6th Air Landing Brigade (Glider). On the D-Day flights in 1944 he had brought early editions of the *Evening Standard* with him so that *en route* the men could read anticipated accounts of what they were about to do. Such conduct endeared him to all ranks. Now as the first attack stalled, he took charge of the first company of his battalion and rushed the village where resistance was firm. The impetus of the charge was such that, within relatively few minutes, they took 500 prisoners, about equal to their full battalion front-line strength. Given a further objective that day, Crookenden again led the rush and secured another 200 prisoners.[25]

Meanwhile, Hugh Clark had opened the forward and rear doors of his glider while still in flight in order to ensure quick exit. With the resultant rush of cold air 'we could feel, hear and smell' the heavy anti-aircraft fire. In addition to direct shrapnel bursting around them, their No. 1 glider was hit, blew up and showered them with debris, adding to the murk of smoke with which pilots were contending. No. 2 glider lost a wing and plunged towards the ground. Their pilot saw a 20-mm enemy gun pointing directly at them but managed to slew to the right, hitting the ground at speed and crashing through hedges, which helped to slow and halt the glider. The time was 10.20. As he exited, Hugh had time to notice both glider wings clipped off short, the undercarriage forced through the floor and the tail pulled off by the arrester parachute. Otherwise, all safe and sound!

This was no time to linger. As the men piled out under the glider, enemy machine-gun fire was peppering the top of the craft. Seeing a river bank ahead, which ought to be their first objective, they ran towards it and waded through it, realising that it was too small a river to be the objective. Time to get serious!

We took off our steel helmets and put on our red berets which were a recognition sign particularly with the 17th US Airborne Division who were landing alongside us. Each of us in the platoon had an anti-tank mine tied to an entrenching tool and hanging down our backsides. I decided we could get rid of these to our great relief. Looking back we saw our glider hit by mortar bombs and catching fire. There went all our spare ammunition and our small packs containing spare clothing and washing kit. Later we were able to make up this loss from other empty gliders. Word was passed that section leader Cpl Durbridge had been shot through the head and killed. As there was nothing we could do for him, we had to leave him there and head for wooded cover. At this point our two glider pilots left us and went to the help of other wounded pilots.[26]

Confusion was endemic to this kind of landing operation, involving 8,000 parachutists and 2,355 gliders and tug planes. Hugh Clark found that the Americans had set up a first aid post within the British target area, a useful facility for all nationalities. He then encountered another officer leading a mixed group of men from various units. He agreed to use his own platoon as cover whilst the other troops were sorted out and sent in their respective directions. They were quickly down to their last box of .303 ammunition. Good contact was made with the artillery, which responded quickly to requests for help. Unfortunately one of the guns in one of the batteries was consistently firing short. So every accurate 'stonk' intended to support the troops caused them to dive for cover as one shell landed directly amongst them. There was no time to identify which gun was firing short. It was about 12.30 before everybody was more or less in the required formation and position.

A group of Royal Engineers appeared with instructions to mine the bridge over the river in case of a successful German counter-attack. The airborne men gave them covering fire. Then shells began to fall on the area of the bridge. Everyone dived for cover again. Hugh jumped into a slit trench on top of an engineer who then shouted to him, 'I hate to tell you, sir, but there is a trailer loaded with half-a-ton of explosives just a few yards from your head.' After the barrage an enemy tank was observed approaching the bridge. The battalion's 6-pounder anti-tank gun began to shoot at the turret of the tank, which was visible above the hump of the bridge. The shots bounced off the tank at short range. Fortunately the enemy commander decided that discretion was indeed the better part of valour and joined his infantry as they withdrew to reform.[26]

One of the scariest experiences for a higher-ranking officer must have been that of Lt-Col Gleadell of the Devons. His battalion had to capture the dominant and vital village of Hamminkeln. As all open ground was covered by enemy fire the attackers advanced in a kind of leap frog style from house to house, breaking through the buildings and haring across open spaces. The colonel was observed smashing a window, leaping into a house and then exiting from the other side of the building, pursued by his batman and another corporal. Other men followed suit. At one house machine-gun fire poured down from an upstairs bedroom. Other Devons fired back to allow the colonel time to sidle along the wall and toss hand grenades at the offending weapon. When the enemy had been totally subdued officers had time to glance at their watches and observe in amazement that the battle had lasted only thirty-five minutes.[27]

To some extent the confusion of gliders arriving without the rigid formations of powered aircraft proved as much a problem for the defenders as for the attackers. Defenders were constantly surprised by gliders descending at various speeds from different angles. A machine-gunner might be firing at a glider in front, only to find another one coming in from behind. Another gunner might have to switch from a glider falling steeply out of the sky to another drifting in quietly at ground level. There was no consistent pattern to guide the defenders as to what might occur next.

While the airborne men encountered extreme danger in one element the Commandos were at risk in another. The storm boats in which they would be crossing the Rhine were very fragile. One boat was overloaded. Lt-Col A.D. Lewis saw that, 'when the driver took off, the thing dove straight into the water. Many of the men had their rucksacks still on their backs and some were drowned with the weight of them'. Once across the 300 yards of river, in natural darkness exacerbated by smoke, they employed a trusted Commando tactic. The route was opened by a tape party laying hundreds of yards of white tape along which others could advance. This involved the leaders in taking compass bearings, reading maps, laying tape, stamping it flat into the ground and returning any enemy fire along the way. Surprise was complete and the large town of Wesel, which could have been the scene for costly house-to-house fighting, was taken quickly and with light casualties.

Gliders, parachutes, amphibious Buffalos and storm boats could only convey a minimal amount of troops and supplies across the river. The main bridge was the essential pivot of Operation Plunder. Peter White's company was placed in support of engineers working on the bridge. He was shown a 'long, narrow, petrol-driven canoe used', he was told, by 'a daft South African recce bloke to patrol up and down the enemy bank the night before the crossing to select the most suitable spot for the landfall of the new pontoon bridge'. Spitfires patrolled overhead and batteries of Bofors guns were placed at the end of the bridge, 'we stood on watch listening to the squeak of the bridge straining against the three and a half knot stream... the dark waters strumming past the cables which anchored the pontoons into position on the pebble and sand bed of the river'.[28]

Beside the river bank were rafts where Maj. H. Warde, MC, 'went down to the river at nine o'clock to start building the rafts and I got my raft which was the first one to get functional... getting going at about nine o'clock the next morning'. There was not much interference from enemy artillery, but clutches of mortar bombs descended frequently about them. His raft took across the first 'normal' tank to cross the river. The Buffalos, the very first vehicles to cross, were not tanks as such, but amphibious carriers too small to carry Sherman or Cromwell tanks.[29]

Also beside the banks, crawling along, were the signallers intent on setting up their intricate network of wiring. R.W. Deans, in front of the first wave of 51st Highland Division, found the lines giving continual trouble:

> It was not a pleasant feeling, creeping along, fearing the cable had caught in an obstruction every time you jerked it. It was a most depressing place, a sea of mud and water everywhere. I felt very confident grasping a revolver in my hand as we crept back – though I doubt very much if I should have known how to fire it if the occasion had arisen; so it was as well that all went smoothly.[30]

Five new bridges were thrown across the Rhine over many miles. This allowed the American armies, farther south, a simultaneous route over the big obstacle. Equipment needed would include 260 miles of steel wire, 80 miles of barrage balloon cable, 25,000 wooden pontoons, and a casualty list of 155 engineers killed or wounded during the work. The main bridge in the area of Emmerich and Wesel, on the most direct route to Berlin, would be a 1,152 feet pontoon bridge built in nine hours under fire. Jack Swaab noticed a sign that read, 'Lambeth Bridge, opened 25 March 1945', and bearing XXX Corps, Royal Engineers and 2nd Army insignia.

Although it was a masterpiece of military engineering it did not immediately evoke confidence in the minds of those destined to cross its narrow, trembling planks. Fred Leary, driving a lorry whilst his 1NY comrades crossed the river in Buffalos, described the area before the bridge: 'what had once been a grass bank on our side of the river, now turned into deep mud like a ploughed field'. Crossing the bridge he saw that it was 'constructed by a line of boats being packed together and the "road" being made of some flexible material that could expand and contract with the swell of the boats'.[31]

Ken Cardy crossed the bridge 'to the usual ya-hooing by the paras and commandos' along the way. As they hit the bridge, 'it bucked and swayed like a ship at sea. We had even been issued with blow-up life jackets'. Beyond the bridge:

> The devastation was chronic, not a building standing. Telephone and electric poles and cables all over the place. Mines everywhere not buried, just laying on the surface. A route had been cleared through by the REs and paras/commandos.[32]

Ian Hammerton's squadron of flail tanks presented a special problem in crossing the 'long, heaving bridge'. Exceptionally heavy vehicles could not process in normal file over the bridge, and had to go one by one. Those on the near bank watched on anxiously as the leaders travelled along the slender planks with inches to spare on either side.

L/Bdr Lowe's turn to cross the bridge came at night, and was a truly hair-raising trip in his large artillery truck:

> After a few do's and don'ts, away I went. What a nerve-wracking drive it turned out to be. Pitch-black darkness and a wide river to cross, no road lights to light the way but small green pinpoints to guide you across to the other side. Please do not ask me how long it took to cross, creeping along,

but I can tell you it was lovely reaching the other side of that river. Do not ask me whether I would like to do it again or you would get an emphatic reply, and probably not a very polite one.[33]

Back with the aptly named Buffalos, Cpl Stan Hilton was sensing that he was in as much danger as if beingchased by a real, raging buffalo. His craft, like others, was equipped with a quick-firing Polsten cannon on a mounting. As it happened, this was never used. Whilst maintaining course and preventing the wallowing craft from sinking, there was no-one spare to fire a gun. Not intentionally, that is. Until, after a successful landing on the far bank, sailing home, with the gun pointing forwards toward the 1NY landing stages... the Polsten started firing. Of its own accord! Nobody had ordered 'Fire!' Nobody had pressed the trigger. It was as though a ghost out of the shadows had taken control. Firing at the regiment's base. There was a mad rush to try to switch off the gun. The rush halted and everybody ducked when the ghost handling the Polsten decided to traverse and fire into the Buffalo. Then to preserve ghostly neutrality, traversed again and shot at the Germans. The hastily assembled gun had swung loose on its mountings and was responding to the swaying of the vessel. In dire danger Stan managed to grab the gun and disconnect it. Then he and the crew crept into the home bank hoping they would not be identified as the renegades who were shooting at their own side. Stan had experience of the untrustworthy Sten gun firing spontaneously, but the Polsten was firing much bigger bullets.[34]

The honour of being the first Highland Division soldier to step ashore from a Buffalo was claimed by Sgt Andrew Imrie, of the Black Watch, an Edinburgh tinsmith in civil life. Only a few minutes behind the sergeant came the general commanding the crossing. Maj.-Gen. Rennie had earned a great reputation in Normandy and later, both for his tactical sense and for his charismatic impact on the troops. Now, as he approached the Buffalo, his red trimmings clear in the gun flashes, one yeoman joked from the dark depths of the craft, 'Sail at attention', to which the general replied, 'I heard that. Never mind the bull. Just get me over this bloody river.' He sat like an interested tourist, squinting in the fluctuations of blank darkness and startling fire flashes.

The crew unashamedly tried to eavesdrop on the conversation between the general and his aide. He was heard to say, 'I had a peculiar feeling, something between pessimism and dismay about this plan. Wondering if it would be another Arnhem. But our Yeomanry friends seem to be delivering on target.' At the far bank he and his small retinue ploughed through the mud into the wilds of mist, smoke, nocturnal black and flaming explosions. One well-read crew member was heard to quote from Henry V, 'a little touch of Harry in the night'.[35]

When Les Carr drove his Buffalo to the loading ramp he was surprised to see a very long 17-pounder anti-tank gun awaiting him. This appeared to be far too large for the Buffalo. Engineers fixed two large baulks of timber on top of the open iron box, ran the gun up onto these baulks and wedged it in place with kapok-filled floats. In Les's words, it rode upon the Buffalo 'like a huge parasite bird on a real buffalo's back'. Les drove slowly down to the water, the craft rocking on the carpet laid over the uneven earth.

As they hit the water there was a loud cracking sound as one of the baulks broke. The weight of the gun tilted the Buffalo over so that water was shipped from one side. The craft went into a spin in the river as though in the vortex of a whirlpool. Fortuitously, in the darkness another craft slammed into Les's. There were cries of 'Stupid ruddy imbeciles! Mucking oafs!! Where d'ye think y'er flooding are – at the Dodgems?' But then the second baulk snapped and the gun settled down more or less level across the righted vessel. Again, in Les's words, the gun now 'looked like a gigantic eagle in the mating position on the Buffalo'. Mercifully, as the craft struck the far bank and halted, the gun rolled off and away, apparently on a mission of its own towards Germany.

On the route from the Normandy beaches to the Rhine, many of the 1NY lads had suffered at the gentle hands of Capt. Harfield, Army Dental Corps, attached to the 51st. They were consoled to know, however, that he had also inflicted his skills upon no less a person than Montgomery. Now, on crossing the river, 153 Brigade (HD) was without its usual medical officer, and so Harfield volunteered to serve as temporary MO. As a Bren carrier was leaving a Buffalo it was hit by a shell and its various occupants were scattered, wounded in an open space laced by machine-gun fire. It is perhaps relevant to observe that a single *Spandau* machine-gun fired at a rate

of 1,200 bullets per minute or twenty bullets per second. And there
would have been several guns, either on fixed lines or in discretion-
ary firing at perceived movement in the dark. It was into such a
maelstrom of fire that Harfield walked to tend the wounded and
help them, one by one, to gain cover in a Buffalo. Later, his former
patient Montgomery was delighted to pin the Military Cross on the
dentist's chest.

Even after the completion of the main bridge near Emmerich,
it was necessary for the Buffalo shuttle service to continue due to
the mass of troops and material needing to cross the river. Sgt Eric
King, 1NY, watched his second load of Highlanders disembark; their
boots churning further the deep mud on the bank. His ramp operator, Charlie Broadbent, stood at the bottom of the ramp. 'Don't go
farther, Charlie. Get back on the ramp. There's always mines, even
however many had trodden there already', the sergeant shouted.
Charlie stepped back onto the ramp. Almost as though scheduled in
a drama, an incoming shell exploded under Charlie's feet, blasting
what was left of the man out along the *Bund* and spattering Eric and
driver John with unspeakable mess. Still on his hands and knees Eric
muttered, 'Find your own way home, son'. There was no time for
mourning.[36]

The regimental diary on all this was laconic:

> 2104 hours 'A' Squadron left troop landed 7 Argylls on East bank of
> Rhine. 2107 hours 'A' Squadron right troop landed and at 2108 hours
> 'C' Squadron reported the assault wave of 7 Black Watch landed on both
> routes. By 2118 hours both Squadrons had landed reserve Companies.

Other diaries, such as that of 44 Brigade (part of 15th Scottish Division
who rode the Buffalos of East Riding Yeomanry to the north), were
a little more graphic. They watched the water-proofed DD tanks of
44 RTR, 'Diving Ducks' to their crews. 'The DD tanks, like strange
canvas boxes, dived into the water and swam slowly across, emerged
on the far bank, shook themselves, deflated and then miraculously
appeared as Sherman tanks again.'

It was, of course, routine for the returning Buffalos to carry back
the wounded and, if space and time permitted, those who died near
the ramp. It has already been noted that, as in the case of Lt-Col

Crookenden and his airborne men, hundreds of prisoners were taken very early in the enterprise. These men were a burden to the attackers in a very small bridgehead, as there were no easy holding cells available. Traffic over the bridge was one way and would remain so for some time to come. Therefore much of the prisoner traffic was directed back to the Buffalos, together with others garnered by the Highlanders and Commandos, despite all the front-line NY crews being hard at work on the outward traffic.

A call went out to all ranks – cooks, clerks, waiting lorry drivers, signallers and any spare lingering troops of other units. The sappers took charge. With huge bales of barbed wire the 'odds and sods' erected instantaneous POW camps, shepherded the often stupefied prisoners into the enclosures and quickly worked out guard schedules until such time as the prisoners could be sent back. The hard-working military police were there. Bane of the soldier in training and arriving back late from leave, the conspicuous red-capped, white-blancoed MPs stood heroically at crossroads on traffic duty whilst their positions were often prime targets for enemy guns. The villains had become saviours. Even on the temporary tracks of the Allied side of the *Bund*, MPs had to sort traffic so that it was mainly one way except for ambulances and staff cars.

On the same day that Operation Plunder commenced, the Canadian prisoners of war, mentioned in a previous chapter, ended a horrific forced march. On 8 February they had been called out of the prison barracks into the severe winter dawn far to the east. Now, as the traffic rumbled eastwards over the new Rhine bridge, they arrived westwards at a *Stalag* near Fallingbostel. The Germans had evacuated their original camp which stood in the line of the advancing Soviet armies. For weeks they had been herded along. Their march coincided with the bombing of Dresden and they were heckled and sometimes stoned by furious civilians. There was no standard issue of rations and food consisted mainly of potatoes and other root crops grubbed from farmland under the bored eyes of the guards. Fortunately it seemed that the guards themselves had only one intention, that of moving as far away from the Russians as possible. Some deserted. Most of the soldier prisoners had kept themselves as fit as possible during their time in incarceration, and were able to survive a final diet of herbs, weeds and grass. Nobody counted the number who fell out and died on the way. But now, at Fallingbostel, they were on the line of the British, Canadian and Polish armoured divisions.[37]

Looking back in history, Operation Plunder was the long delayed substitute for the failed airborne venture at Arnhem half a year earlier. The purpose of the Arnhem operation was to cross the Rhine at a point which would give easy road and rail access to the northern German plains; ostensibly good country for massed armoured advances. In the town itself civilians had given heroic support to Allied wounded and escaping servicemen. Now the focus was on the Emmerich area to provide the desired Rhine crossing point. Arnhem itself remained isolated, still awaiting the joys of liberation.

Back at the Rhine, a 1NY Buffalo nudged into the far bank of the river and waited briefly for the beachmaster, Maj. Rollo, to indicate any return cargo there might be. A stretcher party approached at the trot, accompanied by a staff officer shouting orders. On the stretcher lay the body of the Highland general. He had just had time to congratulate the first troops he met on the far bank. Then his jeep was at the centre of a clutch of falling mortar bombs. As so often happened with mortar fire, Rennie's aide, inches away, survived. The general died almost immediately. Now, irrespective of rank, he lay under the regulation grey blanket which the medics seemed to use on such occasions. A clumsy utilitarian Buffalo had become the general's funeral barge.

From a human point of view there is no reason to mourn a general more than a private. The point of view of the frontline soldier is different. Men die in battle and are often anonymous. Sometimes it is a friend or a known man from another squadron with whom guard duties may have been shared. Otherwise the sheer number of dead causes the observer to pass on his way with relatively scant regard for the unburied. However, encountering a general in action is different. Merely to see a red-tabbed general in the frontline is unusual, surprising and can be inspiring. But to see a general killed in action is a unique experience and brings an unexpected degree of shock to the ordinary soldier involved. If a general can be killed, where does that leave me in the face of the enemy daily? And when the general is the charismatic Rennie?

Soldiers deal with such matters in their own particular way, but the bluff, kindly First World War soldier, RSM George Jelley, superintended the unloading of the general's body on the home bank. Aware of the visibly shaken troopers around him, George bawled at the Buffalo crew, 'Tomorrow old Churchill's coming over. Don't you dare bring that bugger's body back on a stretcher.'

Other witnesses pondered silently. One of them, Rex Jackson, began to form in his mind lines of a poem; the dark river was the mythical Styx, and Rex saw himself as the boatman ferrying dead souls through the Stygian darkness. Later he wrote it all down.

Slowly, like ancient reptiles scenting water,
the lumbering craft move towards the river,
with each its little group of men, each its own small world
close wrapped in secret thought, not looking beyond the hour...

Straining eyes peer... ahead... then left... right: 'Are we keeping station?'
Still the reassuring engine throbs, still the streaming pumps:
'Will the landing be opposed? How much farther can it be?'
Time seems fixed, a different plane.

Then: 'What of the men crouching behind me?'
Waiting for the touchdown, waiting for the practised leap,
the leap to bank: on mines? perhaps to death?
WE only have to touch the bank, wait for them to clear, then back.

But they must stay... perhaps only to return
among those we later carry back with stained bandage,
or under the grey blanket, silent and unknown,
with no coin for the Ferryman,
no coin for their Last Crossing![38]

CHAPTER SEVEN

DALEKO DO DOMU

They would not return to become slaves to the tyrant… but would sail away and found a colony in another land.

(Herodotus, 440 BC)

It was not possible to hold an opinion poll amongst British troops in action in early 1945. Had it been possible, a pertinent and popular question could have been 'Why did we start this unending war?'

Answers could have varied considerably:'to destroy the Nazi regime', or 'to get rid of Hitler', or 'to gain revenge for them bombing our families', or 'to get our own back for throwing us out at Dunkirk', or a dozen other reasons. The correct reply would, of course, have been because Germany invaded Poland with whom we had a mutual defence treaty. Amid the confused politics of the late 1930s the French army commander, Marshal Gamelin, had declared that if Germany invaded Poland, Anglo-French forces would attack Germany within two weeks.

German troops advanced into Poland on 1 September 1939. Britain and France declared war on 3 September. However, nothing would occur for an eight-month-long period, later coined 'the phoney war'.

Left alone against the largest battle-ready army in the world, Poland resisted for seventeen days. Then Russia's dictator, Stalin, sent in the second largest battle-ready army in the world (at that time) in one of history's largest stabs in the back. The main part of Poland's army could do no more than surrender with full honours. However, a significant element of that army was ordered to escape, find its way to the west and continue the fight. Thousands of Poles did this in the hope of one day celebrating victory and returning home.

For those who survived it would be *Daleko do domu* —'a long way home'. For many who were fortunate enough to survive the shells and bullets there would, even then, be no way home whatsoever.

To Polish Warrant Officer Alexander Leon Manka-Jarzembowski, standard bearer of the 2nd Armoured Regiment, it seemed as though he had been fighting for most of his life. Already in the 1914–18 war he had been in the frontline as an Austrian infantryman, his home town having at that time been part of the disintegrating Austro-Hungarian Empire. With the coming of Polish independence after the war, there followed two campaigns against the Bolsheviks of Russia to preserve the newly revived independent state. Promptly on 1 September 1939 he was in action again. Now in 1945 he stood at the western frontier of Germany, ready to advance in the compass direction of his home city – an objective which would never be attained.

In the changing politics of Eastern Europe over the twentieth century, Alexander was often separated from other members of his family. For many years they were living dispersed under hostile regimes. The fact that one member of the family was serving a potential enemy meant that the remainder of the family could fall under suspicion. As Stalin's Russia, in the throes of continuing ethnic oppression, was one of the countries involved, this made for precarious family relationships. So Alexander chose to hide his background by abandoning the second part of his name and using only 'Manka' which, to some extent, lessened the risk to his relatives. It was a time and region of suspicion, treachery and repression.[1]

Warrant Officer Manka was typical of many soldiers who now comprised the Polish Armoured Division, a unit of skill and experience unique among the Allies by 1945. His background also had much in common with other Polish soldiers, Polish airmen, Polish seamen, Polish Resistance fighters, and the Free Polish civilian government in London, who continued the battle for liberty whilst the soil of their homeland was again partitioned between Germany and Russia.

In the early hours of the morning on 1 September, the Polish Armoured Division's predecessor, the 10th Cavalry Brigade, was ordered to counter-attack German armoured columns pouring over Poland's western frontier. The brigade was commanded by

Col Stanislaw Maczek, originally a university philosopher. Both German and Polish armies were still using horses in cavalry units, but the 10th Brigade was now fully motorised. Its most powerful section consisted of a mere nine Vickers tanks. These were light tanks of about 5 ton, each armed only with one machine-gun. They were confronted mainly by the Pz MkIII, a 15 ton tank carrying a 50-mm gun plus machine-guns, and some of the even heavier MkIV with the 75-mm gun. To make matters worse the 10th Brigade faced a fully equipped enemy armoured division and a light division, equivalent to six brigades, and each were more powerful than the 10th.

The tactics used by the 10th were similar to those deployed by the overwhelmed German units at the end of the war: surprise counter-attack, withdraw, repeat counter-attack in a different fashion, then back to a strong defensive position. The German *Blitzkrieg* rolled forward in Poland in 1939 as it did against the Anglo-French forces before Dunkirk in 1940. However, the tactics of the 10th Brigade and other Polish units restricted the advance to a mere 3 miles a day. As Maczek, when a general, summed up later:

> We had to resign from long distance observations and fire, as in such circumstances the enemy will have excellent conditions to demonstrate his superiority in artillery fire and use of armour. It was better to accept battle in a terrain with limited horizons, drawing the enemy into gorges and defiles in which he will be unable to deploy his troops without long delays and in which he will fight us with individual fingers and not with his whole fist… and seek occasions to 'bite back' with short sorties…[2]

It was at this time that Stanislaw Maczek first displayed the bravery and concern for his troops which distinguished him throughout the war. Three enemy tanks were driving into the market place of Wisnicz town. They were engaged at point-blank range and knocked out by two anti-tank guns of the 24th Lancers, commanded by another Stanislaw, Lt Ziolkowski. Having to report to HQ for further orders the lieutenant mentioned the incident to his colonel. Maczek immediately jumped into his vehicle and drove to the firing point to congratulate the gunners on their feat. Yet a third Stanislaw, Lt Martynoga, remembered shouting to the commander, 'What are you doing here, colonel? Please get into the ditch', as bullets 'whizzed past'.

For sixteen days the Polish Army conducted an orderly withdrawal whilst inflicting significant casualties. Then on 17 September Stalin ordered the Soviet Army to attack the Polish rear, squeezing the smaller force between two larger armies. Whilst a treaty existed between Germany and Russia, Stalin's main concern was not so much to conquer a slice of Poland, but to establish a buffer zone in the event of a German attack on Russia. The Polish Army had no alternative but to surrender. At the same time the government took two extreme measures. It packed up its essential bureaucracy and moved to London to become a government in exile. It also ordered that any Polish group able to escape to the west should do so. The Polish navy sailed away. Polish merchant ships headed for Allied ports. Polish pilots flew to join the continuing fight. The mobile 10th Brigade was ordered to detach, leave the country and find its way to France as the nucleus of a new Polish Army alongside its dilatory allies.

So on that epic night of 17 September Maczek's brigade commenced forced marches through the narrowing gap between Nazi and Soviet forces. They were not a moment too soon. Furthermore, had they tried to make a stand along the river Dniestr they would have been overwhelmed from both sides. However, their orders on 18 September were clear: Evacuate!

The units gathered near Tatarow and on 19 September, despite losses amounting to a third of its strength, were in full battle order. With its arms fully operational, and under command, the brigade crossed into Hungary (a friendly country) through the Tatarska Pass. The campaign was lost, but its soldiers were definitely not resigning from continuing the struggle for the freedom of their country.

Hungary allowed the brigade to pass through intact, making its way as a unit towards France. Other Polish servicemen were making their way to the same destination but by many separate routes to a common rallying place, some passing through Africa, Scandinavia or Siberia. When nearly two years later Germany crossed the Polish buffer zone to attack Russia, the Russians opened prisoner of war camps to allow Polish prisoners to find their own way back into battle, some with the Russian army but many making an even more precarious journey back to Britain. During the same period in April 1940, in one of the worst atrocities of the war, Stalin ordered the execution at Katyn of thousands of Polish officers who had surrendered on 19 September.

Later research would also discover that, in less than three weeks of battle in Poland, the German losses in men and armour were higher than those suffered against the Anglo-French forces in the better-known 1940 *Blitzkrieg* which, over a somewhat similar period of time, caused the surrender of the main French Army and the evacuation of the British Army from Dunkirk.

In September and October 1939 the officers and men of the 10th Brigade were determined to join the Anglo-French armies in France. They hoped that a combined offensive would force the Germans to come to the negotiating table and agree to return Poland to its rightful owners. There was a period of frustration during which the Allies argued about the most appropriate ways of re-arming and re-equipping a Polish unit of whatever size. For the Poles the frustration was made more unbearable because the Anglo-French armies continued to stand almost motionless on the German frontier.

When at last the weight of German might was loosed through the Ardennes, throwing the Allied armies off balance and causing disruption which would never be corrected, the 10th Brigade had become the 10th Armoured Cavalry Brigade and its leader had become a general. They were manoeuvred just in time to try and defend Paris, which was by then a hopeless cause. The 10th then fought a delaying withdrawal all the way back to Dijon. By that time the remnants of the Anglo-French forces were in total disarray and the 10th Brigade was surrounded. Maj.-Gen. Maczek was once again gathering his remaining men and seeking a way out of France to continue the fight in Britain. One of the battalion commanders, Col Chabowski, received a handwritten order which said:

> If you are unable to embark at Bayonne, leave the vehicles to the French authorities and try to get troops through Spain to Portugal. From there, with the help of the Polish consular service, try to reach England.

There the survivors from all routes were eventually concentrated in Scotland. With reinforcements from many sources, it was possible to develop the brigade into a fully equipped armoured division, consisting of an armoured brigade of four regiments, an infantry brigade plus artillery, engineers, signals and other necessary arms.

It is worthy of note that, as this story follows the trail of the 1st Polish Armoured Division to Germany; Poland made other important contributions to victory in the Second World War. Polish Intelligence had acquired the secret of the Enigma coding machine, which enabled the Allies to read coded German messages through to the 1944 assault on North-West Europe. The 'Polish mine detector' was indeed a Polish invention; a simple implement something like a carpet sweeper which saved the lives of thousands of infantrymen treading through unidentified minefields. During the Battle of Britain one out of every six Luftwaffe planes destroyed was shot down by a Polish pilot. Polish ships were used to transport Allied troops to Normandy on D-Day. Other Polish army formations fought in Norway, the Middle East and Italy.

Now ready for action and hearing the news of D-Day, 6 June 1944, 1st Polish Armoured Division made its way southwards to take its place on landing ships in early August 1944. By this time soldiers like WO Alexander Manka had a battle history of twenty-seven years and were now setting out on their sixth campaign. In Normandy they would come under the command of Lt-Gen. Guy Simonds, of II Canadian Corps, over the battlefields where bitter fighting had taken place after D-Day. The German defences south of Caen along the Bourguebus/Verrieres Ridge had proven impregnable so far. Ominously, a previous attack by almost 800 British tanks had seen approximately 400 knocked out. Now Operation Totalize was tasked to assault the same ridge.

Fortune did not smile on the Poles as they went into action in Normandy. Due to FM Montgomery's insistence on too early a start to Totalize, there was insufficient time for proper preparation. Polish tanks had to squeeze their way through the still chaotic ruins of Caen. Then the American air attack which was designed to destroy enemy units along the Polish attack route, bombed the Poles (and allies), causing them more disruption than that inflicted on the enemy.

Overnight on 7 August the German defences along the ridge were breached. At midday on 8 August the 2nd Armoured Regiment and 24th Lancers rolled forward. Lt Tony Faulkner, of 1NY, sitting on a forward position captured during the overnight penetration at Saint-Aignan-de-Cramesnil, watched in horror as the lead tanks advanced towards hidden German guns. Apart from vainly waving his beret, Faulkner had no means, no common code signs, to alert the foremost tanks to the danger. The rushed plan had allowed no time for liaison.

In the first hour the two regiments suffered grievous casualties, which only reinforced their determination to get to grips with the enemy after a five year wait.[3] They had their opportunity a few days later. The converging Canadian corps, from the north, and American armour, from the south, began to close the Falaise Gap and enclose most of the German Army. At the moment of crisis the Polish tanks were leading the charge towards the village of Chambois, which they knew the Americans under Patton were nearing.

After ten days of incessant fighting, the tired and battered Polish tank brigade HQ received a dramatic and inspiring order:

> Special Assignment. By request of the Supreme Commander of the Allied Forces your assignment has been altered as follows:
> By crossing the country and avoiding roads seize the area of Chambois to block the enemy retreat. Infantry to be carried on your tanks and all other available vehicles. Leave unnecessary material behind. This order to be carried out immediately on receipt. Trun is in enemy hands. The Americans have taken Foret de Gouffron.

The great master plan of D-Day was coming to its climax. The vast trap was snapping closed on an entire army. This time it was the Germans inside the vice and the Poles sealing the exit.

There exists a photograph of a Polish tank crashed into a German tank on the slopes of Mont Ormel overlooking Chambois. It reflects the incredible final struggle which took place between elite German SS forces, trying to break out from one direction or break in from another and, for many hours, the Poles on the dominant natural feature in between. Meanwhile, other American, Canadian and British units fought their way to complete the encirclement. The division's history recalls the climactic day of 20 August when 'the Germans, realising that their last road of retreat had been blocked, directed their attacks in concentrated fury born of desperation on each and every unit of the Division'. On 21 August the fighting began to abate. Maczek himself observed that 'the soldiers, cut off for two days, without fresh supplies or an opportunity to evacuate the wounded, showed great hardiness of spirit by repulsing the furious attempts to break out...'. It was some kind of vengeance for the evacuation through the Tatarska Pass, almost five years earlier.

For the Poles, there were days of exhilaration to come. Together with other allies they drove half the length of France, followed up retreating enemy units and prevented any prolonged defence through most of Belgium. While the division rested temporarily, Polish paratroopers experienced disillusionment when the Germans displayed their ability in reorganising defences at Arnhem, and hopes of victory were quickly dashed. They also experienced glory when, in a sudden flanking movement, 1st Polish Armoured Division liberated the important Dutch city of Breda without extensive damage. The inhabitants of the city had anticipated a terrifying climax of demolition and ruin.

In France the division had no opportunity to liberate occupied communities. Saint-Aignan and Chambois in Normandy were deserted, ruined villages with no civilians remaining. Now the tanks were rolling into a large inhabited city and being greeted by citizens, delirious with the joy of liberation after years of foreign occupation and also aware that the speed of Polish advance had saved their lovely city from ruin. The division's band was able to unload its trumpets, the standard bearers to unfurl their flags and the troops to march in triumph through a city which miraculously had displayed welcome notices in Polish in almost every house window.

A somewhat amusing incident now involved the division's commander. Like the Polish government, the Dutch government had been in exile in London. Queen Wilhelmina had become a symbol both of continuing resistance to foreign domination and hope of the restoration of democratic government. Now the Queen was back in Holland and located not far from the Polish HQ. A royal invitation came for the commander to visit the Queen. As Maczek donned his best uniform and medals, his aides speculated on what kind of sumptuous banquet the Royal court might purvey for their commander's delectation. They were disabused of that notion when the general returned with the news that, in sympathy with her subjects of *de Hongerwinter,* Queen Wilhelmina had entertained him with frugal tea and biscuits.

With trumpets packed, flags furled, guns cleaned and after a month of stagnation on watch for intruders over the wide River Maas, the reinforced 1st Polish Armoured Division now stood beyond the River Rhine on the western frontier of Germany. At that moment there occurred an event which no fiction writer would dare to invent.

It related to an uprising by the Polish Resistance in the capital Warsaw almost a year earlier. As the gap was closing around Chambois, and as Russian troops closed in on Warsaw, an entire underground army of Poles had risen against the Germans. Men and women put on uniforms and took up arms, striking at the enemy lines of communication. The hope was that this would enable the Russians to accelerate their drive into Warsaw. Cynically the Soviets halted and watched as the Germans gradually fought off the resistance fighters, taking many of them prisoner and sending them westwards to prisoner of war camps. One section of one camp housed the strength of two battalions of women soldiers, civilly treated by their captors.[4]

On 12 April 1945 Lt Henryk Papee had been interrogating both German and Dutch civilians about German troop dispositions ahead. They had reported a prisoner of war camp, thought to contain Polish soldiers, somewhere in the vicinity. Papee reported to his colonel, Stanislaw Koszutski. The latter immediately alerted those standing nearby and formed a small task force consisting of himself and his tank, two scout cars, a jeep and a motorcycle. They were the first Polish soldiers to probe into Germany, a truly mixed batch: two lieutenant-colonels, three lieutenants, six OR soldiers and a war correspondent who happened to be lurking. With Lt Barbarski's scout car hitting top speed at the front, they raced along the roads, firing their guns at random in the hope of scaring off any enemy. This was what British troops would have called a 'Fred Karno's army': totally without a formal plan.

Suddenly they saw a barbed wire fence surrounding the barracks of a large camp. A few rounds of machine-gun fire from the tank produced white flags from German defenders. Motorcyclist Leopold Witkowski roared through the gates into the square. Then the small task force stared in amazement: 'What the hell? Who is that?' A tiny creature runs across. She is a very attractive young girl, dressed in a long military coat and wearing a cap displaying the Polish eagle and the colours of the 7th Lancers. 'English, Francais, Americano, Canada sind Sie?' she shouts. 'Polish troops, Miss. 1st Polish Armoured Division, darling!' replies Witkowski. 'And we are here from the Home Army from the Warsaw insurrection', she shouts, running back to the barracks to call out others.

Still in a state of surprise the liberating group watched in amazement as all the doors opened and they saw 'women, like a hive of bees, running out wearing uniforms or rags of uniform. Their commander then calls the parade.' With the women formed up in straight lines facing the liberating force, Lt Maria Milewska reported to Lt-Col Koszutski, 'Sir, battalion of the defence of Warsaw, one thousand, seven hundred and sixteen women soldiers, twenty in hospital, seven babies'. This was possibly the most remarkable parade report of the entire war.

The tough tank colonel struggled as his eyes misted with tears and he tried to make an appropriate little speech for the occasion. While he spoke the woman adjutant pulled a piece of white and red material out of her pocket and waved it as a Polish flag. And as the colonel ended his brief 'you are free' speech, from among the women the patriotic tune of 'March, march, Dabrowski' began to swell into a spirited choral response.[5]

The liberation of the Warsaw girls was a tremendous boost to Polish morale, a boost which was greatly needed. Poland's western nemesis, Hitler, might be nearing the point of self-destruction, but their eastern nemesis, Stalin, was in a very strong position. In negotiations with Roosevelt, who trusted him, and Churchill, who was now in the weakest bargaining position, Stalin had drawn up his own plan for bringing Poland into the Soviet empire. Britain would have to withdraw recognition from the Polish government in exile in London. Soldiers fighting under the auspices of the government in exile would now be facing the reality that rather than it being *'Dalek do Domu'*, a long way home, there might now be no way home ever.

Be that as it may, there was now consolation in fighting across the German border, and also bewilderment. It was an area of small rivers, canals and intervening floods. An advance could start in Germany, cross a canal back into Holland and then find a way across another waterway into Germany again. However, there was no mistaking the local geography. Maczek himself remembered:

Dutch villages, mainly spared from destruction, were filled with flowers and decorated with national flags of the Allies; on the German side there was devastation everywhere. The only decoration was, here and there, a white flag on some habitation which had survived ruin. The joy and gladness on the faces of the Dutch crowds thronging the streets was in stark contrast to the emptiness, the shuttered windows, the closed gates and the few pale-face Germans sidling in the streets. Later the crowds of people from all over Europe, who had been deported... greeting us with joyful laughter mixed with tears.[6]

Not as emotional as the liberation of the Warsaw girls, but unique in its own way, was the day when the Polish vanguard captured a huge stud farm near Lubeck. There they found more than 2,000 Polish horses requisitioned by the Germans after the fall of Poland. It must be remembered that, even at this stage of the war, there still existed horsed German cavalry units and also infantry divisions with horsed transport. Now in a brief moment of free time Polish soldiers enjoyed riding on their liberated steeds.

April 1945 was to be the last month of fighting, which for the Polish soldiers stretched back to 1 September 1939. For older soldiers like WO Alexander Manka, it had now been twenty-eight years since their first taste of enemy fire. But this present enemy was still defiant and skilful in defence. For the frontline soldier, the danger and the apprehension were undiminished by any sense that the war might soon be over. The odds were always against the attacker. The reality concerned today's bullets and mortar bombs. Regimental diaries of 20th Mounted Rifles and 24th Lancers spoke of 25 and 26 April as being 'a time of particularly heavy fighting' which, from the survivors of the Armageddon at Chambois, is a very significant statement.

Among other actions 'at the price of considerable casualties, under unrelenting enemy fire, the Engineers built a bridge on the Hault-Fehn Canal during the first night'.[7] Then the advancing infantry found themselves in difficult, rugged and easy to defend country. Polish Dragoons, supported by tanks of the Lancers, guns of 2nd Motorised Artillery Regiment and rockets from RAF Typhoons, fought a classic all-arms battle to force their way into the town of Pothausen. Again and again the engineers were called upon to repair or replace bridges. Village after village still had to be attacked, cleared and consolidated – Pothausen, Stickhausen, Rhaudemoor, Bakemoor, Bokelsch, Bollingen, Brinkum and Brunn.

On 4 May the division was still in action. In the ruined village of Astederfelde the Germans, as so often in this campaign, profited from the destruction wrought by Allied artillery and bombers. They dug in deep into the ruins as the attackers tried to find their way through the chaotic streets. The leading infantry were forced to halt again, dig in and wait for a planned combined attack. This was never to develop. At 22.15 hours the order was received to stop firing, but only at 08.00 hours next day. An exchange of artillery fire continued in the night as men sheltered one more time from the threat of explosions and shrapnel. Only at 07.39 hours did the Polish guns, ordered to open fire on 1 September 1939, at last fall silent.

It was still necessary to formally occupy designated German territory. Now the erstwhile Colonel Maczek, who had to lead his battered 10th Cavalry Brigade over the Polish border into exile in September 1939, would, as Major-General Maczek, direct the 1st Polish Armoured Division, progeny of the old 10th Brigade, to occupy the important city and naval base of Wilhelmshaven. A moment of vengeance and justification!

The 2nd Armoured Regt, with WO Manka bearing its colours, and 8th Rifle Battalion, commanded by Col Grudzinski (second-in-command of the old 10th Brigade) formed the vanguard. At the entry to the fort they were met by the commanding officer, *Kpt zur See* Mulsow, in formal surrender. British naval officers arrived on HMS *Royal Rupert* to receive the formal surrender of the navy.

It was no doubt a day of legitimate triumph for the Poles when they calculated the surrendering forces and their equipment, which included two admirals, one general, 1,900 officers and 32,000 other ranks; three naval cruisers, including the redoubtable heavy cruiser *Prinz Eugen*, a command ship, eighteen U-boats and 205 smaller ships; not to mention eighteen heavy fort siege guns, 159 artillery guns, nearly 1,000 machine-guns, masses of ammunition and rations intended for 50,000 servicemen for three months. Undoubtedly more than one of the veterans would have allowed himself a quick flashback of memory to the Tatarska Pass.[8]

Sadly, Wilhelmshaven was still a long way from Warsaw or Lwow. In between stood the massed Soviet armies and for the Poles it would still be '*Daleko do domu*'. Those who wished to retrace the tortuous 1939 escape routes would find no hero's welcome in the new Poland, which would virtually become a Soviet province. The moment hostilities ceased, the eastern and western Allies began a quick drift into mutual hostility. In the immediate post-war politics, the rush to appease Stalin was even hastier than the efforts to appease Hitler in 1939. Chamberlain's politics of appeasement are well remembered (as are forgotten his efforts, if belatedly, to prepare Britain for air war). The appeasement policies of Attlee (and Truman) in regard to Stalin's rape of Poland are often overlooked.

At this point it might be relevant to refer to a letter written by the British Foreign Secretary, Ernest Bevin, to all Polish servicemen in the British forces. Himself a socialist, Bevin must have been aware of the murderous ethnic policies of Stalin and the fact that Stalin's word was worth no more than Hitler's. Yet he advised the Polish personnel to return home to the new Soviet Poland. He was, he declared, satisfied that the new Polish 'Provisional Government has furnished His Majesty's Government with a statement setting forth its policy on this question' (Chamberlain arrived home in 1938 with 'a note'). He then continued, 'speaking on behalf of the British government, I declare it is in the best interest of Poland that you should return to her now'. This declaration would ring hollow in the ears of Poles who were by now aware that almost their entire officer corps who surrendered to the Russians in 1939 were murdered in one punitive operation at Stalin's command at Katyn.

From the time of the evacuation of British troops from Dunkirk in 1940 until D-Day, Polish troops had trained mainly in Scotland. Firm links had been formed with the local population. The two cultures seemed to empathise. Local girls married foreign soldiers, children were born, homes set up. Local authorities were well disposed to the temporary guests. Scotland, and indeed any part of the British Empire of the day, might seem an ideal place for a wandering soldier to relocate. A future they had been led to expect! Then came the words of Ernest Bevin, as inhospitable as disingenuous, 'Nor can the British Government offer to the members of the Polish Armed Forces under British command any guarantee that they will be able to settle in British territory at home or overseas'. In other words, 'Thank you for your help and now be gone!'

This cruel policy has to be set in contrast to the previous British policy towards Polish servicemen, quoted by Bevin himself in the same letter: 'In the execution of the policy announced by Mr Winston Churchill, the British Government will give… such assistance as is in its power to enable those who fought with us throughout the war to start a new life outside Poland with their families and dependants'. How Bevin's new policy can be seen an 'execution' of the original policy beggars belief.

After victory in Europe the new regime in Poland promptly deprived Polish generals and senior officers, who had fought with the western Allies, of their citizenship. Any lesser officers who returned home were viewed with suspicion. Less than 10 per cent of Polish servicemen chose to return to the tyrannical and discriminating regime. Not until the rise of a new Polish president, Gomulka, in 1956 did the outright antagonism towards the 'western Poles' begin to lessen. Full reconciliation had to wait nearly fifty years after the entry into Wilhelmshaven.

Meanwhile, the distinguished active war service of the 10th Brigade, later 1st Armoured Division, came to an end in almost anticlimax with the formal occupation of the tiny islands of Spiekerog and Wangerooge.

CHAPTER EIGHT

NOW *WHO* DIES LAST?

Their fear was not so much that they be worsened in open fight as lest
some trick be practised on them

(Herodotus, 440 BC)

With the last great defence barrier of the River Rhine pierced; there
would still be pitched battles to come. The German strategy would
have to change as overwhelming numbers of attacking troops stormed
from both east and west towards Berlin. However, the Germans were
masters of the military craft: 'craft' in more than one sense of the word.

Many British and Canadian infantrymen were impressed by the
German tactic of waiting for the advanced enemy troops to pass by
and then either attacking the rear echelon or counter-attacking the
leaders from behind. Stan Whitehouse remembered a German group
hiding in a dugout during the night in a forest behind his position.
Then at dawn the hidden men rushed the Black Watch positions
from behind, virtually wiping out the entire section which was taken
by surprise.[1]

Capt. Hugh Clark, MC, recorded an exceptional example of
German craftiness during these last battles. German tanks penetrated
the defences of the Cameronians during the night. The tanks had
entered the village street with their headlights on, which normally an
attacking force would never have done. The leading German commander, speaking perfect English, convinced the guard that his was
a British tank, and once the suspicions of the guard were allayed the

tanks opened fire with fatal results.[2] Ken Cardy found that 'Jerry was burning every building that they left and letting cattle, sheep and pigs loose on the roads. And if a building was left, it was booby trapped to some of the [Guards] infantry's cost'. British troops were generally reluctant to drive tanks over live animals.[3]

The more physical tactic of booby-trapping was rife as the Germans reluctantly yielded patches of their Fatherland. Canadian brothers Hans and Harold Neumann were well aware of this. Hans 'got hell from an officer' for savouring a jar of peaches left on a German breakfast table. The officer yelled, asking him how he knew that the peaches were not poisoned. Weakly Hans replied, 'Well, I'm still alive'. Harold agreed. 'They used to pull tricks like that. You had to be careful all the time. Even some dead people they'd booby trap. When you touched them – BANG! You were gone too!'[4]

Ken Cardy further observed that the Germans were now laying the mines too deep to be detected. The mines were then primed so that one or more tanks or vehicles could pass over, but a later vehicle would trigger the explosives. This meant that vehicles following a leader could no longer be reassured of their own immediate safety if the leader blew up on a mine. In a sense each vehicle had to advance as though it were the leader. Peter White with 4th KOSB encountered minor devices in unexpected places:

> The enemy occasionally secreted these with devilish cunning in a wide variety of positions which ranged from explosives with an anti-lifting device under his own or our dead or even wounded men, to booby trapped vehicles, door-handles, WC chains and so on. Battalion HQ were later fortunate to evacuate a building in Bremen which had been mined [with a time fuse] and which subsequently blew up.[5]

L/Bdr Bill Lowe saw one mine explode 'killing the sergeant outright, and an officer and one of our drivers died from injuries, another sergeant was severely injured and evacuated, and several more of the party wounded and needing treatment'. His gun position had not been swept for mines due to a lack of engineers to do the job.[6]

The problems of following a cleverly managed enemy were exacerbated by ground conditions. In some places units were lucky enough to encounter a wide autobahn, one of Hitler's new wonder roads, but in other areas the patchwork of waterways continued to be a hindrance.

Maj.-Gen. Maczek reported that:

> ...the last phase of fighting along the Dutch-German border and then in north-eastern Germany took place in very difficult terrain.... It was rarely suitable for tank action. It is a low-lying region, parts of which are below sea level.... A network of marshes and fenland cut by the larger rivers: the Ems, Leda, Jumme and their tributaries, by canals both large and small...with sluices and drainage ditches. The roads were of necessity on embankments and it was impossible for heavy equipment to leave them as their tracks or wheels immediately churned up the thin layer of turf and they sank into the boggy ground below. The terrain was full of well-camouflaged ambushes...

Engineer Ernest Egli, coming up in a brigade echelon, was surprised on crossing the Rhine to find what was virtually a vast flood plain stretching on both sides of the river, making transport difficult both for heavy vehicles and men on foot. The movement through the area was also complicated by numbers of crashed aircraft. The nature of the new fluid warfare was illustrated when, at his point in the long queue of advancing vehicles, he beheld a German *Kubelwagen*, a kind of jeep, approaching blithely from a side road and driven by a man in smart German field-grey uniform. He obviously had no idea of where he was nor had he been intercepted by Allied troops.[7] At this juncture something like a million troops, British, Canadian, Polish and American, were rushing through a few bottlenecks across temporary bridges and then dispersing urgently in all directions, often leaving gaps. It was not a time for a 1918-style solid, regulated line of troops advancing across a defined no-man's land.

To add to topographical and logistical difficulties there was a renewed problem of personal fear and apprehension in men who, for so long, had adjusted their minds to the possibility of wounding and death. After D-Day, with interminable months of battle stretching ahead, men developed either an almost fanatical trust in a Supreme Being, or a sufficient everyday fatalism, or they collapsed and disappeared under the strain. Now, with the remaining calendar days of battle obviously flicking down into hours and maybe ticking down into minutes, men remembered that bullets continued to wound and kill up to the last moment of 'Cease Fire!' Nobody wanted the dubious honour of being the last man whose name was indeed on a bullet.

A further dimension had also developed. Short leave to Antwerp or Brussels or longer leave back to 'Blighty' did provide a time for relaxation, but also broke the self-imposed hypnotism which had countered personal fears and horror for most people. Canadian George Blackburn, a Normandy veteran, found it disturbing to have to forsake his gunner's OP on strict orders to take his regulation leave in England. He found it difficult to join in the mad jollity of London's West End and galling to see some civilians making a profit and staff officers obtaining promotion out of war. On returning he found he had again to go through a mental adjustment to war. This was made even more difficult because any sense of adventure, novelty or purpose, experienced when landing on the exciting sunlit D-Day beaches, was missing when returning to the dismal reality of a German bog.[8]

Leaving his mine-sweeping tank, Capt. Ian Hammerton went on leave to England but 'although I thought myself lucky, I was not able to throw myself heart and soul into enjoying myself at home... but it took a lot of will power to return to Holland... a number of our troops found it very demoralising to have to return to the fight after a week at home, some even refusing to take their leave'.[9]

Some soldiers thought that the 'name on a bullet' syndrome was more than a barrack-room tale and that premonitions could be well founded. Richard Carr-Gomm with the Coldstream Guards confessed to a certain lack of imagination himself, but cited two brother officers. After breakfast one morning they both called their soldier-servants, telling them how to divide up their belongings among family and friends in the event that they did not return from action that day. Each officer set off with his crew of five in his tank and each was killed during the day. Carr-Gomm also censored a letter home from a guardsman who told his parents he was going to die and thanking them for a loving upbringing. He then went out into action and was killed.[10]

Pte Charles Dunesby, who served with both the Somerset Light Infantry and the Seaforth Highlanders, experienced a similar tragedy. His pal, signaller Jimmy said on 23 March, 'I'm going to die tomorrow'.

Dunesby countered, 'What are you talking about? We've come all the way from Normandy. Why should you die now?' But Jimmy was deadly serious and gave instructions for the disposal of his belongings. He then went off to D Company. After breakfast on 24 March, Dunesby was sitting at the battalion wireless set when ominously a strange voice gave D Company call sign. The voice requested another signaller as their signaller had been killed by a random shell: Jimmy![11]

As to personal fear Carr-Gomm, who won the French Croix de Guerre, thought that the really brave man was the one who knew he was afraid. And the bravest of all was 'the man who returns to the fight having been several times wounded and knows what it is like to be hurt'. He also admitted that he did not think about fear or bravery until the very end. Just as the disintegration of the German Army indicated that peace was imminent he was ordered to clear a road where a Tiger tank may have lurked, not the first such battle experience. Then 'for a few minutes I felt fear but not bravery'.

Artillery FOO Jack Swaab was another soldier who thought, 'I wish leave were not so near – it doesn't do one's fighting spirit much good!' Neither was he impressed when senior officers started talking about the last battles being only small ones. As his friend said, 'There is no such things as a small attack when you yourself are involved'. One man in battle is all of the battle for that one man.[12] However, Stan Whitehouse, who earlier in his career considered himself a bit of a rebel, found that eventually a kind of 'experienced professionalism' took over. At the point of crisis a kind of 'madness takes over, driving you on'.

Discussing fear is of great importance, for the outcome of untreated fear was often mental illness and this reduced the number of soldiers available to a unit. Expert Ben Shephard calculates that in normal frontline life '10 per cent of casualties were psychiatric and whenever there was serious fighting, the number of exhausted soldiers shot up'.[13] Canadian Bill McAndrew, in one of the most exhaustive studies, found neuro-psychiatric cases rising from 15 per cent to over 30 per cent of all battle injuries in the worst fighting. In one battle he found that there were 1,871 wound casualties but 570 neuro-psychiatric cases.[14] These statistics omit the number of deaths caused directly by psychiatric aberration, such as a commander 'freezing' at the moment of giving an urgent order.

Shephard found that some soldiers were haunted by bogey weapons. A common example of this was the German Tiger tank which dominated much of tactical thinking in Normandy. The report of a Tiger tank approaching could cause 'hysterical fear' because it was known that shots from the smaller Allied guns would bounce off the Tiger's armour at point blank range.[15] For tank crews it was often the 'Moaning Minnie' mortar bomb which could drop vertically down through the open turret of a tank.

Shephard also points the finger of accusation at bad leaders, including those who were too ready to sacrifice their own troops. He cites the 43rd Wessex Division, commanded by a general nicknamed 'Butcher', and that very few of whose wounded ever 'showed any desire to return to their units'. In contrast, wounded men of the 15th Scottish Division 'were keen to rejoin their own units and doctors came to inquire about their well-being'. Shephard praises the army psychiatric service which had developed services according to post D–Day requirements to such an extent as to 'produce a dramatic improvement in rates of men returned to units – from 10 per cent to 65 per cent'.

Whether men were adversely affected by the approach of peace and a growing sense of apprehension, or not, it was those who had poured across the River Rhine in Buffalo amphibians or had braved the rickety new pontoon bridges that now had to advance into the mists beyond and finish the whole business of war in Europe.

Leading the way along one route was Sgt Richard Brew of the Somerset Light Infantry. He had already endured the river crossing in a Buffalo, 'how they were going to float I had no idea. About the scariest thing I had ever done'. On 29 March his unit had to break out of the bridgehead, fighting 'with stubborn and fanatical rearguards', gaining two villages and then digging in for the night. After about an hour's sleep:

> … my section was given a house… beyond a cornfield and as we crossed a barbed wire fence I got caught and I reckon it saved my life because by the time I got myself free all the others were dead.
>
> I ran back and got a tank to fire at some trees where I thought the Germans were, then out they came, 30 odd Germans. I went among them, looking for sniper badges. I don't know what I would have done if I had found one. When I went back to that house the tank crew were

already there having a cup of tea. Suddenly there was a ping as a bullet came through the window, killing the tank driver. It could have been me or Johnny Martin who was nearby, but it was that driver's turn. The crew were very upset… together since Normandy. Put the body on the tank to go back and bury him.[16]

Although the Rhine crossings had come to an end, the Buffalos of 1NY were still required. The 'vast flood plain' viewed by Egli now required the services of 'Hank's Ferry'. Maj. David 'Hank' Bevan, MC, was directed to set up a ferry taxi service of Buffalo amphibians at the beck and call of any troops needing to cross stretches of water which were not passable for ground troops. This presented Buffalo commanders like Rex Jackson with another problem, as the flooded stretches bore no relation to the maps or aerial photos on which navigation normally depended. It was a case of pointing the Buffalo in the general compass direction and asking the way from the next military policeman, or infantryman, or sapper you met. It was a fraught situation and Rex's green reinforcement driver, seeing 'grossly bloated bodies of German soldiers floating on the waters', shouted, 'You've come the wrong way. You'll get us all killed', refusing for a moment to drive farther. For the only time in his war career Rex drew his revolver to persuade his driver that it was the right way.

Amid all the serious strife soldiers constantly entered into, some unexpected situations remained in the memory when other routine events vanished into oblivion. XXII Dragoons despatch rider Duchene, the top hat humorist, found himself across the Rhine having breakfast with the Highlanders. In the queue he was asked, 'Porridge?' and replied eagerly, 'Yes, please'. It was 'my first experience of the Scottish variety'. In his own squadron porridge came up 'hot, creamy, wet and sweet'. Now 'this variety came out flat on a tray, grey, solid, about three inches by four, and a quarter of an inch thick. And for seasoning I was offered salt!' For once Duchene was not laughing.[17]

Nor did the omnipresent fear and pain blank out a person's sensitivities to the changing scenes around them. Poet and musician, as well as artillery FOO, George Blackburn, his life at risk crossing one of the many canals, was still aware of the breadth of nature wrapping around the human turmoil:

Though clearly every man in the boat you are in is white with apprehension, having waited so long for the boats to be brought up, no shots ring out, no mortars flutter down to crash about the boats, and no air-bursting 88s crack overhead. It is uncannily quiet since the 72 guns of 2nd Division finished firing the smokescreen and the diversionary shelling on the left near where the bridge used to be.

Paddling over the still water, glowing blood-red from the stunning sunset now in progress, with only the gentle sound of dipping paddles and gurgling waters breaking the silence of the balmy spring evening, it is as though there are no Germans anywhere within miles.[18]

The new war of movement still required the intervention of the bravest of the brave. Ted Chapman, the 25-year-old son of a Welsh coal miner, was with the 3rd Monmouthshires when his section was strafed by heavy machine-gun fire from a concealed dug-out. Ordering his men into cover, Ted marched forward firing his Bren machine-gun from the hip, overawing the enemy crew and forcing them to withdraw. Then lying flat in a shallow fold in the ground he fired over his shoulder to keep the enemy away whilst others went back to fetch more ammunition. Finding his company commander lying wounded, he tried to carry him back for first aid, still amid heavy fire. As he went, the officer was killed in his arms and Ted was badly wounded in the thigh. Refusing treatment he returned to his front post and held the ground for another two hours before reinforcements could be brought up into line with his isolated section. The Victoria Cross (2 April 1945) was awarded to Cpl Edward Thomas Chapman, who later became a sergeant-major and was awarded the MBE.[19]

There were heroes and there were cowards, or at least people whose susceptibilities rendered them more likely to collapse psychologically under the strain of killing and avoiding being killed.

Capt. Charlie Robertson came back from homeland leave to find his 7th Black Watch lost in the mists beyond the waters. He took advantage of Hank's ferry 'to the edge of that oblivion'. He found his men at yet another small bridge over yet another small stream.

His men had rushed a vital bridge at Empel. Massed German counter-attacks had tried to wrest the bridge back again. Lance-Corporal McBride, with only five men, had held the bridge for twenty-four hours against odds of more than a hundred to one. But another [more senior] commander, nerves wracked by months of fatal battles, and judgement dulled by entire days without any sleep, had failed to support the gallant corporal. Charlie launched himself into action, muttering to himself, 'it will be a Distinguished Conduct Medal for one, and home in disgrace for the other'.[20]

Whilst the armies 'bashed on', with Berlin the prize to be gained, a forgotten town lay far behind the leading tanks of the armoured divisions – Arnhem. It had proved impossible to liberate the area by airborne endeavour more than six months previously. During those intervening months it had become a backwater, not now affecting higher strategic considerations. However, the German Army never retreated from a post unless forcibly pressed to do so. Someone at long last had to complete the task.

According to Maj. Hugh le Messurier 'that was quite a good operation. It wasn't expensive in casualties'. With 56th Brigade he had crossed the Rhine and 'started to move into the outskirts of Arnhem over the River IJssel, arriving in the middle of Arnhem at night'. Le Messurier's main crisis had occurred prior to the actual operation when he and others ascended into a church steeple to view the line of advance. They had to stand on a wobbling plank with the church pews a hundred feet below. 'The plank actually moved every time you moved... nobody actually took much interest in the scenery', they were too busy balancing. Then, as they left the church, they found that the smoke from a generator, which was supposed to hide their exit, was blowing the wrong way, exposing them to nearby enemy snipers so that colonel and staff 'were left running like hunted stags across the fields'.[21]

Maj. Harry Warde, MC, of the Royal Engineers, saw the Arnhem fight as rather tougher. His unit was using petards. It was Shakespeare who coined the joke about 'the engineer' being 'hoist with his own petard'. Originally just a simple bomb, by 1945 the petard was a firing device mounted on a tank. This could discharge a bomb or mine sufficient to cause damage to the strongest of walls on impact. Warde recalled, 'we fired more ammunition in two days at Arnhem than we did in the whole of the rest of the war as a squadron, because the people that were holding Arnhem were a Dutch SS Division, and therefore they had nothing to lose and they obviously weren't going to give up'. The relatively small number of soldiers from Allied countries who fought with German SS divisions could expect prisoner of war treatment different to that accorded to ordinary *Wehrmacht* soldiers, and possibly summary execution by their own restored governments.[22]

After Arnhem, Harry Warde was to win a bar to his Military Cross at Otterlo. He and his men were in bed asleep when an almost panic-stricken Canadian runner burst into the billet, stating that the Canadians had been cut off, the village was 'swarming' with enemy troops and help was urgently needed. The normal duty of a troop of engineers was to stand off and fire their petards in a combined all-arms attack on buildings or fortifications. It was not their role to counter-attack enemy tanks or personnel. However, Warde roused his men and within 8 minutes he had five of his vehicles on the road, counter-attacking the 'swarming' enemy. They were 'German infantry. Very heavily armed. They had machine-guns. Russian machine-guns. They were on wheels which they were towing around the village.' The infantry were astonished and stupefied by the volleys of huge mines crashing into buildings. Although Warde's own tank was hit three times and disabled, he was able to dismount, link up with the Canadian infantry commander and work out a more normal plan to continue herding the enemy out of the village.

As in the case of Harry Warde, the exigencies of battle often required a commander to undertake a task which had never figured in his training instructions or been tasked in unit conferences. Ken Cardy, effectively a mobile repair man with the Welsh Guards, found himself in a similar quandary when no other more appropriate force was available. His duty, of commanding his armoured recovery vehicle up to any broken down vehicle and repairing or removing it, was dangerous enough. But he would now need to take risks beyond the normal duty of after-battle repairs.

Ken saw a tank ahead hit by a high explosive shell and beginning to burn. The crew jumped out and were hit by a second shell. Ken ran to the burning tank and helped the crew into a jeep which was passing by. He then grabbed a fire extinguisher and put out the flames so that the tank could be quickly put back into service. All this happened under heavy artillery fire from the enemy. Later that night a tank was reported missing. Suddenly a wireless call came in from the tank gunner saying that the engine was out of action, the tank crew were wounded, but the guns were still firing. The only vehicle near the HQ wireless set was Ken's ARV called *Ajax*. He volunteered to go and see what the situation was.

Ahead there appeared a lurid scene. The disabled tank stood near a blazing farm and between two smaller houses which were also alight. Into this small illuminated space the enemy poured shells and heavy machine-gun fire:

> Traversing his turret around by hand, the gunner had no power for hydraulics but he was loosing off the big gun a couple of times and machine-gunning. Jim England and I baled out and started getting crossed cables attached. Using the tank's infantry phone I said 'We are towing you back'. He replied 'Get under cover. You are under observation. That's what we are shooting at'. Shells were falling all around. One fell on a large shed and blew it to pieces. We were showered by wood and chickens and blood and feathers. I shouted to Jim to get back to the ARV and for 10 seconds I grabbed and slung chickens on to our engine covers. How we never got hit I will never understand. Anyway we took up the slack and started towing.

Ken has never said what pleased him most: the luxury chicken supper he was able to provide for the troop that night or the Distinguished Conduct Medal which he was later awarded. This was the only such award made to a member of his parent arm, the REME, during the entire war.[23]

Now that the Allied armies were driving deep into Germany, some frontline units were required to take on temporary military government roles in the vacuum left by the German police. Civic leaders who had been dedicated Nazis were quietly disappearing and there was no established opposition party ready to step into the void. Troops also had to adjust their attitude to civilians in Germany after being welcomed into French, Belgian and Dutch towns with flags, girls' kisses, flowers and wine. In many places released prisoners, both military and civilian, as well as forced labourers from other countries, wandered without guidance in search of the basics of life: food, shelter, travel arrangements and identity.

On 5 April 1945, Lord George Scott, now lieutenant-colonel, addressed his squadrons of 1NY on the subject of behaviour towards civilians, explaining the non-fraternisation policy, and warning against temptations which might be offered by the opposite sex in a defeated country. The padre also, somewhat bashfully, pronounced his regulation platitude on venereal diseases, ending with the forlorn joke 'you may call it "the clap" but you certainly won't clap if you get it'. On 6 April Lord George was ordered to take temporary control of the town of Calcar, near the launching sites of the Buffalo fleet across the Rhine. Eventually more formal military government units would take over this responsibility.[24]

The regiment had no official translators and few of the officers or men had even a basic knowledge of German. Lord George appointed Lt Redfern as temporary liaison officer with Tpr Midgley as his interpreter. After reference to the local priest and one or two well disposed civilians, Redfern proposed a man as temporary Burgomaster whom Lord George then authorised to handle local administrative and disciplinary matters. The remaining German police constables were instructed to deal with looting. A central bakery was established. Curfew, blackout and general behaviour notices in German were prepared and posted. Lord George reported the population as 'very submissive and, once our wishes were known, no trouble was experienced'. This was in addition to the regiment's current task of handing in their Buffalo craft and fitting out their Sherman tanks again.

Rumour had it that sometimes the troops themselves caused more trouble than the civilian population. Certainly there was a temptation for the conquering soldiers to exact some kind of retribution on the civilian population. Tpr Don Foxley remembered that in Calcar on the first night of occupation, some of his friends found inexhaustible supplies of strong German beer and, in an alcohol-fuelled anger, wrecked a local china shop. Don, although a teetotal Baptist, was also drawn into this brief expression of revenge. In retrospect he did not feel that the woman who owned the china shop should have had to pay such a high price for being born and living in Hitler's country.[25]

There was a very thin line between the simple spoils of war and criminal looting or persecution. Wounded or abandoned animals were regarded as fair prey by hungry soldiers. Tpr John Stenner, 1NY, thought that pigs always ran faster when they saw a military vehicle approaching. Some officers had a firm idea about instant reparations. Stan Hicken, 1NY, was surprised to be reminded by tough but humorous Capt. Bill Fox, MC, that he could play the piano. 'I want a pianist to help me, Hicken', he said. Stan's job was to drive a large truck as Bill Fox visited certain local houses, often identified by Nazi insignia within, aiming to find pianos which had been confiscated from Dutch people. Later a number of pianos were taken back to Holland. Stan was never sure of the legal propriety of his mission but it seemed morally justifiable at the time.

Capt. Ernest Egli went on a similar mission but benefited from the authority of a brigadier. Having heard from Dutch friends that many bicycles had been stolen by German troops, the brigadier ordered a brigade initiative to collect civilian bicycles from the brigade area and ship them back to Holland. As Egli spoke German he was sent out with a party of men to organise the reparation programme. As with Bill Fox's piano campaign it might have seemed justified at the time, but Egli recorded, 'I must confess that it was a task which we did not particularly like'. Another task was more to engineer Egli's taste. The main bank in Bocholt had been bombed and the door to the vault had jammed. At the request of the bank officials, he, Capt. D.G. Morgan and Cpl S.J. Raggett used plastic explosives to blow open the door. But, conquerors or not, they were closely watched by the German bank officials, zealous for their cash. Their success led to another similar request the next day. Unfortunately for the three helpful REME men, no cash exchange was involved.[26]

The difference between undisciplined revenge and customary soldier's plunder was neatly observed by the valiant Sgt Richard Brew of the Somersets. His wife and son had been bombed out of their home in England and he found himself sheltering in a ruined farmhouse from which the bodies of five of his friends had just been taken away:

> It was brutal reality....We found the headquarters of the local SS headman. We smashed every single thing in that house and not one thing of any use or value remained. I remember having a lot of fun in there. We also found an egg-packing plant and we put out the word for everyone to come and help themselves. We had them boiled, scrambled, even raw and every which way. We all had wind for a few days which gave us all a laugh.[27]

Although the Allied armies from north to south were now advancing beyond the Rhine with speed, it was becoming obvious that if this was to be a race to Berlin then the Russians were going to win. The Allied goal would have to be foreshortened. Much has been written about why the western Allies did not at least attempt to reach Berlin before Marshal Zhukov's men, which would have had a profound effect on post-war politics. But for the frontline soldier the final surrender of the German forces just along the road was far more important than any vision of a triumphal entry into the German capital.

On the contrary, the Russian dictator Stalin had a paranoid passion to be the first to reach Berlin. In addition to future political advantage there was the compulsion to settle old scores with many enemies. An instance of this was the manner in which Marshal Zhukov was made responsible for the conquest of Berlin. The armies directly facing the German capital had been brilliantly commanded by Marshal Konstantin Rokossovsky who could, perhaps better than anyone, have continued through to the eventual triumph. However, Rokossovsky was half Polish. Stalin had nursed a hatred of all things Polish since the war with the Poles in 1920 and he did not wish Berlin to be won by someone with Polish blood. So he moved Rokossovsky to another command and appointed the very Russian Zhukov to lead the final sprint.[28]

Berlin, Bremen, Berchtesgaden or wherever: all units were caught up in the urgency of the last days of war. Ken Cardy had been through the shambles of Operation Goodwood in Normandy in July 1944, the hard combat of the Falaise pocket, whipped into the hectic race across three countries in hardly more days and then the deadly struggle to cross the Rhine. Now his division, the Guards Armoured, were let off the leash and told to 'bash on regardless'. He noticed that the Household Cavalry 'used their scout cars like sports cars, always driving flat out, that was their defence really'. In the same division Richard Carr-Gomm joined in 'an impressive, unexpected and very welcome "gallop" from the Rhine to the Wesser, a distance of 140 miles. The Brigade Group, long accustomed to "waddling along" at 15 mph, advanced fifty miles in six days... had taken 2,000 prisoners'.

Signaller R.W. Deans and his Highland comrades were both amused and delighted when, in a fast forward 'recce', they had burst from the woods and found the next bridge blown, but 'lo and behold! our carriers caught the Germans right off guard – they were in fact swimming naked in the river when our people arrived', fully clothed and with guns loaded.[29] Deans also noted a change in radio circumstances due to the rapid advance. In Normandy and southern Holland a battalion's wireless communications could be limited to as little as 500 yards. During his experience in Operation Totalize some 400 vehicles were transmitting within a 2-mile range, not including the artillery and other transmissions of four divisions. Now they had to adjust and 'here on one occasion we did manage to contact over a range of about 12 miles'.

Bursting from woods into clear country, as Deans did, the advancing troops sometimes seemed to have rolled right out of the war. Ernest Egli found it all unreal:

> We drove through small towns and villages, which were undamaged, neat and tidy, on roads that were smooth, not broken up by shell fire or tank tracks, with fields on either side, with grazing sheep, cattle and horses. Just as if the war had never happened, and people were going about their business and taking no notice of us… the officers and men of the Brigade were to maintain law and order and to clear up and dispose of all dangerous material.

On 12 April Jack Swaab wrote down 'Quakenbruch: lovely country-side – almond and cherry trees in their first blossoms, already dusty from the convoys, the trees budding'. As they hurried on, 'we went into 3 positions today, reaching this one towards sunset, following the rapid advance of the 154th Brigade'. Houses and hamlets were 'bedecked with white flags'. Whilst there were 'old folk with their disillusioned expressions' there were also many 'girls with flaxen pig-tails and tough-looking little boys'. But the 'tough-looking' image of the boys only reflected that in this apparent haven of peace and beauty 'even the budding of the trees holds menace here, deep in Germany, for the forests are still sheltering deserters, saboteurs and other dangers'.[30]

Inevitably the illusion of peace and quiet was shattered from time to time as the 5th Inniskilling Dragoon Guards discovered more than once. On the road to Ibbenburen Tpr A.J. Carder heard that the enemy were elite troops from an officer training corps who had been resolutely resisting other units for two days:

We got to our start line and proceeded at cautious pace… not more than 100 yards before the tank in front of us was hit by a bazooka. Our gunner traversed on to the offending foe and put a 75-mm shell into them… then our crew commander was hit and wounded. Nothing to do but reverse out. A neutral turn took care of that… only to find that some snipers had been busy shooting the crews of our tanks to our left and right. A friend of mine who was hit was sitting on the side of the road. Sadly he died while I was comforting him. We had not advanced that day and had suffered many losses.

Day 2 – we started a bit more spread out and we had infantry. Wasn't long before we were in trouble again, we started to lose men and tanks mainly due to snipers, who seemed all around. My own tank got bogged down in some soft ground. A large hole [from artillery fire] appeared about 100 yards away, then another at 50 yards, then the 3rd striking the ground beside our tank. The force of the explosion lifted the tank up and a lot of armour plating dropped off. We were the sixth tank in as many minutes to be disabled. Our commander and operator got out but when the gunner and myself tried to get out the bullets came whizzing past our ears so we stayed in the tank and used our guns to good effect.[31]

Carder was impressed by the quality of the enemy troops. 'The fighting was intense – house to house, cellar to cellar. It seemed the only way to overcome them was to burn down the houses. They had fought to the last man. I saw only one prisoner, a German Sgt Major, a right Prussian bastard.'

Moving on to Wildeshausen the crew hard-boiled twenty eggs to eat during the day, 'as well as keeping the bowels under control as you can't always choose your time to go to the toilet'. This time they were facing German paratroopers, another elite unit. They had just found 'a warehouse full of booze' when:

…our tank on guard at the front was hit and practically exploded. We were outside into our tanks in about 30 seconds. Their leading tank appeared to be knocked out but not before he had knocked out 6 of our vehicles. All hell broke loose. Our own artillery had been called down on our own positions. We ducked down and hoped our infantry had been able to find cover. Finally the enemy cleared out and retreated back to where they came from. But all that night we stayed awake. We never did get an evening meal or a chance to have a drink…oh, so weary!

As the war approached its end Carder calculated that he had had, since June 1944, twelve crew commanders, eleven of them evacuated as battle casualties and one relieved of duty after a psychological breakdown. He had also served on eleven tanks, ten of them knocked out along the way. There were always replacement tanks available, but often five man crews had to go into battle with only four men available.

Meanwhile, in the sky the strife continued unabated, and, in some cases with more enemy forces than had previously been experienced. Frank Gutteridge saw mixed forces of Focke-Wulfs and Me262s from his tank, 'the latter being the first jet aircraft I ever saw flying', as the Luftwaffe joined in the desperate last days of resistance.[32] Flying his Typhoon John Shellard noted, 'the flak stayed with us until the very end of the war and could be very frightening indeed, but it was a matter of pride to have flown through it.'[33]

Some men felt that their luck was now running out, in later parlance they felt they were past their 'use by' date. Don Ward, MM, who had the hard landing from the stricken glider over the Rhine, suffered a direct hit on his Tetrarch tank. He managed to bail out into a ditch of water. The enemy then peppered the area with air-bursting shrapnel. One large jagged piece shattered his foot just two weeks before the end of hostilities.[34]

Canadians Bud Jones and 'Red' Jeannette of the Royals had been friends for long enough. In odd moments they had sat in a two man slit trench whilst Red tried to teach Bud how to play the guitar. Red was so nicknamed because of his striking red hair which framed a face full of boyish freckles. Having slept in a house which was their defensive position, on 4 April Red was shaving when Pte Bellingham, on watch outside, screamed, 'Here they come'. Bud reacted:

> …with suspenders a-hanging and foam on his face Red went barging by me and on his way grabbed my Sten gun off the door knob, leaving me with his rifle which was leaning on the wall. As I reached the door there was a splatter of machine-gun bullets that hit the door in front of me. There was a large tree outside behind which I took cover. Red was exposed on the front cement step. Even though I was ordering him off the step he rose on one knee and aimed in the direction the firing was coming from. Suddenly a small hole appeared just below his left eye. Then he turned a bluish white and collapsed with his head down on top of the Sten gun.

It was a scene which Bud knew well and had seen many times since his arrival in Normandy. But he still had the rest of his section for which he was responsible:

> Sudden rage seemed to sound a horn of defeat and set me thinking about getting out of there. As luck would have it my platoon commander came spinning around the corner of the house and ordered me to pull my section back across the railway tracks. However, I still required my Sten gun. When I tried to pull it out from under Red's head I noticed that Red's blood had spread all over the gun and it was soaked from barrel to handle and still dripping. It was Red's blood and I would not clean it off. But we managed to drive the Germans away and, being under orders to keep driving on, we had to leave our own casualties behind for others to bury. He was just a red-headed, freckle-faced kid who had done nobody any harm – Henry Joseph Jeanette.[35]

Norman Ford, with 2nd Devons, on 26 April believed that the Germans were making probably the last counter-attack of the war at Vahrendorf; a 'place too small to appear on any map' and insignificant in the history of the war. 'No one wanted to be a dead hero at this stage of the War'. The fire of a lone bazooka almost provoked 'an ignominious rout on our part'. Imminent peace brought a new dimension of fear. 'Death seemed more certain the night we defended Vahrendorf than at any time since Normandy'.

Ford had a rare experience when a lone soldier stepped into his line of sight. Ford fired and the soldier fell. As they advanced Ford was able to examine the dead man who was about 17, 'a very new recruit with minimal training, who carried a brand new rifle, its woodwork unstained and unpolished'. He then realised that the Germans were in so much worse a situation than the Devons:

> All went quiet. Germans started coming in from all directions, hands raised in surrender. Our casualties were few but enemy dead and prisoners totalled well over eighty. The reason obviously lay in the poor quality of the troops. Though the officers were experienced SS men, the soldiers consisted chiefly of young boys (one only 14) and old men in civilian clothes bearing the armband of the 'Volksturm'. They were clearly just a little more frightened and confused than we were. We had survived the Reich's last kick![36]

On the enemy side the problems of setting up any continuous defence system and mustering sufficient trained personnel were becoming insuperable. Jan Munk found supply problems in his SS unit, even though the SS normally had priority in its demands:

> There was an acute shortage of brass in Germany at this time, so the identical shells for M-Gs and rifles were no longer made from brass but steel. To prevent them from rusting these were then varnished. I had an excellent M-G, plenty to shoot at but inferior ammunition. It was normal to control our firing, giving only short bursts... longer bursts were needed which resulted in the barrel over-heating. It jammed. A cartridge could neither enter or leave the barrel because the varnished empty shell could not be withdrawn.[37]

By this time the German Army was relying heavily on non-German speaking soldiers like Jan Munk from occupied countries. This in itself caused problems. There had to be daily repetition of all spoken commands in German, as well as terms and names of weapon parts and so on. For many soldiers there was no further conversation in German except perhaps to be able to order a beer. Misunderstanding easily arose and militated against the easier compliance and comradeship possible where commanders and rankers were from the same linguistic background.

One encouragement the ordinary German soldier received was the frequent sight of high-ranking officers leading from the front. Jan Munk observed one such apparition as he followed his colonel, Klingenberg, on a frontline check. A car appeared and a small man emerged from it. To Munk's astonishment it was Germany's top tank general, the famous Guderian. General and colonel stood talking in the middle of the road and quickly drew heavy artillery fire:

> 'Take cover', shouted Guderian, which everyone did, but Klingenberg wasn't finished and carried on saying what he wanted to say as shrapnel fell about his ears. I shot a glance at the two men – didn't they hear or feel the detonation of shells getting closer and closer? Once more the general shouted 'take cover' and Klingenburg politely said 'after you, general, please, after you'. Klingenburg then gave the general his hand and, after giving each other a slight bow, only then did Guderian take his place in his car.

Manfred Thorn and his tank unit encountered a different problem in the dying hours of the war. Whilst there was a shortage of supplies generally, they still had two tanks and enough ammunition for the day. However, the constant loss of manpower meant that they did not have enough tank men to crew the two tanks. At that point two girls, Inge and 'Calamity Jane', cycled up to the tank and, learning the position, asked to be allowed to join the crew. Cpl Thorn said that it was no job for a woman and, in any case, they were not in uniform, which meant that if taken prisoner they could be shot. Turning to another task he then found that within minutes the two male crew members had found spare overalls in their kit and the girls were transformed into tank soldiers. With some brief instruction Inge was able to fire the fixed machine-gun, but Thorn lived in suspense in case one of the girls answered a radio call and betrayed a prohibited feminine presence inside the fighting machine. After doing what was to be the last day's duty on those tanks the girls cycled away, to the commander's relief.[38]

Allied troops noticed the change in age among defending troops with boys and veterans comprising the *Volksturm*, the German 'Home Guard'. George Blackburn always vividly remembered an exhausted white-haired prisoner who had been a bank manager a day or two before entering battle (indeed a 'Dad's Army' in reality).[39] Similarly, Stan Whitehouse never forgot German women shaking fists at his platoon and shouting, 'You've killed an old man'. To which they could only reply by pointing out that the corpse still had a *Panzerfaust* held tight in rigid fingers.[40]

Any sympathy for boys and old men, or any empathy with a chivalrous frontline foe, on the part of Allied soldiers was about to be sullied and then burned from the mind. As in the case of Tpr J. F. Elliott of XXII Dragoons:

April. Saw something today I will never forget, came across a camp called Belsen, some of our troops were already there, got out of the tank to have a look, if there is an hell on earth then this is it. How could humanity sink so low in bestiality? I was only there for an hour, but that hour was a lifetime. Now I know that power gives strength but absolute power corrupts absolutely.[41]

And that comparison of 'hell on earth' came from a man who had himself been blown up four times in a highly combustible tank.

Lt P.M. Hedley-Prole, Royal Artillery, was driving his jeep 'in warm sunshine, birds singing overhead, no signs of enemy, emerging blossoms and aroma of heather'. What happened next was like a sudden descent from heaven into hell:

> I followed the track... ending up outside the main gate of a camp. By now I was aware of a VERY unpleasant smell and saw, moving among the huts, some incredible beings – stick thin, unsteady, mostly in rags, heads shaven – and one was quite unable to tell what sex they might be. Faces skull-like and skins yellowish. I was conscious of eyes sunken and lacklustre... some were just lying against huts scratching occasionally. Overall was that simply awful smell. I was also aware of what to me seemed to be a kind of 'mist' hanging over the camp.[42]

Tank gunner Alf Gritton was another person first alerted by 'a terrible stink'. An officer in another armoured car drew up alongside and said, 'What's that stink?' Gritton replied that he did not know but observed that the wind was blowing from a wood. This led the officer to decide 'that's where the camp is'. They circled round the wood and found themselves at the front entrance of Belsen. Unprepared by any training or specific orders, at first the sight made no sense to them:

> We couldn't quite puzzle out what it was, all the people in stripes, bodies on the floor. Thousands of people in there... Colonel Kramer, the camp commandant, was there. He was a big man about 6ft 4 and he came over with hand extended to shake hands, which we refused to do because we couldn't take our eyes off all the corpses.... I think I smoked about half a dozen cigarettes in 10 minutes. My stomach was rolling over... About three days later there was another concentration camp ahead. I thought, 'Oh this is all I want'. We saw one of the guards come out of the gate and try to make it to a little wood. The commander said 'bring him down, bring him down' and I swung the turret round and fired a burst. There was a poor old horse standing in my line of fire. The horse dropped and I brought the SS bloke down with another burst.[43]

Things got even worse for Alf. Later, strolling to smoke a cigarette he found the place where he had accidentally shot the horse. There was 'just the tail and a big pool of blood left'. The starving prisoners had stripped the body and eaten the raw meat. He was then part of a group trying to round up the prisoners who had gone on a mission of vengeance, murdering some German women on small farms and taking cats, dogs and other animals. They then lit small fires on the parade ground to cook and eat the animals.

Even people like the amiable despatch rider Charles Dunesby of the Seaforths were caught up in the atmosphere of horror and vengeance. They had found a small outlying camp of Belsen and taken a dozen prisoners. One was a tall man in SS uniform. The remainder were *Volksturm*. They were standing beside the road guarded by 'a quite diminutive Scots soldier'. An Intelligence Officer drove up but, after a moment, drove away again, saying he would be back soon. The Scot then told the prisoners to sit down. At that, the SS man barked an order at the *Volksturm* telling them not to sit down. He then spat in the face of the Scottish ranker. The diminutive man 'in a flash brought up his rifle and hit the SS man between the eyes with the butt of his rifle, felling him like a log'. He then told the other prisoners they could sit down, which they did 'giving the impression that they would have liked to hit the SS man themselves'. The enemy had become a darker influence.[44]

All across Germany Allied troops were encountering similar camps. Also being liberated were many prisoner of war camps containing Allied soldiers and airmen. For the prisoners it was often a complicated time. Typhoon pilot Derek Tapson had found himself in a camp near Nuremberg with two old friends; pilots Allan Smith and Ken Trott. Although they were hoping for liberation from the west they were summoned to pack up and move. They were made to walk further into Germany for two weeks in order to reach another camp at Mooseberg. There they were eventually liberated by the Americans coming from Italy in almost the opposite direction. No explanation was given for this totally unnecessary forced march. The Americans produced flour and margarine which Derek mixed and fried up into a kind of celebratory pancake.[45]

Also released on Easter Sunday were the Canadian prisoners at Fallingbostel who had endured a two month forced march from the east. They had bypassed Dresden after the infamous bombing raid, been threatened by German civilians and on one occasion carried a chicken, stolen and hidden for nine days before they could safely cook it. They too were liberated by American tanks. After their near starvation march many of the prisoners had proved incapable of eating more than a few spoonfuls of soup before suffering violent stomach reactions. Their special treat from the liberating Americans was tinned peaches.[46]

A Typhoon pilot still in action, John Shellard, was still being given targets even when it was clear that the war was to end imminently. Prime targets still included troops dug in. He remembers:

> ...my last sortie, four aircraft to attack a train on the German/Danish border when our [flight] leader force-landed. The three of us were bounced by two ME262 jet fighters. We shot down their leader and came home. David, our leader, ended up at the same MEs' airfield before going to prison [fortunately only for a day or so] and found their pilots surprisingly like RAF pilots. When I joined 263 Sqn in Dec 1943 I brought the number of pilots to 27. Of that number 16 were killed and 4 were shot down but evaded capture and returned home. The number of *replacement* pilots was 37, of whom 13 were killed, 3 were POW and 1 escaped.[47]

The 8th Kings Royal Irish Hussars sensed something between amusement and frustration when, within a month of the end of the war, they were at long last issued with new infra-red gun-sights for night fighting, a piece of equipment the enemy had long enjoyed. Capt. Bill Bellamy, now wearing the MC ribbon, found everywhere in ruins, 'everything drab and dusty. Everywhere sullen people slinking about with averted faces'. The exception was the children who were always on the lookout for kind soldiers with chocolate to spare. Then seeing the bombed shambles of Osnabruck Bill had profound thoughts:

> ... the worst large-scale devastation that I had seen....I was stunned by the totality of it and, despite my anger, horrified at the suffering which it had brought in its wake. Whatever the German people had done, I couldn't gloat over their anguish, or get satisfaction from a feeling of revenge, and already the healing process of recognising 'selective' as opposed to 'corporate' guilt was at work in my being.[48]

Next day, 18 April, he met up with his friend Titch Kirkham and mentioned these feelings about collective guilt. However, Titch had been involved in liberating a POW camp at Fallingsbostel and then had gone into the horrors of Belsen. He was not swayed by Bill's gentler considerations saying, 'Don't waste sympathy on the bastards'. Bill was also deeply affected when Titch told him of the death of Richard Anstey, who had suffered a strong premonition of impending death and was blown up by a huge concealed bomb.

Some Allied units were still liberating Dutch towns. Capt. Ian Hammerton enjoyed the 'shaking hands and laughing with joy', although the tank crews had to be alert for enemy counter-attacks even whilst delirious local people scrambled over the tank. As civilians emerged from the horrors of the *Hongerwinter.*

> ...we noted the ragged clothes, the pinched faces, the thin children, many shoeless, the cycles without tyres, and we dug deep into our tank larders to hand out tins of sardines, soup, chocolate, sweets and cigarettes.[49]

Hugh Clark was another person who noted the sullen response of local civilians along the way as they passed farmhouse after farmhouse with white sheets draped from the windows. His 2nd Ox and Bucks (Air Landing) covered 332 miles in thirty-nine days:

> Some of the German women offered us milk to drink but this was refused as we thought it might have been poisoned. All organised defence by the enemy to our front was now gone and it was only isolated pockets of resistance that had to be dealt with. However, some of these were fierce and determined.[50]

If anything the last ditch defenders were resorting to even more subtle modes of deception and more powerful means of obstruction. Ian Hammerton and his mine-sweeping tanks tried to drive into Bremen, but found the streets blocked by railway wagons of various sizes. The squadron lost time pushing these aside. Then they came to a thick concrete wall extending on both sides of the street with a huge concrete block rolled into the gap. Ian's tank shot AP (Armour Piercing) and HE rounds at the obstruction but only succeeded in knocking

bits off it. An AVRE with a petard then took over and, using its powerful bombs, eventually reduced the block to small pieces. The AVRE
then trundled forward to climb over the rubble, followed by a jeep.
As they passed through the gap there was a terrific explosion and the
40 ton AVRE was lifted into the air. The jeep simply vanished. The
assumption was that a naval mine, or more than one, had been used as
the explosive.[51]

Prisoners were surrendering in droves to Allied vanguards and
presented a variety of facial expressions and mental expectations.
Maj. Bill Close, MC, who had led the first tank squadron into
the carnage of Operation Goodwood in July 1944, witnessed the
reversal of fortune. Descending from his tank, his overalls naturally
dishevelled by the rigours of tank battle, he prepared to accept the
surrender of a German battalion. From a group of officers accompanying a white flag a smartly dressed adjutant stepped forward and
said, 'My colonel will only surrender his unit to a British officer of
field rank!' Bill assured the man that he himself was indeed of field
rank, but also pointed out tersely that he had seventeen tanks also
of 'field rank' lined up behind him. It is not known if the German
appreciated the pun. In the end both colonel and adjutant accepted
a ride into captivity perched on Bill's tank.[52]

Ian Hammerton's experience, though similar, was not quite so courteous. He took the surrender of a major and ten soldiers. The major
pompously quoted the Geneva Convention and refused to ride on the
back of Ian's tank with the rankers. Before Ian could remonstrate, Staff
Sergeant-Major Bob Butterfield intervened, 'It's all right, sir. I will
arrange for him to go back alone with my tank'. It was 2 miles back to
the collection point and Ian's tank clanked along at a reasonable speed.
However, there was then a considerable pause and Ian wondered if
Butterfield had taken the law into his own hands after recently losing a
close comrade. Then they heard the sounds of Butterfield's Cromwell
slowly approaching, the tank pursued by the usual cloud of filthy dust
and smoke, and by the German major. He had indeed travelled alone
with the SSM's tank. Ian was careful to look the other way.

Meanwhile, special flights (infantry platoons) of the RAF regiment
were racing ahead to secure airfields, especially in Denmark and later
in Norway. Numbers of German planes were now coming in from all
over Germany to land at such locations; the crews only too anxious

to surrender to the British rather than the Russians before the war had even ended.

As the fighting diminished strange occurrences of a cloak and dagger nature became apparent to some people of humble rank. Cpl Reg Spittles, 1RTR, involved in the accidental shooting of an officer, had been offered a Mention in Despatches for rescuing wounded crew, but the award had then been withdrawn by his brigadier as a *quid pro quo* against the admittedly accidental wounding of the officer. Reg was not too worried about losing the award because, after being wounded, he was now downgraded as unfit for tank service. He found himself working as a driver to a pool of interpreters in Brussels. One day a major required his services saying, 'You will address me as Major Harry Smith and go where I tell you but ask no questions.' For some days they visited various headquarters and areas of the frontline. Then one morning the major took his seat saying, 'If you keep your eyes and ears open you may one day find out what we were doing today.'

Their route took them along a road which was clogged up with military traffic of all kinds. The major instructed Reg to drive ahead on the wrong side of the road. At a road junction a red-capped military police sergeant was directing traffic, his motor bike perched at the side of the road. The sergeant advanced menacingly towards Reg, waving his hands furiously and shouting. The major leaned out of the car and showed something to the sergeant. To Reg's amazement the sergeant slammed to attention, gave the major an immaculate salute and then barked at Reg, 'Follow me!' He mounted his motor bike and roared away, leading them to a large country house where the major disappeared for most of the day. Another military policeman had approached the car as Reg parked, shouting, 'You can't park there'; again the major's sleight of hand trick convinced the guard to allow Reg due preference. Although he kept eyes and ears open and saw various high-ranking officers entering and leaving the building, Reg never worked out who or what 'Major Harry Smith' was. He also refrained from joking to his imperious passenger, 'I know you are not Major Harry Smith because the real Major Harry Smith is my brother-in-law'.[53] He did learn later that FM Montgomery had more than one 'major' who travelled and acted on Montgomery's own authority. The war ended a day or two after the country house meeting.

The conclusion of the war appeared to be producing even more horrific scenes, and soldiers like Peter White found it increasingly difficult to differentiate emotionally between friend and foe. This was especially so when Peter's infantry unit needed to call in the flame-throwing tanks:

> Despite Uphusen being an enemy village I felt sick at heart to see house after house blaze up in flames and towering sparks and smoke as the jets of trickling fire ate into them. Some had women and children in them, as we could soon tell from the screaming and shrieking misery, piercing in pitch above the hell of other noises of war. ...some grey-green clad figures materialised...they had their hands up...dog-tired, sallow with fatigue and ill feeding and fright; bloodshot in the eyes and smelled of singeing, fire and smoke.[54]

Bereavement was bitterly poignant where soldiers had fought together through the entire campaign from the D-Day beaches onward. By 18 April Ken Cardy, DCM, and comrades were hoping that they would all 'make it' through to the end. It was not to be. Their tanks had halted on the road to Visselhovede:

> Jim England, Lewis and myself had got out for a stretch and a smoke. Jim Mills was standing on his seat, half in, half out, all of us side by side. Three shots rang out. One shot clipped my epaulet. One spun off the visor in front of Jim Mills. But Jim England had dropped like a stone. Of course we had all dropped down but Jim was pumping out blood. Some Scots Guards stopped and we told them we had been sniped at. They ran forward and blasted the nearby treetops and out fell three snipers. The large barn beside us was burning and by its light we dug a grave. We rolled him in his blanket and buried him. We had just finished patting it down, put the cross in, when Padre Payne arrived in his jeep. He said, 'Is he a Catholic?' I said, 'Yes'. He said, 'Take him out again, please. I will take him to a Catholic centre'. So with big lumps in our throats we lifted Jim out again and on to the jeep stretcher. And that was the last we saw of our mate.[55]

The continued resoluteness of the sporadic enemy resistance is exemplified by the fact that the last Victoria Cross of the campaign was won as late as 21 April by Guardsman Edward Colquhoun

Charlton of the 2nd Irish Guards. At Wistedt the defenders, officer cadets supported by self-propelled guns, knocked out three of the four tanks of the Guards troop. Co-driver Charlton was ordered to dismount the heavy 50-mm machine-gun from the turret top and support the infantry.

With the Germans attacking in overwhelming numbers, Charlton decided to march towards the enemy and fire the gun from his hip, which was in itself a very difficult task. He was wounded in the arm but continued forward and stopped the enemy attack. The wound made it impossible to continue holding and firing the 50-mm machine-gun so he fixed it upon a fence and continued to fire at the enemy as they regrouped for attack. He was wounded again and eventually, still firing, fainted from loss of blood. Charlton later died from his wounds. Unusually his award was based on German accounts of the battle as for much of the time Charlton had no senior leader within sight of his action.[56]

At the very last Peter White, at a forward post, saw a tragic incident. A jeep which had been ordered to stay some hundreds of yards back from White's slit, suddenly and inexplicably started up and raced forward. As it came to a bridge there was a great explosion and the jeep was blown up, disintegrating totally, obviously on a concealed mine. 'Many feet above it small bits and pieces spun back to earth'. One man was killed instantly. Remarkably 'a bundle of crumbled khaki near the still smoking crater' proved to be still alive, but was borne away unconscious. It was assumed that the jeep crew had heard something on their wireless about the war ending and were rushing forward with the good news. Shortly after the incident the 'cease fire' came through officially.

Capt. Bill Bellamy was shocked when his good friend Lt Wally Ryde, 8th Hussars, was killed two days before the ceasefire. Cpl Ken Jordan and the rest of the crew carried Ryde's body into the local church and laid it decently before the altar. Ken then went to a neighbouring *Hausfrau* and asked if he might have some flowers from her garden to place beside Ryde's body. Ryde, Ken, the crew and their squadron leader Tim Piersen had all moved to 8th Hussars when their own shattered regiment, 2NY, was disbanded in Normandy.[57]

To Sgt Jock Stirling and his XXII Dragoons crew, it also looked as though the war was virtually over (in fact only about 40 hours remained). The crew and troop leader Ian Hammerton watched while 'a column of very beaten-looking Germans, an unkempt, ill-clad *Volksturm* mix of old men and untrained boys – shambles past' their flail tanks, as Alan Walkden the operator/loader remembered. Cameron Highlanders infantry ushered the prisoners along. 'Jim Taylor (our gunner) and I simultaneously spot an SP some distance ahead on the right-hand verge. It's an ugly customer, low and squat, but it's leaning sideways and not looking very hostile'. Gunner Jim Taylor trod on the 75-mm firing button and a flash on the enemy's glacis-plate indicated a hit. It began to burn. But 'there's something odd about the emptiness of the road':[58]

As the burning SP recedes, the road, rising slightly, stretches ahead, very straight, in unnatural quiet. Then speculation is abruptly shattered. A jarring metallic impact makes the whole tank shudder. Jock is up top – maybe he knows what's happened.

'What the hell was that, Jock?'

No reply from the commander. He seems to lean forward resignedly against the cupola. I look properly at him and I see why he isn't answering. Where his head used to be, there's something out of a slaughterhouse – bloody, shapeless, obscene.

'Let's get out of here,' I bellow over the intercom, and in reply comes the voice of Baz, our driver, 'I can't move, man! The bloody 75's traversed over my hatch'. Jim's presence of mind hasn't deserted him: he switches to manual traverse and the turret swings in response. Baz wastes no time. He's out of the hatch and diving for the roadside ditch.

Jim and I heave at the dead commander: his cupola is the one way out of the turret. The tank shudders to another impact. And I am tugging at a second inertly indifferent, horrendously butchered corpse: Jim. There are neat three-inch holes in the turret's front AND rear armour where Jim's 75-mm executioner shot has passed right through… steel armour and human flesh.

I heave at the bloodied bodies. I'm climbing towards freedom when something yanks at my neck, impeding escape. My pistol lanyard has caught in the jagged, shell-blasted flap of the cupola. I tug, in crude desperation, and something gives. Spiteful cracks are still sounding from the enemy 75 at virtually point-blank range. The top half of a telegraph pole splinters into matchwood. Our tank surprisingly does not burn: just sits there sullenly, smoking. In the ditch Baz and I look round dazed and unbelieving. A number of Camerons are moving around a farmhouse. We climb out of the ditch and make our way towards the Scotsmen.

A Cameron corporal stares at my gory tank suit with sagging jaw. 'Ma Gawd! Whit the hell happened tae yous?'

No fully adequate answer is possible. Baz and I stand dumbly staring in a kind of stupidity at the Scot. The Highland corporal's own blackened face loses something of its dourness as he leads us towards the nearby farmhouse.

'You laddies juist aboot had enough', he says. 'C'm on in the hoose an' let's hae a wee drenk o' tea!'

CHAPTER NINE

VICTORY! – OR FURTHER STRIFE?

They took the citadel six years from the time the strife first broke out.

(Herodotus, 440 BC)

CIPHER MESSAGE FORM   d/84

350

From: EXFOR MAIN   042050b

To: FIRST CDN ARMY, SECOND BR ARMY, L OF C, GHQ AA
TROOPS, 79 ARMD DIV, EXFOR REAR

Info: 2 TAF, EXFOR TAC, 22 LIAISON HQ

GO 411 A (.) SECRET (.) All offensive ops will cease from receipt this
signal (.) Orders will be given to all troops to cease fire 0800hrs tomorrow SATURDAY 5 MAY (.) Full terms of local GERMAN surrender
arranged today for 21 ARMY GROUP front follow (.) Emphasise these
provisions apply solely to 21 ARMY GROUP fronts and are for the
moment exclusive of Dunkirk (.) ACK

EMERGENCY   042050B

Thus the signal of 4 May 1945 indicated the end of the war in North-
West Europe. But there was as yet no release from the disciplines
of war. And men would still die. The terse message from EXFOR
MAIN filtered down to individual units. At 34th Armoured Brigade
HQ signals officer Capt. Ian Carmichael, later to become a famous
film star, translated it for the colonels, including Lord George Scott of
1NY, simply as 'Cease Fire! 0800hrs, 5 May'.

Cpl Stan Hilton and Sgt Falconer of 1NY had found a pleasant billet with a Dutch family. Returning from duty in the tank laager they found the family sitting at the table, ready to eat, heads bowed in prayer. Respectfully the soldiers waited and then, as heads rose, Stan tried a gentle joke, 'praying for the liberation?' (parts of Holland were still in German hands). The father laughed and shouted, 'Praying FOR, friends? THANKING for! The Boche has capit... capul... *zich overgeven*... overgiven! Ask for, you say, armistize? We hear BBC. Thank you God! But thank you, you, our great brave friends!' And Stan thought how often he had been scared stiff rather than being a big brave hero.[1]

If the Dutch family knew of the German surrender before Sgt Falconer's crew, numbers of German troops were the last to learn of the order to cease fire. When a vanguard of Seaforth Highlanders approached the last bridge before a seaplane base they were halted by a somewhat puzzled German guard. The Highland colonel came up and demanded to see the German guard commander. He in turn stated that his last order was to blow up the bridge if threatened and he knew nothing of any surrender. The colonel persuaded the German to phone his HQ, which confirmed that surrender was the order of the day. The colonel then moved on to the seaplane base HQ and entered.

Matters became even more bizarre. The colonel, emerging with his interpreter, told his despatch rider, Charles Dunesby, to stay where he was in the entrance and then went back to conduct the rest of the battalion forward. A moment later a German officer came out, saluted the DR and, speaking perfect English, requested him to enter the building. Dunesby found himself in a mess hall full of airmen. The officer barked an order bringing all the men to attention. He then asked Dunesby's permission for the men to eat. The bemused Seaforth Highlander, formerly a Somerset Light Infantryman from Bournemouth, gave permission to proceed with all the authority of Supreme Allied HQ. The almost farcical formalities continued. Outside the building the DR found a German guard of honour, in full uniform, assembling and quickly mounted to receive and surrender to an incoming Seaforth guard of honour.[2]

If this story from a ranker should appear a little over imaginative it is corroborated by other sources. Capt. Peter White, adjutant of his KOSB battalion, encountered a similar situation. His first intimation of peace was a firework display of coloured Very lights from another frontline position. Then his wireless operator on a weak 38 set managed to tune in to the BBC and heard very faintly the confirmed announcement of the ceasefire. However, a German officer and fourteen men on Peter's left flank, and in front of 7th/9th Royal Scots:

> ...could not be convinced the war was over for a further forty-eight hours and repulsed with fire any attempt made to contact them. This seemed to demonstrate to what extent the enemy communication and control had deteriorated. Our orders were meanwhile to carry on with normal stags and alertness just as though nothing had happened![3]

In rather more picturesque language, Canadian hero Bud Jones described the Germans cut off in Friesland as 'frazzled'. Bud's Royal battalion had celebrated peace in Groningen but continued patrolling into Friesland and encountered German groups also unaware of the end of war. The Royals had to send out a white flag carried by a platoon commander with escort to negotiate their own ceasefire with the confused Germans. Canadian FOO Capt. George Blackburn also remembered a discussion with a lone German soldier in Groningen, who had come forward, as to whether the war was over. When the Canadians had convinced the man, who had worked in Detroit and spoke English, he returned to his post and, after a while, his entire battalion surrendered.[4]

Meanwhile, other frontline soldiers were, like Reg Spittles, witnessing strange goings-on involving high-ranking enemy officers. Bob Taylor and Ron Harrison, two ex-2NY men and now with 11th Hussars, were patrolling near Hamburg in their armoured car when a German staff car with two motorcycle outriders came over the hill, one motorcyclist waving a white flag. The leading man explained to the surprised Hussars that the car contained Admiral von Freideburg who had come to surrender the German forces in the west. This was somewhat beyond the remit of the Hussar patrol, so they radioed Capt. T.O'B. Horsford at squadron HQ who came forward to escort the Germans back to regimental HQ. Thus ended Bob's and Ron's brief brush with history.[5]

Lt Frank Gutteridge, 1RTR, on patrol had been advised that emissaries were approaching from the German side. The 1RTR interpreter, an East European, using a loud hailer, shouted in German that a black sedan would be allowed to cross the battle lines. Frank remembered the exact words:

> *Es gibt in eurer Linie ein schwartzer Sedan…* An open tourer Mercedes arrived and travelling in it were German officers and a civilian. The officers were immaculately dressed and I imagine they were not impressed by our scruffy appearance. They complained about the loudhailer message, saying that there were SS troops in the vicinity who were opposed to any surrender. This was prophetic as the Mercedes car was later blown up on a mine on the enemy side. Incidentally we called the SS 'Sugar-Sugar Men' as our radio code was S for Sugar, BUT they were, of course, anything but sweet![6]

On Luneberg Heath, scene of FM Montgomery's acceptance of German surrender, signals Sgt F. Cooper saw 'a gaggle of German officers' arrive, but could not stop to watch as he and a Welsh lad had been ordered forward to lay lines. Coming to their appointed village and rounding the bend they:

> …had the fright of our life because there coming towards us was a column of Germans. There were 3 officers in front, the Colonel in charge and 2 Aide de Camps and about 200 troops fully armed and what could we do? We just sat there in our jeep and the Colonel in front, whoever he was, halted his troops and came over and saluted us and said in fluent English 'We are your prisoners'. Well, I thought to myself 'I don't want any prisoners at the moment'. The Colonel went on 'My troops are about finished. They are very, very hungry and very, very thirsty' Well, I didn't know and so I just thought to say 'About 3 kilometres back is a reception centre and you will get something there'- not that I knew anything was 3 kilometres back. And he said 'Thank you very much' and off they went.[7]

Capt. Richard Carr-Gomm and his Coldstream Guards had been given more precise instructions about an active search for particularly evasive Germans. Two Dutch students had been allocated to them as interpreters. It was not until 22 May that they accomplished their mission, taking by surprise a train standing near Bokhorst station. Inside sat the surviving German government and its head, Admiral Doenitz. The train had to be taken by surprise in case of hidden weapons or explosives. About 160 high-level personnel were counted and Carr-Gomm had the task of checking that no vitally important papers were destroyed in the melee.[8]

Formal surrenders also took place at corps level. Nearly six years after the start of his incredible odyssey on the Hungarian border, Maj.-Gen. Maczek was present at the surrender of German forces in Ostfriesland. As he sat next to the Canadian general, Guy Simonds, the Pole noted that there were no chairs in front of the table. The German delegation entered. Gen. Straube began to speak, but Simonds immediately interrupted. 'You have not come here to negotiate with us. You are here to listen to the terms of the unconditional surrender'. He then began to read the terms. This included the disposition of which Allied forces would hold absolute authority, for the time being, in which area. Then he came to 'Wilhelmshaven…' and with quite a dramatic pause, no doubt aware of the history of 1 September 1939, Simonds stated, 'First Polish Armoured Division'.[9]

At less exalted levels, Allied officers and men were struggling to cope with the increasing chaos on the roads and in urban streets. Hugh Clark, MC, was ordered to reconnoitre for billets near Luttersdorf:

> It was a day I shall never forget. All day long as we drove east we met, coming in the opposite direction, a whole mass of humanity in an endless column some four or five wide. Among them were German troops, looking dejected and having thrown their weapons away. There were German civilians and also many released slave workers. Some had managed to commandeer a horse and cart, others were pushing handcarts…waiting for the regiment in a house, there was a knock on the door. We found a rather bedraggled man in uniform who said he had thirty hungry soldiers. I sent him away saying that WE had not eaten all day. It was only afterwards that I realised that they were Hungarian troops wanting to surrender.[10]

Also with the Guards in his ARV, Ken Cardy had a fascinating chat with some *Volksturm* prisoners who had all served in the First World War and had great respect for 'Tommy'. 'They told us why they were anxious to surrender. It was because of the Hitler Youth squads, if the Volk didn't toe the line they were reported to the nearest Gestapo, the swines that they were'. Directed to the Cologne area, Ken's unit took more than three days to cover 350 miles due to the problems of congestion on the road (normal cruising speed about 30 mph).[11] Ken found it still 'disconcerting to see the familiar field-grey uniforms standing in fields and farmyards, watching us pass by. Freed Russians were roaming about all night and we expected some trouble but all went well'.

There were still pockets of German troops who had not yet surrendered, as artilleryman Jack Swaab noted, 'a small patch on the Baltic', in Czechoslovakia, Norway and Denmark. While his Highland infantry comrades towards Bremerhaven were collecting prisoners by the thousand, Jack saw that 'some of them looked literally 14 years old'.[12]

As advancing troops accepted more formal surrender and disarmed large units, a sense of bewilderment continued. Hugh le Messurier's Duke's infantrymen were disarming the elite 6th Para Division, the famous *Fallschirmjaeger*. The system was so organised that at night there were patrols of three different armies: the Duke's, the White Brigade (Belgian/Dutch) and the German Paras. The latter were still armed 'so as I stood at the garden gate there they were [the Germans guards] with their Schmeissers walking past and guarding'.[13]

Even more astonishing was Typhoon pilot Derek Tapson's encounter at a forward airfield:

> We saw a squadron of German fighters land at Mooseberg, except that the CO of the squadron did a final air display before landing. What surprised us most was when he got out of the plane he took off a panel behind the cockpit where we assumed the radio equipment was kept. However it was his girl friend who had been in the space and she got out to join him [rather than being left behind to be liberated by the Russians].[14]

Lt Bill Bellamy discovered why some Germans were nervous about surrendering. His 8th Hussars troop accepted the surrender of a *Kubelwagen* bearing a large white flag. He said, '*Guten Tag*' to the senior officer who was immediately 'blindfolded and whisked away' to divisional HQ. Later he learned that the senior officer, Dr G.A. Link, had served on the Russian Front and said that if they had tried to surrender to the Russians they would have been shot on sight. Bill intercepted another *Kubelwagen* which carried a grievously wounded German officer. Again essaying his schoolboy German Bill said,

'*Mochten-sie ein cigarette?*' to which the man replied, 'My dear fellow, nothing would be nicer'. He was a Classics graduate from Oxford. Taking a camera from under the blood-stained blankets he offered it to Bill, who refused. The German insisted, 'If your bloody second-line troops are anything like ours, I shall soon be robbed of this. And I would rather see it go to a fighting soldier', handing a *Zeiss Super Ikonta* to Bill's driver, Much.[15]

By now peace had been confirmed almost everywhere and Allied troops celebrated appropriately, even more so where they were still among liberated Dutch civilians; other columns continued on towards Denmark. Using a commander's discretion, Harry Warde's squadron commander of 617 REs, noting that they were just beyond the Dutch border, sent Harry back across the border to find a Dutch town in which to celebrate. Harry succeeded in finding 'a lovely little town called Coevorden and the whole squadron set out and went over to Coevorden, where they were in time to hear Winston Churchill's victory speech broadcast in the village square'.[16]

Fred Leary and 1NY comrades joined civilians 'singing and dancing in the streets' until the early hours of the morning and 'anyone wearing a uniform was common prey to be carried aloft as if they were personally responsible for winning the war'. Brian Carpenter, the lone guard who had been alerted during the Ardennes emergency, had been sent back to hospital for treatment on his foot problems caused by frostbite in the Ardennes snows. Now well again he took several days passing through various holding units to get back to 1NY. Arriving at the regiment's tank laager at long last he found it practically deserted. Everybody had gone into Zwolle town to celebrate, leaving a few bad-tempered guards on prowler duty.[17]

A more formal brigade celebration involved Capt. Ernest Egli:

We lined up ten tanks we had in workshops and warned everybody we were going to fire a victory salvo. We fired our salvo and I was pleased to be one of the gunners because it is exciting to fire a tank gun [His normal task was in workshops]. You smell the cordite fumes, which raises the adrenalin level, and increases the excitement. The salvo blast unfortunately broke a number of windows. At night we illuminated the night sky with tank Very pistols. The red, green and white flares made a good show.[18]

Ken Cardy, also REME, admired the Welsh Guards to whom he was attached. Now they obtained dark grey paint from the Cuxhaven Naval Base, together with the necessary brushes, and set to work in preparation for a formal victory parade. Three ARV sergeants carried welding equipment around the tanks to weld up bullet holes and slits caused by shrapnel. 'Typical of the Guards the tanks were going to be like parade-ground order'. Ken had 'borrowed' a Leica camera from a knocked-out enemy tank (officially British combatants could not carry cameras) to take photos of himself and the crew. A German chemist developed the prints free of charge as he was 'glad the war is over'.[19]

It is a British eccentricity to celebrate victory by beating the retreat. Highland division pipes and drums had done this across France, Belgium and Holland to the wonder and delight of civilians. Now, Ian Hammerton noted with a chuckle, the German spectators were not too sure about the significance of this warrior display. The sky had been filled with 'every conceivable missile from revolver shots to Bren. It was quite dangerous':

> But not as dangerous in German eyes, apparently, as the sight of the Regimental Pipe Band of one of the Highlander regiments, dressed in full ceremonials of kilts, sporrans, plaids, white spats and cockaded bearskins, counter-marching to and fro in a neighbouring field, an extremely proud Drum-major at their head as they 'Beat the Retreat'.... As the lines of returning prisoners and civilians approached this field they edged over cautiously to the farthest side of the road, as far away as they could get from the extraordinary but stirring sight and sound of the bagpipes and drums of the 'Ladies from Hell'.[20]

George Blackburn watched his own artillery guns roll past in celebration and found his pride in their smartness and efficiency. He was, however, troubled by thoughts of the damage they might have caused to friends as occupied countries were liberated and desecrated:

> Remembering the revulsion you felt on first being introduced to the death-dealing capacities of an old 18-pounder by an enthusiastic lieutenant at summer camp, you marvel at your feelings. Has time, training and experience perverted you? Can it be right for a man to look with affection on killing machines? But as you stare at those passing guns,

you decide that a man would truly be perverted if today he was unable
to feel gratitude for those trustworthy old weapons that unquestionably
saved the lives of many, many men, including your own. D Sub's gun is
going by, and you look for the holes in the shield through which the
bullets came that killed Sgt-major 'Lefty' Phillips. Its breech shines like
silver in the sunlight.[21]

For some servicemen victory day hardly provided a break in the continuing routine of war and war's impact. There was no holiday for the
crews and ground staff of Lancaster bombers. Many planes had been
converted to carry as many as twenty-five passengers and were destined to carry released prisoners of war back to Britain. During this
Operation Exodus the 'Lancs' totalled 3,000 round trips in the first
month and carried 74,000 personnel back to England. The operation continued until September and also reached out to Italy and the
central Mediterranean.

Allied troops continued to find and liberate concentration camps
and prisoner of war camps. Many shared the experience of Capt. Tim
Piersen of 8th Hussars. His recce troop had liberated a huge camp
'full of all nationalities of Europe', some slave labourers and some
prisoners of war. Generally the occupants appeared dirty and bedrag-
gled. Then they came upon a camp of British prisoners of war, seeing
first of all 'through a gap between two trees a khaki-clad figure wearing a maroon-coloured beret, clinging to a fence and jumping up
and down'. As the camp came in sight both the wire fence and the
barrack roofs were black with excited men. 'The sounds of welcome
from the crowd… grew into a roar that penetrated our earphones
above the noise of our engines'. However, 'despite the enthusiasm
of the men inside, you could see at a glance that there was order and
discipline'. The troops were clean and smart even in well-worn uniforms. Typical was a Highland SM with 'creases in his tartan trews and
shining buttons on the jacket'.[22]

The liberation of camps took place on an ad hoc basis and was
not always well organised. Maj.-Gen. Maczek was compelled to write
directly to FM Montgomery with a serious complaint:

I have been informed by Polish officers formerly PoW in Sandbostel
Camp that, in spite of being liberated by Allied units some 12 days ago,

their conditions of life have not altered. The only difference is that the guard has been changed. They continue to sleep on the floor without paillasses [sic], covered with lice and receiving the same starvation rations which they used to get from the Germans. Should units of Second British Army, in whose sector this camp is situated, be unable to do anything, I could request that my Division [part of First Canadian Army] might help….I enclose MO's report on conditions prevailing in this camp.[23]

The war might be over but casualties continued. Amid the rejoicings on the official VE Day, George Blackburn was shocked and grieved when his friend Capt. Jim Else, a veteran of D-Day 1944, ran over an undetected mine in his vehicle and was killed.[24] Hugh Clark's unit had been sent to collect weapons discarded by surrendering Germans. 'One accidentally went off, hitting a young soldier who had recently joined us among the reinforcements – such an unnecessary waste of life when all the fighting was over'.[25]

Despatch rider Dunesby was shepherding a convoy of vehicles sent to disarm a naval base. He saw a gun carrier ahead of him swerve off the road and cartwheel onto the verge. 'It was a flame-throwing type and the tank in which the napalm was stored split and engulfed the crew in flames many feet high. All of them died, including a friend from the Somersets, George Hearman…. They had lost their lives just when they thought the danger of death was over'.[26] Life in and around fighting vehicles and munitions was always dangerous. 1NY lost three men killed in the months after VE Day.

With hundreds of thousands of displaced persons of many nations wandering aimlessly or still confined to camps, and some of the oppressed former slave labourers bent on revenge against the Germans, the confusion and disorganisation everywhere was beyond the control of any temporary government system. Military units had to be switched quickly from battle action to police routines. Field officers took the reins of local government in unit areas.

Notes from the 1NY war diary show the kind of duties to which the troopers were ordered and for which their former Sherman tanks or Buffalo amphibians were of no use:

– B Sqn reported arrest of two German ex-soldiers alleged to have threatened the local burgomaster.

– A Sqn reported stealing and burying of a pistol by a young boy. The family were evicted and forbidden to return within 10 kilometres.

– Convoy sent to the Ruhr to fetch coal for Military Government.

– Checks of civilians and vehicles were carried out and unauthorised vehicles and equipment impounded. An inlying picquet of 1 officer and 12 ORs provided by each squadron nightly.

– Four men arrested for failing to observe curfew regulations.

– Patrol from B Sqdn intercepts armed Poles raiding a farm and take one prisoner.

– German girl arrested for being out 15 minutes after curfew.

Bill Mosely remembered that A Sqn's area included a German POW camp commanded by a German brigadier who took his orders from 1NY's Lt Owen. The camp was surrounded by an electrified fence which, if tampered with, sounded a Klaxon alarm. This was not entirely successful as prisoners would simply short-circuit the fence by using an iron bar. With the Klaxon sounding and the guard squadron turning out in force, individual prisoners would slip through the wire. Surprisingly, next morning the roll call showed no absentees. Prisoners were breaking out to go home and then returning because, compared with conditions outside the wire, Bill says, 'they were too well looked after behind the wire' on British rations.[27]

The raid by armed displaced persons on a farm, reported by B Sqn, was a fairly frequent occurrence. Occupying troops had some sympathy with homeless ethnic labourers. Many of them had no prospect of returning to their pre-war homes. They therefore felt that they had the right to exact retribution on their former oppressors. Furthermore, many German soldiers were of non-German nationality and some German nationals now found that their home towns were no longer a part of Germany. On cessation of hostilities many German soldiers simply laid down their arms and disappeared into the transient crowds. In this fluid situation, organised, armed crime had to be dealt with summarily and decisively.

On 20 August, erstwhile artillery FOO Jack Swaab was involved in a General Military Court concerned with civil crime. For crimes ranging from concealing arms to actual armed robbery two displaced persons were sentenced to seventeen years imprisonment, one to fifteen years, and six to ten years. Jack found this a difficult moral issue because most of the displaced persons were only youths when they were dragged from their homes and sent to Germany to work as slaves in appalling conditions. At the same time he realised that 'one must make it clear that highwayman tactics just don't pay in an occupation zone'.[28]

Even among the Allies, all was not peace and concord. Russian troops advancing from the east, passing through Berlin, were now face to face with armies of other nations advancing from the west. Frontline officers and ORs from the west now found their Russian 'friends' to differ widely in attitude as they gazed over a new frontier which would soon become the frontline of a new Cold War. Often the actual border line was at the centre point of a bridge over a river, with watchful guards lining both banks. At the sharp end of confrontation there was often no clear guidance as to behaviour; no training had been possible for such a deployment and certainly no adequate interpretation services were available in most places. Probably like many other units 1NY had nobody who spoke Russian sufficiently for a detailed conversation.

For some the first encounter with the Russians was of mutual suspicion, but not aggression. Although their Buffalo amphibians were about to be handed in, Stan Hicken and Les Carr, finding themselves on the banks of the Elbe, ventured across:

> I pulled up onto a large sandy beach. The reeds parted and two Russian sentries came out and gave me a fine military salute. They couldn't speak any English and I couldn't speak any Russian so we used German. They came from south-west of Leningrad. One had fair hair and the other brown. They were just privates with rifle and 4-bladed bayonet, which I'd read about but never set eyes on before. We exchanged cigarettes, one of our Players for one of theirs containing black tobacco, which nearly put me flat on my back. They liked the Players. Then they said it was time for them to go, otherwise they would get into trouble. As people saw that I managed to get over and back, one or two others copied me. But next day in place of the two civilised privates we had some short-legged Mongolians riding on ponies and whooping. They had mounted a huge machine-gun on a tripod pointing at us, which we didn't think was very welcoming.[29]

For a day or two forward troops like Stan Hicken were able to test the new frontier informally, armed with nothing more lethal than a packet of Players cigarettes. Conversely, officers like Ian Hammerton of XXII Dragoons, having handed in their clumsy flail tanks, were given a more specific task:

> Our new job was to see to the adjustment of the frontier with the Russian Army. At each road crossing over the new frontier we set up a bell tent manned by half-a-dozen men armed with pistols, together with a simple barrier across the road. As soon as people living in the zone to be occupied by the Russians got to hear about their imminent arrival, they fled towards our side of the new border. Old people, nuns, children, farmers and, above all, patients from several German military hospitals. When the Russian troops appeared, they came fully armed and with tank support and proceeded to dig and occupy slit trenches.

The flood of evacuating Germans caused the detachment of Dragoons a problem as the local Burgomaster was not happy to have to find accommodation and food for the new arrivals. However, Ian's sergeant-major 'was good at persuading people to do things they did not want to do' and turned his peculiar kind of charm on the Burgomaster. A German tank sergeant-major was put in direct charge of local logistics and discipline.[30]

There was nothing remotely humorous about an incident involving Alf Gritton in a town shared by the Russians and British. Alf had already been forcibly invited into a house where Mongolian troops were carousing, only to find a girl dead on a sofa and the mother and father with throats slit in the kitchen. Next day he heard that his unit was withdrawing to a new border. Whilst packing his armoured car he was approached by an old couple who asked, 'Would you take our daughter with you?' Alf said, 'What daughter? I haven't seen her'. They said, 'She's down in the cellar'. They had been trying to keep her safe from the drunken foreign troops.

Alf went to his lieutenant and started to explain, but the officer simply said, 'Don't ask me! You haven't asked me. Just go away'. On the strength of that, Alf asked the old couple to hurry and pack a bag for the girl who could be smuggled down into the turret of the armoured car. When eventually the frightened girl appeared and climbed up onto the turret he was surprised to see his mates hurriedly helping other girls into their turrets. Once the cars had arrived at their new position, Alf found a friendly German policeman who said that there was a reception centre nearby. The policeman then took charge of the bevy of girls. Alf said, 'She was about eighteen, quite a pretty girl, first time I'd ever seen her and I'd been there a couple of weeks.'[31]

Frank Gutteridge, appointed a staff captain at brigade HQ, found his contacts with the Russians difficult at another level. He was working with a Russian liaison officer 'in reality an NKVD (later KGB) man; a smooth and devious individual'. The Russians' duty was to repatriate Russians imprisoned or forced to work in Germany. Many of these displaced persons were women who gave a party to Frank's staff for liberating them, 'Which was sad because they were all doomed for the Gulag, having been "contaminated" by contact with the West'. Indeed one Russian prisoner escaped forcible repatriation by jumping out of a lavatory window with the connivance of one of Frank's colleagues.[32]

A more serious incident was seen by Bill Bellamy. His 8th Hussars was one of the relatively few British units to actually reach Berlin, which had passed into a system where four Allied armies controlled separate zones of the city. (Many British drivers had painted 'Berlin or Bust' on their vehicles, very few arrived.) On arrival he was amazed amid 'mounds of rubble, tottering walls, blocked side streets… everything drab and dirty' to find that some German civilians were applauding the British armoured cars as they drove past. The Hussars were under strict injunction not to become involved in any Russian-German dispute.

Then one night, following a Russian truck packed with soldiers near Spandau, Bill's driver had switched off his headlights and dropped back about 75 yards:

Suddenly the Russian truck swung out into the middle of the road, braked sharply and stopped… A Russian soldier leapt out of the back of the truck and then we saw that there was a woman with a bicycle at the roadside. The soldier wrenched the bicycle from the woman's hands and she was dragged after him as she struggled to hold on to it. There was a sound of a shot, the woman slumped to the ground, the soldier threw the bicycle and himself into the truck which was already on the move. By the time we got to her they were roaring off down the road… She was dead. An elderly frau, harmless…Some German civilians appeared, took the body to an adjacent house and reported the matter. We heard no more of it. Life was cheap.[33]

Other soldiers had more friendly encounters with Russians. Reg Spittles was driving an interpreter to Berlin as the Russian zone was being set up. He was instructed not to make any voluntary stops as they were 'very trigger happy'. A Russian lorry, sliding out of control on a temporary surface hit Reg's car and holed the petrol tank. Reg stood by the roadside, waving at other vehicles in the hope that someone would tow them to some place of repair. Along came a Russian staff car with two motorcycle outsiders. The car stopped:

A short, stocky, bemedalled staff officer got out of the back of the car and strode across to Reg. To the latter's surprise the Russian touched Reg's divisional arm badge [7th armoured] and said 'Desert Rats! Good soldiers!' saluted him and shook his hand. He then ordered his driver to bring two jerry-cans of petrol and Reg was able to stuff up the hole well enough to drive to the nearest workshop. Meanwhile, Reg's interpreter had also got out of their car and had a brief conversation in Russian. As the motor-cyclists revved up again and the Russian convoy drove away, Reg's officer said, 'You know who that was, don't you?' To Reg's shake of the head, his officer grinned, 'the one and only Marshal Zukhov'.[34]

Looking much farther east even than Russia, 1NY diary stated curtly:

20th June – first draft from the regiment for SEAC [South East Asia Command] to be eight Sgts and two Cpls between age and service groups 27–75… Lt W. Skipper C Sqn to leave for SEAC having volunteered under 'Pickford' scheme.

This scheme allowed ambitious or adventurous officers to volunteer for the continuing war against Japan. 'Sgts' and 'Cpls' would be sent whether they were ambitious and adventurous or not.

Ralph Hill, 1NY, C Sqn, and this author found themselves on VE Day emerging from a hospital and rehabilitation camp via Catterick depot.

They then had the prospect of long monotonous durance in a static holding regiment before probable posting to SEAC. Like most soldiers, desiring to return to their own regiment, they wrote to Maj. 'Hank' Bevan, MC, asking his intervention. Hank's reply was disappointing, stating that any soldier under age 23 and 'Y' listed from his regiment (away more than three weeks) must now be posted automatically to the Japanese war; there was nothing that could be done about it.

Sometimes the postings to SEAC involved large groups rather than individuals. Hugh le Messurier's entire company of the Duke's were advised of a fascinating future:

> We were going to America for three months training and re-equipping and then, with a British Empire Corps, consisting of an ANZAC Division and a Canadian Division, we were going to assault the shores of Japan. Happily or unhappily we didn't get our three months in America, which we were rather looking forward to, because the atom bomb came… My rank at that time, because of leave and demob, was as a corporal-acting-company-sergeant-major.[35]

Airborne Capt. Hugh Clark, MC, had been in a guard of honour the day after VE Day as FM Montgomery met Russian Marshall Rokossovsky. But on return to Bulford camp his unit was re-equipped with 'new kit all of which was jungle green, right down to underwear, towels and even our housewife [pouch] and steel mirror'. Individual companies were sent off for a week of simulated jungle fighting. Hugh's B company marched 70 miles to find their own 'jungle' on Esher Common.[36]

In Frank Gutteridge's tank regiment nobody wanted to go to the 'forgotten' war against Japan. 'It seemed unfair for those who had borne the brunt of the fighting in Europe to be sent there whilst those who had remained in the UK enjoyed the benefits of peace'.[37] However, because few heavier tanks could be used in the jungles and Frank had experience of lighter vehicles, he was selected for Asia and sent to Catterick depot for medical examination. Fortunately for him it was discovered that, due to long exposure to oil, grease, dirt and ammunition, his hands had developed a kind of eczema and he was downgraded to 'B non-tropical' and sent on exchange to a US cavalry regiment.

Whilst many troops were engaged in policing lawless areas of the new Germany, and others were confronting the dug-in Russians from behind simple signposts, some technicians were allocated special duties of a different kind. Engineer Ernest Egli joined a team of civilian experts in examining a factory where V2 rocket bomb parts were made. At another factory they found a special machine for making 20-mm gun barrels. The wonders of German technology were being made available to the Allied countries a little too late.[38] Ian Hammerton went with a team of experts into the Focke-Wolf factory to secure and examine aircraft production drawings.

Other duties were more mundane. Capt. Joe Brown had to organise parties of men who went into German forests and cut down trees for shipment back to Britain as a part of war reparations. This led him into a situation of droll gamesmanship. An RAF unit refused to move out of the hutments allocated to army tree-fellers. Suddenly the army commander arrived in the vicinity and sent for Joe, enquiring about the hold-up. Once advised of the problem the general seized the phone and commenced a round of calls berating various colonels and air commodores because no action had been taken.[39]

Canadian Bud Jones was 'riding shotgun' on an army truck carrying 'all sorts and sizes of freight' from Germany to the Channel ports as a part of the reparations programme.[40] Ken Cardy had been removed from his ponderous ARV and given a two-seater open Adler 10hp car. His job was to scour the countryside within 50 miles of Cologne, carrying side arms and accompanied by an interpreter, and commandeer civilian trucks. These would be used in the battle to provide food and other essentials for the hundreds of thousands of wandering people still caught in the chaos of disintegrating national and local services. Each night Ken reported to the Daimler-Benz works so that the requisitioned lorries could be converted back to petrol engines. Much German transport had been running on 2-inch cubes of pinewood fed into a firebox, producing a resin gas. This accounted for the frequent piles of wood blocks seen by Allied troops beside German roads.[41]

There also began an interchange of soldiers between national armies. Cpl Stan Hilton was sent to an American unit where he enjoyed the easier discipline and also had the opportunity to fly an aeroplane with minimum instruction, unthinkable in a British yeomanry unit. The American cookhouse was well supplied with food and staffed by local kitchen workers. Some of these, on basic rations themselves, could not resist the temptation to smuggle out excess food of which there was plenty. The Americans had lighted upon a simple punishment for a simple crime: if a cookhouse worker was found smuggling food, as in the case of one who stole three large loaves of bread, he or she was made to stand and eat all the food at the guardhouse before leaving.[42]

The contrast between Stan Hilton's American facilities and those of his own unit was a continuing cause of dissatisfaction among non-American troops. Infantrymen who had slogged from the Normandy beaches to the Baltic coast in rough clothes, on basic rations, earning poor pay and with a very modest gratuity at the end felt that it was unjust that equivalent men in another Allied army (some American divisions were in action for a relatively brief time) should enjoy much superior uniforms, lavish rations, higher pay, frequent medals and many other advantages.

The same sentiment was attached to medals and certificates of merit, which were still being issued after VE Day. As distinguished Canadian battalion and brigade commander Denis Whitaker observed:

> ...decorations often appear to have been issued strictly on a ratio system. For every decoration awarded to men at the sharp end (and those were awarded on a monthly or quarterly basis) a proportionate number would be made to headquarters-based men. The British appear to have been equally cavalier. Of 12 men of 153 Brigade (51st HD) recommended for decorations in the Reichswald/Goch battle, none received a medal.[43]

Major 'Hank' Bevan later recalled the colonel saying to him, 'There's a Military Medal available, David. Is there anybody you could give it to?'[44]

Whilst the war in Europe had now ended, many younger soldiers would have to serve for another two years. Such disparities in conditions and rewards were still a thorn in the flesh for those moving from the dangerous excitement of real action into the monotonous round of military routine, for which they had not signed on. Frank Gutteridge noted one incident typical of the peacetime army. An inspecting general noticed clean sections on the tank track painted red as a warning that they were not to be loosened or removed. The general asked, 'Why haven't they been greased?' After the question had been passed down through the ranks to the driver, the latter replied, 'They don't have to be greased, sir', to which the irate general snapped, 'Then grease them anyway!'[45]

Not all service immediately after VE Day was unimaginative or unproductive. Ken Cardy, while still working on battle clearance and vehicle recovery at a large reception depot near Sennenlager, suggested to his commander the idea of setting aside an area where one example of each vehicle, machine or piece of equipment could be preserved in good state. The REME commander agreed, thus collecting the initial exhibits for what became a permanent war museum.

The worst duty which continued for some time after the ceasefire was carried out by crews of flame-throwers. Concentration camps had proved to be places of permanent contamination. Corpses could be buried and survivors treated in hospitals, but the filth, vermin and bacterial infestation of the empty barracks proved insoluble. The flame-throwers were therefore called into the continuing stench and, as more than one observer described, into a kind of mist of indescribable filth hovering in the camps. One by one barracks were burned down and open spaces treated to the all-consuming power of fire. The fighting crews had neither been trained nor prepared psychologically for this task. Soldiers did what they were ordered. 'Do it now and complain later' was the watchword.

Men were also being sent into the camps to organise the final evacuation of detainees, although the country lacked adequate facilities for the reception of refugees. Typical was the experience of American tank driver Joe Solarz.[46] He had driven a Sherman all the way from the Normandy beaches, usually looking out through a small periscope, and never remembering the name of any village passed through along the way until the last. He remembered that last name: Buchenwald. Quietly sitting in his tank he was called by his commanding officer. 'Joe, you're half Polish. You can speak some Polish. Colonel says you stay here as an interpreter. Hundreds of Poles in this camp'. So the humble tank driver found himself with hordes of clamouring, distressed prisoners in the ultimate Hell of one of Hitler's worst concentration camps.

Whilst many photographs were taken of concentration camps in April and May 1945, the prison inmates were not allowed cameras. Joe Solarz met three Polish prisoners, Tadeuse Wasowice, Josef Kachel and Stefan Dziwlik who, at grave peril to themselves, and also with the utmost difficulties in obtaining materials, had contrived to make watercolours and drawings of atrocities carried out by prison guards. And had hidden and preserved them by devious means. They presented one drawing to Joe in appreciation of his help. The camp was still infested by rats, lice and other vermin. Joe was bitten more than once but, the tough soldier that he was, shrugged it off. Like many in the camp, he caught typhus, prompt medical attention soon had him back on his feet. He thought no more about it.

James Sims, a British prisoner of war, had missed the 8th Hussars' liberation of Fallingsbostel camp because he was one of a group marched off eastwards a day or two earlier. He was a witness of a heavy raid by American Flying Fortresses on Uelzen station in the last hours of the war. He and fellow prisoners were put to work on clearing up the damage, picking their way 'through a lunar landscape'. There occurred a memorable encounter:

> After the devastation of the town the Germans moved a Flak train in and it was commanded by a stocky, good-natured German warrant officer. Red-faced, with a chest full of decorations and a cigar always in his mouth, he was a complete realist. When we asked him how much longer the war would last he replied, 'It all depends on the speed of your tanks'. He was not upset about the idea of losing in 1945 and said something I, for one, have never forgotten.
>
> 'Ten years from now you'll be paying me to help you keep out the Russians' – prophetic words.[47]

CHAPTER TEN

KRIEGSGEFANGENGESELLSCHAFT

Then the men, when they heard that all the towns were taken, scattered this way and that to their own homes.

> (Herodotus, 440 BC)

'Ah, Hicken. I've got some bad news for you. I'm afraid we're going to lose you. You are being posted.'

'But I don't want to go. I've been with C squadron all the way,' Stan Hicken argued.

'Can't do anything about it. Army HQ have found your records, that you learned German at school, also did some clerical work. You're going as an interpreter and administrator. It means promotion to sergeant. Affects your gratuity. You are going to…'

A mysterious grin spread across the face of Maj. Richard Courage, now commanding C, 1NY, as he handed a slip of paper to 'Hickie'. 'What does your schoolboy German make of that?' The slip of paper said, *Kriegsgefangengesellschaft,* Bruges.

'I think that works out something like a prisoner of war company, sir.'

'I believe it's a demob centre. Not for you yet. For Germans.'[1]

As for the British, a regimental war diary stated, '10 July 1945. The first move under the Age and Service Group Release scheme, Class A, started with L/Cpl Innes, Group 7, being despatched to England for demobilisation…. 13 July. The regtl educational scheme was started….

20 August the first four Class B (Essential Industries) releases were received but two refused to accept this alternative owing to their low A&S Gp in Class A.'²

Demobilisation after the First World War had been hurried and chaotic. Now, after the Second World War it was to be much more ordered and fairer. As the title suggests, the Class A release under Age and Service allowed soldiers who had served six years or more and were over thirty years of age to leave the armed forces before younger men with lesser service. Class B allowed some specific experts or highly skilled workmen to be moved from routine soldiering into designated essential industries or agriculture. Later the B system would also allow young servicemen whose higher education had been interrupted to resume their studies. The B scheme had one snag: the demobbed person had to remain in the designated job or study centre or be returned to complete his service in the forces. It was not a quick way out of discipline.

At the same time a quickly organised army education scheme provided refresher classes in basic subjects for men who had had no opportunity to improve their civilian skills for several years. At first this was accomplished in an ad hoc fashion by regimental personnel with some teaching experience, but later it was completely taken over by the rapidly developing Army Education Corps.³

So some departed and some soldiered on. Cpl Doug Gardner moved from commanding a 1NY tank to serving as the guard on a demobilisation troop train from Arnsberg to Lubeck, and the return (although most passengers had no desire to return). Due to the successful air bombing of German railways, Doug's guard's van was just an empty goods truck into which they installed a 'liberated' coal-burning stove with a rickety flue pipe which gave off smoke into the open air.⁴

When S/Sgt Ken Cardy's number came up he took a train like Doug Gardner's and was put in charge of fifteen men, carrying all their release books in his haversack. On departure their CO told the men they must accompany Ken to Aldershot and if they did not they would be posted absent without leave. Ken felt his last army duty was as a nursemaid. At this late hour there could still be a temptation for a man to desert and join the flourishing black market in Europe.⁵ At the moment of demob many found it difficult to restrain a last comment. Fred Leary's Sqn

Ldr lined up a demob squad and said rather pompously, 'It is men like you who have made this regiment what it is today'. Fred's instinctive response was 'Don't blame me!'[6]

Whilst career officer Joe Brown intended serving on, he suddenly found himself charged with the demob of his entire battalion, although most of his men were not yet due for release. As battalion adjutant he was ordered to place his wartime-only unit into 'suspended animation'. This entailed 'posting all our officers and men to other units and returning all our arms, transport and equipment' to store. Being then without an appointment his role was reversed and he became a staff-captain, posting reinforcements coming from the UK to regiments still serving in Europe.[7]

On the German side many soldiers simply disappeared into the multitudes of unidentified people. Units with stricter discipline surrendered to the Allies in formal manner. Manfred Thorn, still only nineteen, had similar sentiments to other tank men. 'One cannot say that you love a tank, but when you have spent three years in one, feeling protected, knowing all of its tricks and that "she" will respond at will, then you cannot escape feeling a heel when tipping her into the river', which, on orders, was his last farewell to his steed. Then, having served with an SS unit, he was separated from ordinary *Wehrmacht* prisoners, arrested pending possible trial (for atrocities) and, although exonerated, had to spend two years being 'denazified'.[8]

In some cases the return of a soldier from Europe appeared to be a resurrection of the dead. Roland England had been taken prisoner in 1NY's battle to cut off the final German retreat bridge over the River Maas. Thought to have been burned to ash in his tank he had fallen into a deep drain. A German surgeon had skilfully inserted a metal plate in Roland's shattered skull. Now he had been released from a prisoner of war camp and flown back to Britain. Awarded long leave he was on the train homeward bound to Rotherham. A pal from the same squadron, Phil Swaby, passing along the corridor, noticed the NY badges, stopped in disbelief and stared at Roland in something like awe. Then he shouted, 'Ruddy Hell, Roland, you're dead. We buried you at Raamsdonk'. With some effort Roland assured Phil that he was not a ghost.[9]

Some soldiers returned to civilian life and greater fame. From the Guards Armoured Division a certain Capt. Robert Runcie, MC, eventually became Archbishop of Canterbury, whilst his colleague Richard Carr-Gomm founded the notable Carr-Gomm homes for the socially deprived. Others continued in uniform. L/Cpl Rex Jackson, MM, found that he could sign on for a further two years after due demob date, rise to SSM and move into work with the War Ministry. The irrepressible Bud Jones volunteered for the Korean War with another Canadian Royal Regiment and did not retire until 1975 when his rank was Warrant Officer.

It could not be said that the army was too kind to heroes who wished to continue serving. Like many successful warriors Maj. Harry Warde, MC and bar, had to come down from field rank and served for years before regaining his wartime rank. Brigadier Harry Scott, DSO, who commanded the unique Night March of 33rd Armoured Brigade up the Bourguebus Ridge in August 1944, was offered a squadron leader's role three ranks down; he refused.[10]

Perhaps as sad as any was the fate of Maj. Bill Close, MC. After an odyssey which took him through Calais in 1940 and the Middle East, he was promoted from the ranks with a promise of a regular commission after the war. He rose to major and was fated to lead the first squadron into the carnage of Operation Goodwood, July 1944, moving from tank to tank as they were knocked-out under him. Successful in every action, he applied for a permanent commission and passed the Selection Board, but was only offered a short five-year commission or a return to the ranks as an RSM.[11] Someone must have decided that he was not permanent officer material.

A hard and hopeless future awaited some of the now stateless Poles of 1st Armoured. Some younger men were able to prosper. Capt. Erwin Mazurkiewicz became president of the Firestone tyre giant. Tank driver Sgt Lenik excelled as chief chef at the Dorchester Hotel. But Gen. Gatowski survived by washing cars. Col Koszutski found himself shovelling coal into the boilers of an industrial laundry.

Even more tragic, Col F. Skibinski accepted Stalin's offer to return to Poland in 1949, but almost immediately realised that he was under constant investigation by theNKVD. In 1951 he was tried on trumped-up disloyalty charges and sentenced to death. With a lessening of tyranny under new president Gomulka in 1956 he was reprieved, but not exonerated until the Waleska era in 1995: after his death.[12]

Similarly Stanislauw Maczek, professor of Greek philosophy and outstanding armoured general, declared a non-person by Soviet Poland and shunned by the British government and universities, gained some kind of livelihood as a barman in Scotland. It was not until the old hero reached his 100th birthday that Lech Waleska, president of Poland, arrived on a visit to Glasgow and restored Maczek to the rank of full general, awarding him an appropriate pension.

War tends to reach far into the future. Tank driver Joe Solarz, appointed interpreter for Polish survivors of Buchenwald camp, was bitten by lice in 1945. In 2010 he is registered blind due to his war experiences. He is also diagnosed with Brill-Zinsser disease; a relatively rare condition in which typhus, with its rash, fever and delirium, recurs after a long dormant period of time: in Joe's case now 65 years after the initial bites.[13]

Recently arrived at his *Kriegsgefangengesellschaft*, Stan Hicken was walking between two wire enclosures when a prisoner waved furiously, shouting, 'Do you remember me?' It was a gunner from an 88-mm crew taken prisoner by Stan and Rex Jackson many months before in Holland. Stan worked directly under the courteous senior German officer, a Lt Goertz, the nephew of an American general. Stan's main assistants were two ex-*Wehrmacht* mechanics who had been involved in car racing at the famous Nuremburg Ring. They awakened a racing instinct which led to Stan eventually becoming a champion rally driver and hill climber. Before D-Day, Stan had planned with his mate, Bill Rawlins, that after demob they would pool their resources and open a motor car repair business. They spent hours working on their plans.[14]

On 30 June 1944 Bill Rawlins was killed in one of many minor skirmishes among the confusing high hedges and tiny fields of the notorious *Bocage*. His tank remained burning throughout the night in the disputed zone. Next morning Capt. Bill Fox went to find the knocked-out tanks and bodies of the missing men. Stan begged to be allowed to go as the captain's driver. To their surprise the Germans had buried the British dead with military dignity and left identity disks hanging on simple wooden crosses. The blackened tanks remained deep in the hedgerows.

On Bill Rawlin's tank a German had scrawled a rough message in charcoal, '*Du wast gewerdet*'. Stan's schoolboy German could not cope with the brief phrase. Until VE Day and long beyond, the phrase tormented him. After overseeing the release of many German prisoners Stan's own demob number eventually came up. As he said his last farewells to the Germans about him, it occurred to him to ask Lt Goertz the meaning of those haunting words, '*Du wast gerwerdet*'.

After a brief pause the lieutenant's translation came as an appropriate memorial, not only to Bill Rawlins, but for many who had been thrust to the forefront of some hopeless battle on the long road to an end of war:

'You never had a chance.'

EPILOGUE

The volunteers and pressed men who went from Germany to fight the Japanese arrived too late to reinforce those of the so-called 'forgotten army', who had been fighting and dying in that theatre of war for years. After the dropping of two atom bombs in August 1945, Japan surrendered. The peace treaty officially ending the Second World War was signed on 2 September 1945. Reporter Hugh Crumpler witnessed the event. Extracts from his version follow.[1]

The crown of a black, silk top hat came slowly into view at the narrowest point of the veranda deck of the battleship Missouri, which was anchored like a gray, steel island in the middle of Tokyo Bay. At that moment, General of the Army Douglas McArthur stepped from the shadows of a bulkhead and up to a microphone that was standing behind a wardroom table covered with green baize. On the table were two originals of the Instrument of Surrender – one bound in leather for the victors, one in canvas for the defeated.

The Missouri's guns were elevated and menacing, as if they had found the range on some distant and doomed target. At sea and out of sight, battle-ready American carriers and other warships had guns trained on strategic points ashore. Carriers faced into the wind with aircraft engines running and pilots in cockpits. The 11th Airborne division and the 1st Cavalry division were ashore.

The opera hat bobbed and wavered, and then the head and shoulders of Foreign Minister Mamoru Shigemitsu appeared. Clumsily and painfully [with an ill-fitting prosthetic leg due to a terrorist bomb in 1930] he climbed the last few steps of the gangway to the deck. Following Shigemitsu was wooden-faced Gen Yoshijiro Umezu, chief of the Imperial General Staff.

MacArthur stood at the microphone, a sheet of paper in his hand. He spoke: 'We are gathered here, representatives of the major warring powers, to conclude a solemn agreement whereby peace may be restored'. His voice was strong, each word clearly enunciated and carrying to every corner of the decks. Shigemitsu fumbled inside his cutaway coat, searching for a pen. He stared at the surrender documents as though he did not understand why they were before him. He appeared to be confused or dazed. Adm. William 'Bull' Halsey wanted to 'slap his face and snarl "Sign, damn you, sign!"'

MacArthur barked an order to Lt Gen. Richard K. Sutherland. It was the only time during the ceremony that MacArthur switched his delivery from the voice of the statesman to the voice of the commander. . . 'Sutherland! Show him where to sign!'

Sutherland pointed to a line of the document. Shigemitsu signed his name in Japanese characters. Umezu, the sullen, was next. MacArthur turned next [for signature] to Gen. Sir Arthur E. Percival who wore a toothbrush moustache, a Sam Browne belt and a stiff British staff hat that gave him the appearance of a British colonial police officer. Admiral of the Fleet Chester Nimitz, a white-haired Texan, then signed the documents.

Nimitz was followed by representatives of the other Allied powers that had fought Japan: the United Kingdom, Union of Soviet Socialist Republics, Commonwealth of Australia, Dominion of Canada, Provisional Government of the French Republic, Kingdom of the Netherlands and Dominion of New Zealand.

MacArthur stepped to the microphone and said, 'Let us pray that peace be now restored to the world and that God will preserve it always. These proceedings are now closed'.

The Japanese delegation departed from the surrender deck carrying the canvas-bound copy of the Instrument of Surrender. They would deliver the document to Emperor Hirohito, who, in 1929, had selected a name for his reign:

'The Era of Enlightened Peace'.

GLOSSARY

AP	armour-piercing shot
ARV	armoured recovery vehicle
AVRE	Royal Engineers armoured vehicle
bn	battalion (of several companies)
brig	brigade, usually three battalions
Buffalo	amphibious armoured tracked carrier
Capt.	captain
CO	commanding officer
coy	company (of several platoons)
Cpl	corporal
Crab	mine-sweeping tank
Crocodile	flame-throwing tank
CSM	company sergeant-major
DCM	Distinguished Conduct Medal (ORs)
DD tank	tank waterproofed to 'swim'
div	division (two or three brigades)
DSO	Distinguished Service Order (Officers)
Duck	Light amphibious vehicle
Firefly	Sherman with larger 17-pdr gun
FM	field marshal
Fl Of	flying officer
FOO	artillery forward observation officer
'Funnies'	tanks adapted for various purposes
Gen.	general

HE	high explosive shell
Hongertocht	hunger walk (plural: *Hongertochten*)
Howitzer	gun firing shells in curved 'lobbed' trajectory rather than the flatter trajectory of high velocity guns
HQ	headquarters
Kangaroo	armoured tracked troop carrier
Kubelwagen	light personnel carrier
LAD	Light Aid (repairs) Detachment
L/Bdr	lance-bombardier (artillery) – lower than Bdr
L/Cpl	lance-corporal – lower than Cpl
Lt	lieutenant
Lt-Col	lieutenant-colonel (between major and colonel)
Luger	German pistol
Maj.	major
Maj.-Gen.	major-general (between brig and lt-gen)
MC	Military Cross (officers only WW2, but now ORs in 2010)
m-g	machine-gun
MM	Military Medal (ORs, no longer awarded 2010)
-mm	gun measured by shot size, e.g. 88-mm
NCO	Non-commissioned Officer – SM, Sgt, Cpl
Nebelwerfer	Multiple mortar bomb projectors ('Moaning Minnies')
NY, 1NY	in this book 1st Northamptonshire Yeomanry (tanks) – with apologies to Norfolk and Notts Yeomen
OC	officer commanding
O group	orders group/conference
OP	observation post, usually artillery
ORs	other ranks – non-officers
Panzerfaust	hand-held anti-tank bomb projector
pdr	pounder – gun measured by shell weight
platoon	part of a company, lieutenant's command
POW	prisoner of war
Pte	private, lowest military rank
Pz	*Panzer* – German armoured troops/tanks
QM	quartermaster
RA	Royal Artillery
RAMC	Royal Army Medical Corps

RCMP	Royal Corps of Military Police
RE	Royal Engineers
regiment/regt	battalion of tanks or parent group of several infantry battalions (or parent of tank battalions as in RTR)
REME	Royal Electrical and Mechanical Engineers
RSM	regimental sergeant-major
RTR	Royal Tank Regiment
Schmeiser	German hand-held sub-machine gun
section	smallest formal infantry grouping within platoon
slit	small trench for two men
SM	sergeant-major
SP	armoured self-propelled gun on tracks
Spandau	fast-firing German m-g
Spr	sapper, Royal Engineers
sqn	squadron of tanks (major's command) or aircraft
Sqn Ldr	squadron leader – a rank in RAF, a post in tanks (major)
SS	*Schutzstaffel:* originally Hitler's bodyguard; in war the SS provided frontline army *(Waffen)* units administered separately under Himmler. Also separate police/concentration guard units.
SSM	staff sergeant-major
Sten	British sub-machine gun hurriedly mass produced
SWWEC	Second World War Experience Centre
traverse	tank turret spinning on its hull
troop	usually four tanks or armoured cars, lieutenant's command
Tpr	trooper, tanks
VC	Victoria Cross, highest bravery award
Very	pistol-fired floodlight
Volksturm	German 'Home Guard', sometimes only distinguished by armbands, usually elderly or very young men
Waffen SS	SS combat troops (distinct from SS concentration camp guards and similar units)

Wehrmact	Main German army – apart from *SS*
wing	next higher RAF formation of squadrons
WO	Warrant officer – sergeant-majors' ranks

NOTES AND REFERENCES

Because of the various methods of communication used, personal information given direct to the author is noted only by the individual's name and year. See Bibliography for full publication details of works quoted.

Quotes at the opening of each chapter are taken from *Herodotus* – translated by George Rawlinson, *Internet Classics Archive*

PROLOGUE
1. Northamptonshire Yeomanry (NY) archive.
2. Carpenter, 2010.

1. BRAVEST OF THE BRAVE
1. Citations and W.D. & S. Whitaker, *Rhineland*
2. Cf. Joe Harper in Tout, *In the Shadow of Arnhem*
3. Whitaker, *op cit*
4. Tout, *The Bloody Battle for Tilly*
5. Egli, Second World War Experience Centre (SWWEC).
6. Citation and Whitaker.
7. Author in *By Tank, D to VE Days*
8. Whitaker *op cit* also W.D.W., 1999 and S.W., 2010.

2. WHEN HELL FROZE OVER
1. NY archive.
2. Carpenter, 2010.

3. Swaab, 2010 and *Field of Fire*
4. Clark, SWWEC.
5. Robertson, 2010.
6. Tout, *To Hell with Tanks!*
7. NY archive.
8. Pentelow, 2009.
9. Leary, 2010 and self-published.
10. Upson, SWWEC.
11. Gutteridge, 2010 and self-published.
12. *Heroes Remember,* Veterans Affairs, Canada.
13. Whitehouse, 1996 and *Fear is the Foe*
14. Egli, SWWEC.
15. Thorn, 2010 and self-published.
16. NY archive.
17. Dunesby, SWWEC.
18. NY archive.
19. Swaab, *op cit*
20. Whitehouse, *op cit*
21. Blackburn, 1994 and others.
22. Thorn, *op cit.*
23. Robertson, 2010. Also in Stolte, *The 51st HD in the Ardennes*
24. e.g. the fatal Wittmann decision as in Tout, *A Fine Night for Tanks*
25. Robertson and author at Gordon Barracks, Aberdeen.
26. Deans, SWWEC.
27. Duchene, SWWEC.
28. Clark, SWWEC.
29. Hicken, 2010 and self-published.
30. Carpenter, 2010.
31. Lowe, SWWEC.
32. NY archive.
33. This story brought tears to Stan's eyes 40 years later.

3. UNHAPPY NEW YEAR

1. Cardy, 2010 and self-published.
2. Eaton, 2010. Also Oliver, *The RAF Regiment at War*
3. *London Gazette,* 20.2.1945.

4. Clark, SWWEC.
5. Whitehouse, *Fear is the Foe*
6. Robertson, 2010.
7. Faulkner and La Roche witnesses 1994, 2000.
8. Swaab, *Field of Fire*
9. Egli, SWWEC.
10. NY archive.
11. Tarrant, Ardennes, 2000.
12. Citation for Phil Bonney's Croix de Guerre and Tout, *To Hell with Tanks*
13. Robertson, 2010.
14. Swaab, *op cit*
15. Brown, 2010 and internet.
16. Bennett, 1945 report and 2010.
17. Jones, 1945 and 2010.
18. 21st Army Group report.
19. Gootzen and Connor, *Battle for the Roer Triangle* (and 2010).
20. Brown, *op cit*
21. Gootzen and Connor, *op cit*
22. Gutteridge, 2010.
23. Gootzen and Connor, *op cit*
24. *ibid*
25. Duckworth, SWWEC.
26. Bellamy, 2005 and *Troop Leader*
27. Spittles, 2010.
28. Deans, SWWEC.
29. Gutteridge, 2010.
30. Jones, 2010.
31. Cardy, 2010.
32. Lt-Gen. Simonds' incredible invention and manufacture of the first 72 Kangaroos adapted from SP guns in five days in Normandy, as in Tout, *A Fine Night for Tanks*
33. White, *With the Jocks.*
34. Clark, SWWEC.
35. VC citation.
36. Gootzen and Connor, *op cit*
37. *ibid*
38. Hunt, 2011.

4. THOSE FATAL FORESTS

1. Quoted from Whitaker, *Rhineland*
2. Egli, SWWEC.
3. Carder, SWWEC. The author well remembers the rumours about a tank crushing its crew but has not yet seen proof of such an event.
4. Cardy, 2010.
5. Excerpted from *The Guns of Victory* c 1996 by George G. Blackburn. Cloth edition 1996. Trade paperback edition 1997. Published by McClelland & Stewart. Used by Permission from the Estate and Publisher.
6. Swaab, 2010 and *Field of Fire*
7. Hammerton, 2010 and *Achtung! Minen!*
8. Egli, SWWEC.
9. Bennet, Royals' reports.
10. Jack Williams, via daughter Kim, 2010.
11. Jones, 2010.
12. Whitehouse, 1996 and *Fear is the Foe*
13. Whitaker, *op cit*
14. Shellard, 2010.
15. White, *With the Jocks*
16. Tapson, 2010.
17. Brew, SWWEC.
18. Swaab, *op cit*
19. Upson, per Ian Hammerton 2010.
20. Egli, SWWEC.
21. Hicken, 2010.
22. McCauley, *Soldier Boys*, a semi-fictitious but accurate account.
23. Simonds v. Horrocks in Whitaker, *op cit*
24. Gritton, 2010 – also own website.
25. '*Canada Remembers*' website.
26. Radley Walters, 2010.
27. Hale, 2010.
28. Infamously, when Generals O'Connor and Roberts had requested a Kangaroo-type vehicle for Operation Goodwood, July 1944, the request was turned down on the basis that 'if you once got infantry into carriers

they would never get out' (Roberts, 1947). However, during Totalize, August 1944, they did get out of the new Kangaroos.

29. Blackburn, *The Guns of Victory* as note 5.
30. Whitaker, *op cit*
31. *'Canadian Heroes'*, website.
32. Duchene, SWWEC.
33. Blackburn, *op cit*
34. USA National Archives.

5. DE HONGERWINTER

1. Overliese, per Ger Schinck 2010, and Tony van Vugt, 2010.
2. van der Zee, *The Hunger Winter*
3. Jan Wigard, 2010.
4. Marius Heideveld, 2010.
5. *Hongertocht.org* (Soeters family/Tony van Vugt).
6. Heideveld, 2010.
7. D. van der Burgh, Radio Netherlands.
8. Coutzen autobiography.
9. *Hongertocht.org*
10. *ibid* and succeeding persons, without note numbers.
11. Wigard and Heideveld, 2010.
12. van den Hoek per G. Schinck, 2010.
13. G. Schinck, 2010.
14. Various and http://operation-manna.
15. Author met Greek colonel organiser, Oxfam, 1971.
16. Various and http://operation-manna.
17. *Hongertocht.org.*
18. Author (as consultant gerontologist).
19. University of Leiden.
20. Also University of Amsterdam, University of Southampton and several American universities.
21. Tony van Vugt, 2010.
22. Web – lib.usc.edu.

6. RHINE CRUISES – NO MOD CONS

1. NY History and Tout, *To Hell with Tanks*
2. Toon-Thorn, 2010.

3. 'Plunder' generally – Whitaker, *Rhineland*, also Saunders, *Operation Plunder*
4. Hammerton, *Achtung! Minen!*
5. Clark, SWWEC.
6. Gutteridge, 2010.
7. Dunesby, SWWEC.
8. Mosely, NY archive.
9. Swaab, *Field of Fire*
10. Blackburn, as chapter 4, note 5
11. Schlemm, POW interrogation.
12. le Messurier, SWWEC.
13. Shellard, 2010.
14. Carpenter, 2010.
15. Brew, SWWEC.
16. NY archive.
17. Leary, 2010.
18. Egli, SWWEC.
19. Hammerton, *op cit*
20. White, *With the Jocks*
21. Clark, SWWEC.
22. Veterans Affairs Canada, *Heroes Remember*
23. Citation.
24. Ward, 2010.
25. Airborne div. diary.
26. Clark, SWWEC.
27. Regt. diary.
28. White, *op cit*
29. Warde, SWWEC.
30. Deans, SWWEC.
31. Leary, 2010.
32. Cardy, 2010.
33. Lowe, SWWEC.
34. Tout, *op cit*
35. NY archive.
36. King, 1990.
37. McCauley, *Soldier Boys*
38. Jackson, 1990. and in Tout *op cit*

7. DALEKO DO DOMU

1. Jan Jarzembowski.
2. Material generally from Mieczkowski, 2010 and (ed.) *The Soldiers of Gen Maczek in World War II*, and Maczek, *Avec mes blindes*
3. The author was present at this action in 1NY.
4. Warsaw uprising of Polish Resistance in 1944 is often confused with the German attack on Warsaw's Jewish ghetto two years earlier: see Walker, *Poland Alone*
5. Description due to Capt. Mieczkowski's careful editing of words noted down at the time.
6. Maczek, *op cit*
7. Mieczkowski, *op cit*
8. *ibid*

8. NOW *WHO* DIES LAST?

1. Whitehouse, 1996.
2. Clark, SWWEC.
3. Cardy, 2010.
4. calverley.ca/Part 19 – Veterans.
5. White, *With the Jocks*
6. Lowe, SWWEC.
7. Egli, SWWEC.
8. Blackburn, 1994.
9. Hammerton, *Achtung! Minen!*
10. Carr-Gomm, SWWEC.
11. Dunesby, SWWEC.
12. Swaab, *Field of Fire*
13. Shephard, *War of Nerves*
14. Dr Bill McAndrew, MoD, Canada.
15. Shephard, *op cit.* quotes another authority as saying that British 17-pounder shots bounced off Tigers. In fact the Firefly 17-pounder could destroy Tigers at equal range to 88-mm guns.
16. Brew, SWWEC.
17. Duchene, SWWEC.
18. Blackburn, *The Guns of Victory* as chapter 4, note 5.
19. Citation.
20. Tout, *To Hell with Tanks*
21. le Messurier, SWWEC.

22. Warde, SWWEC.
23. Citation and Cardy, 2010.
24. NY diary and archive.
25. Tout, *op cit*
26. Egli, SWWEC.
27. Brew, SWWEC.
28. See also Beevor, *Berlin*
29. Deans, SWWEC.
30. Swaab, *op cit*
31. Carder, SWWEC.
32. Gutteridge, 2010.
33. Shellard, 2010.
34. Ward, 2010.
35. Jones, 2010.
36. Ford, SWWEC.
37. Munk, 2010.
38. Thorn, 2010.
39. Blackburn, 1994.
40. Whitehouse, 1996.
41. Elliott, per Ian Hammerton 2010.
42. Hedley-Prole, SWWEC.
43. web – alfgritton, with his permission.
44. Dunesby, SWWEC.
45. Tapson, 2010.
46. McCauley, *Soldier Boys*
47. Shellard, 2010.
48. Bellamy, 2002, and *Troop Leader*
49. Hammerton, *op cit*
50. Clark, SWWEC.
51. Hammerton, *op cit*
52. Close, 1995, and *A View from the Turret*
53. Spittles, 2010.
54. White, *op cit*
55. Cardy, 2010.
56. Citation.
57. Eric Thomas, 2010.
58. What follows is in Alan Walkden's own words per Ian Hammerton.

9. VICTORY! – OR FURTHER STRIFE?

1. Tout, *To Hell with Tanks*
2. Dunesby, SWWEC.
3. White, *With the Jocks*
4. Blackburn, 1994.
5. NY archive.
6. Gutteridge, 2010, and self-published.
7. Cooper, SWWEC.
8. Carr-Gomm, SWWEC.
9. Mieczkowski, 2010.
10. Clark, SWWEC.
11. Cardy, 2010.
12. Swaab, *Field of Fire*
13. le Messurier, SWWEC.
14. Tapson, 2010.
15. Bellamy, 2002, and *Troop Leader*
16. Warde, SWWEC.
17. Leary and Carpenter, 2010.
18. Egli, SWWEC.
19. Cardy, 2010.
20. Hammerton, *Achtung! Minen!*
21. Blackburn, *Guns of Victory*, as chapter 4, note 5.
22. Cross, *True Stories of World War II*
23. GOC, 1st Polish AD, 10 May 1945.
24. Blackburn, 1994.
25. Clark, SWWEC.
26. Dunesby, SWWEC.
27. NY archive.
28. Swaab, *op cit*
29. Hicken, 2010, and self-published.
30. Hammerton, *op cit*
31. Gritton, 2010 and website: www.alfgritton.co.uk
32. Gutteridge as 6 above.
33. Bellamy, *op cit*
34. NY archive and Spittles, 2010.
35. le Messurier, SWWEC.
36. Clark, SWWEC.

37. Gutteridge, as 6 above. There were still unused infantry reserves which Churchill had insisted on retaining in the UK.
38. Egli, SWWEC.
39. Jones, 2010.
40. Brown, 2010.
41. Cardy, 2010.
42. NY archive.
43. Whitaker, *Rhineland*
44. Major D.G. Bevan, MC, 1985.
45. Gutteridge as 6 above.
46. Solarz, 2010. The reason for introducing an American (friend of the author) will be seen in next chapter.
47. Sims, in Cross *op cit*

10. *KRIEGSGEFANGENGESELLSCHAFT*
1. Hicken, 1944, 2010, and self-published (author's tank crew).
2. 1NY.
3. On basis of a mere Cambridge School Certificate the author was posted as Sgt Regimental Lecturer to 1st KDG in late 1945.
4. NY archive.
5. Cardy, 2010.
6. Leary, 2010, and self-published.
7. Brown, 2010.
8. Hazel and Manfred Toon-Thorn – SS units were automatically arrested entire down to lowest ranks on suspicion of war crimes, although relatively few Waffen SS were convicted, in contrast to SS units in extermination camps who were almost automatically branded guilty.
9. England, 1994, and NY archive.
10. Michael Scott, 2001.
11. Close, 1993, and *A View from the Turret*
12. Mieczkowski, 2010.
13. Gloria Solarz, 2010.
14. Hicken, as note 1 above.

EPILOGUE
1. Crumper, per Col Hal D. Steward, 2010.

BIBLIOGRAPHY

SOURCES AND FURTHER READING

Beevor, A., *Berlin: The Downfall 1945* (Penguin, 2003)

Bellamy, B., *Troop Leader* (Sutton, 2005)

Blackburn, G.G., *The Guns of Victory* (McClelland & Stewart Inc., cloth edition 1996, trade paperback edition 1997)

Close, Maj. B., *A View from the Turret* (Dell & Bredon, 1998)

Cross, R. (ed.), *True Stories of World War II* (Michael O'Mara, 1994)

Elstob, P., *Hitler's Last Offensive* (Pen & Sword, 2003)

Gootzen H., and K. Connor, *The Battle for the Roer Triangle* (Erskine, 2006)

Hammerton, I.C., *Achtung! Minen!* (The Book Guild, 1991)

Horrocks, Sir B., *Corps Commander* (Sidgwick & Jackson, 1977)

McCauley, G.F., *Soldier Boys* (General Store Publishing, 2003)

Maczek, S., *Avec mes blindes* (Presses de la Cite, 1967)

Mieczkowski, Z., (ed.) *The Soldiers of General Maczek in World War II* (Foundation for the Commemoration of General Maczek, 2004)

Oliver, K.M., *The RAF Regiment at War* (Leo Cooper, 2002)

Saunders, T., *Operation Plunder* (Pen & Sword, 2006)

Shephard, B., *A War of Nerves* (Pimlico, 2002)

Shores, C., and C. Thomas, *2nd Tactical Air Force, vol.3, 'From Rhine to Victory'* (Ian Allan, 2006)

Stolte, P., *The 51st HD in the Ardennes* (per Blockmans, OPT, Bruxelles) *L'histoire du 30ᵉ Corps britannique* (Blockmans, OPT)

Thacker, T., *The End of the Third Reich* (Tempus, 2006)

Tout, K., *To Hell with Tanks!* (Robert Hale, 1992)

    A Fine Night for Tanks (Sutton, 1998, 2002)

    By Tank, D to VE Days (Robert Hale, 1985, 2009)

    In the Shadow of Arnhem (The History Press, 2003, 2009)

    Peace in War? War in Peace! (The Book Guild, 2010)

    The Bloody Battle for Tilly (Sutton, 2000, 2002)

van der Zee, H.A., *The Hunger Winter* (U. of Nebraska, 1998)

Walker, J., *Poland Alone* (The History Press, 2008)

Whitaker, W.D., and S. Whitaker, *Rhineland* (St. Martin's Press, 1989)

White, P., *With the Jocks* (Sutton, 2001)

Whitehouse, S., and G.B. Bennett, *Fear is the Foe* (Robert Hale, 1995)

WEBSITES

www.51hd.co.uk/history

www.BBC-WW2 People's War

www.Heroes Remember (Veterans Affairs, Canada)

www.IWM.org.uk/collections

www.pegasusarchive/Rhine

www.war-experience.org (SWWEC)

INDEX OF ARMED FORCES

INDEX OF PERSONS

GENERAL INDEX